FIRST AMENDMENT LAW:
FREEDOM OF EXPRESSION
AND
FREEDOM OF RELIGION

Second Edition
2011 Supplement

FIRST AMENDMENT LAW: FREEDOM OF EXPRESSION AND FREEDOM OF RELIGION

Second Edition

2011 Supplement

Arthur D. Hellman
Sally Ann Semenko Endowed Chair
University of Pittsburgh School of Law

William D. Araiza
Professor of Law
Brooklyn Law School

Thomas E. Baker
Professor of Law
Florida International University

ISBN: 978-1-4224-9532-2

> ### NOTE TO USERS
> To ensure that you are using the latest materials available in this area, please be sure to periodically check the LexisNexis Law School website for downloadable updates and supplements at www.lexisnexis.com/lawschool.

Editorial Offices
121 Chanlon Rd., New Providence, NJ 07974 (908) 464-6800
201 Mission St., San Francisco, CA 94105-1831 (415) 908-3200
www.lexisnexis.com

MATTHEW◆BENDER

(2011–Pub.3214)

PREFACE

The second edition of our casebook, *First Amendment Law: Freedom of Expression and Freedom of Religion*, was published in the spring of 2010. It might seem odd that the book would require a very substantial supplement little more than a year later; the explanation is that the Supreme Court's 2009-2010 and 2010-2011 Terms proved to be extraordinarily active from a First Amendment perspective. Indeed, it is doubtful that any two consecutive Terms in recent years have produced as many First Amendment decisions with so many implications for a broad range of constitutional claims.

Also striking is the overall pattern in the decisions. The Court strongly reaffirmed its commitment to the proposition that "debate on public issues should be uninhibited, robust, and wide-open." And it went further:

- The Court rejected the Government's contention that "categories of speech may be exempted from the First Amendment's protection" based on "a categorical balancing of the value of the speech against its social costs," thus demoting the oft-quoted dictum in *Chaplinsky v. New Hampshire* (1942) to no more than a "description." (*United States v. Stevens*)

- Revitalizing a largely forgotten 1948 decision, the Court accepted the premise that although the Free Speech Clause "exists primarily to protect discourse on public matters, . . . it is difficult to distinguish politics from entertainment, and dangerous to try." (*Brown v. EMA*)

- The Court endorsed a broad definition of "public concern" that will limit not only state tort actions but also government power to discipline its employees. (*Snyder v. Phelps*)

- The Court overruled precedents upholding regulation of electioneering expenditures by corporations and unions. (*Citizens United v. FEC*)

We recognize that some of the decisions that loom large on first reading may fade in importance as time goes by, but there is pedagogical value in studying recent cases that highlight current issues and reveal philosophical divisions among the Justices. We have therefore opted to err on the side of inclusion.

By far the most controversial of the new cases was *Citizens United v. Federal Election Commission* (Chapter 11), in which the Court (on a 5-4 vote) struck down provisions of the Bipartisan Campaign Reform Act of 2002 that prohibited corporations and unions from using their general treasury funds to make independent expenditures for speech defined as an "electioneering communication" or for speech expressly advocating the election or defeat of a candidate. The Court overruled a 1990 decision that had upheld a similar state law.

Citizens United was one of two cases in the 2009 Term that held a federal statute unconstitutional under the First Amendment. The other was *United States v. Stevens* (Chapter 3), in which the court struck down a law criminalizing certain depictions of animal cruelty. The decision aroused less controversy than *Citizens United*, but its implications for a broad range of novel First Amendment issues may be substantial. We have therefore placed it in a new section on "Other Content, Other Harms." Also in that section is *Brown v. Entertainment Merchants Association*, the 2010 Term decision striking down California's law regulating the sale of violent video games to minors.

In contrast, the Court upheld a federal statute that prohibits the provision of "material support or resources" to certain foreign organizations that engage in terrorist activity. The case was *Holder v. Humanitarian Law Project (HLP)* (Chapter 8), decided by a vote of 6-3. The Court concluded that the statute was constitutional "as applied to the particular activities plaintiffs have told us they wish to pursue." But it left open the possibility of a different result in "more difficult cases that may arise."

Citizens United was not the only decision involving the regulation of elections. In *Doe v. Reed* (Chapter 11), the Court considered the argument that public disclosure of the names of citizens who sign referendum petitions would violate the First Amendment. The Court rejected the broad claim, but noted that a "more focused claim concerning disclosure of the information on [the] particular petition" — involving revocation of a statute conferring benefits on same-sex couples — might yet prevail. The case is part of a burgeoning area of litigation, and we have created a new section on "Political Association and Disclosure Requirements" to reflect this doctrinal development.

Three other decisions represented new variations on familiar themes. In *Snyder v. Phelps* (Chapter 2) the Court held that members of the Westboro Baptist Church were shielded from tort liability for picketing near a soldier's funeral service. The decision emphasized that the picketing involved a matter of public concern; it made no difference that the plaintiff was not a public official or a public figure.

In *Christian Legal Society v. Martinez* (Chapter 18), the Court rejected a free-speech claim by a student religious organization at a state law school. The organization limited its membership to students who adhered to the religious belief that sexual relations should not occur outside of marriage between a man and a woman. The law school refused to grant the organization official recognition and invoked its policies that required recognized organizations to admit all students irrespective of their religious beliefs or sexual orientation. The Court divided 5-4: a majority sided with the law school based on the limited public forum doctrine, but a dissent asserted that the decision rested on the principle of "no freedom for expression that offends prevailing standards of political correctness in our country's institutions of higher learning."

In *Salazar v. Buono* (Chapter 16 Note), the latest decision involving a religious display in a public place, six of the Justices wrote opinions, with no opinion gaining a majority. When the ink dried, the Court voted 5-4 simply to remand the case for still further consideration under the existing line of contested and fact-bound precedents. But the plurality and a dissent engaged in a remarkable legal and philosophical debate over the question: when (if ever) is a cross not a cross?

The Supplement also includes several new Problems. Some of these could well be considered in more than one segment of the course; we have placed them in the chapters where they seemed to fit best, recognizing that teachers may want to assign them at other points in the syllabus.

The 2009 Term was the first for Justice Sonia Sotomayor and the last for Justice John Paul Stevens; the 2010 Term was the first for Justice Elena Kagan. Justice Sotomayor wrote in only one of the major First Amendment cases — a concurring opinion in *Doe v. Reed*. Justice Kagan's first dissent was in the Arizona tax credit case, discussed in a Note in Chapter 16; she also wrote the dissent in a campaign finance case noted in Chapter 11. Meanwhile, Chief Justice Roberts, now in his sixth year on the Court, has continued to play a central role in the development of First Amendment jurisprudence; he authored the

PREFACE

majority opinions in *Stevens*, *HLP*, and *Snyder* as well as *Doe*. Appendix B provides an updated table of the Justices; it replaces the one in the Second Edition.

* * *

In preparing this Supplement, we have continued the approach followed by the Casebook. First, we have concentrated on the main lines of doctrinal development and their implications for future disputes rather than trying to cover every new decision or doctrinal wrinkle. Second, we have edited the cases with a relatively light hand. We have also attempted to keep the decisions readable; thus, some brackets and internal quotation marks have been omitted from quoted material within cases.

A word is in order about the manner in which cases are cited in this Supplement. When an opinion in the Supplement cites a principal case (or a major Note case) in the corresponding chapter of the Casebook, we give only the full name and the year of decision. When an opinion cites a case elsewhere in the Casebook, we add the Casebook page reference. For other cases, we retain the full citation. We think that this approach will reinforce students' understanding of the content and significance of the landmark precedents; it will also help them to master the many different ways in which precedent is used in constitutional argument and adjudication.

* * *

The authors express their appreciation to the staff of the University of Pittsburgh School of Law Document Technology Center for dedicated efforts that made it possible to produce this Supplement under a very tight deadline. As with the Casebook, we welcome comments and suggestions from users and readers.

TABLE OF CONTENTS

CHAPTER 2   **CONTENT REGULATION: THE *CHAPLINSKY* EXCLUSIONS** 1

B.   "THE LIBELOUS" — OR OTHERWISE TORTIOUS 1

[4]   "Outrage" and Emotional Distress 1

     Snyder v. Phelps 1

     Note: Intentional Infliction of Emotional Distress and the First Amendment 12

     Problem: A "Cyberstalking" Prosecution 13

     Problem: An Obsessive Blogger 14

CHAPTER 3   **CONTENT REGULATION: NEW CANDIDATES FOR CATEGORIAL EXCLUSION OR LIMITED PROTECTION** 17

D.   OTHER CONTENT, OTHER HARMS 17

     United States v. Stevens 17

     Note: The Implications of *Stevens* 32

     Problem: Writing a "Crush Video" Statute 32

     Brown v. Entertainment Merchants Association 34

     Note: Violence, Interactivity, and the Protection of Children 50

CHAPTER 4   **TRANS-SUBSTANTIVE DOCTRINES** 53

B.   OVERBREADTH AND VAGUENESS 53

     Note: Clarifying The Vagueness Doctrine 53

CHAPTER 5   **COMPELLED EXPRESSION** 57

B.   COMPELLED SUBSIDY 57

     Problem: Union Camp and Ratification Mondays 57

CHAPTER 6   **FREEDOM OF ASSOCIATION** 59

     Problem: Access to a Gay Pride Festival 59

     Problem: Exclusion From a Gay Softball League 59

CHAPTER 8   **CONTENT NEUTRALITY: THE PRINCIPLE AND ITS PROGENY** 63

B.   *O'BRIEN* AND THE TWO-TRACK ANALYSIS 63

     Holder v. Humanitarian Law Project 63

TABLE OF CONTENTS

Note: Speech Activity as "Material Support" 80

CHAPTER 11   TESTING THE BOUNDARIES OF DOCTRINE 81

C.   CAMPAIGN FINANCE 81
    Citizens United v. Federal Election Commission 81
    Note: (Further) Disagreement in *Citizens United* about Justifications for
    Campaign Expenditure Restrictions ....·........ 100
    Note: Corporations' Speech Rights and the Original Understanding of the
    First Amendment 102
    Note: The Upholding of Campaign Speech Disclosure Requirements in
    Citizens United 104
    Problem: Corporate Contributions to an Independent Spender 106
    Note: Burdening Speech, Encouraging Debate, and Government Assistance
    to Political Candidates 106
    Problem: Encouraging Small Contributors 111
D.   POLITICAL ASSOCIATION AND DISCLOSURE REQUIREMENTS . 112
    Doe v. Reed 112
    Note: Anonymity, Speech and Political Activity 122

CHAPTER 14   FREEDOM OF THE PRESS 125

A.   SINGLING OUT THE PRESS 125
    Problem: Save the Newspapers! 125
    Problem: (Non-)Taxation of Online Information 126

CHAPTER 16   THE ESTABLISHMENT CLAUSE 127

A.   FINANCIAL AID TO RELIGION 127
  [1]   Basic Principles 127
        Note: Standing Doctrine 127
  [2]   The *Lemon* Test as Modified 130
        Problem: Is the National Day of Prayer Statute a "Law Respecting an
        Establishment of Religion"? 130
        Problem: "I Believe" in License Plates 133
D.   DISPLAYS IN PUBLIC PLACES 134
    Note: When is a Cross Not a Cross? 134

CHAPTER 17   THE FREE EXERCISE CLAUSE 145

C.   DISCRIMINATION AGAINST RELIGION 145
    Problem: Dorm Life Versus a Christian Life 145

TABLE OF CONTENTS

CHAPTER 18   **INTERRELATIONSHIPS AMONG THE CLAUSES** . . .   **147**

C.   RELIGIOUS SPEECH   147

        Christian Legal Society v. Martinez   147

        Note: Unresolved and Irresolvable Differences   162

        Problem: "Open Your Hymnals to the First Amendment" — Religious
        Music in the Public Schools   162

Appendix B   **THE JUSTICES OF THE UNITED STATES SUPREME
               COURT, 1946–2010 TERMS** **165**

Chapter 2

CONTENT REGULATION: THE *CHAPLINSKY* EXCLUSIONS

B. "THE LIBELOUS" — OR OTHERWISE TORTIOUS

[4] "Outrage" and Emotional Distress

Page 125: *add after the Note:*

SNYDER v. PHELPS

131 S. Ct. 1207 (2010)

CHIEF JUSTICE ROBERTS delivered the opinion of the Court.

A jury held members of the Westboro Baptist Church liable for millions of dollars in damages for picketing near a soldier's funeral service. The picket signs reflected the church's view that the United States is overly tolerant of sin and that God kills American soldiers as punishment. The question presented is whether the First Amendment shields the church members from tort liability for their speech in this case.

I

A

Fred Phelps founded the Westboro Baptist Church in Topeka, Kansas, in 1955. The church's congregation believes that God hates and punishes the United States for its tolerance of homosexuality, particularly in America's military. The church frequently communicates its views by picketing, often at military funerals. In the more than 20 years that the members of Westboro Baptist have publicized their message, they have picketed nearly 600 funerals.

Marine Lance Corporal Matthew Snyder was killed in Iraq in the line of duty. Lance Corporal Snyder's father selected the Catholic church in the Snyders' hometown of Westminster, Maryland, as the site for his son's funeral. Local newspapers provided notice of the time and location of the service.

Phelps became aware of Matthew Snyder's funeral and decided to travel to Maryland with six other Westboro Baptist parishioners (two of his daughters and four of his grandchildren) to picket. On the day of the memorial service, the Westboro congregation members picketed on public land adjacent to public streets near the Maryland State House, the United States Naval Academy, and Matthew Snyder's funeral. The Westboro picketers carried signs that were largely the same at all three locations. They stated, for instance: "God Hates the USA/Thank God

1

for 9/11," "America is Doomed," "Don't Pray for the USA," "Thank God for IEDs," "Thank God for Dead Soldiers," "Pope in Hell," "Priests Rape Boys," "God Hates Fags," "You're Going to Hell," and "God Hates You."

The church had notified the authorities in advance of its intent to picket at the time of the funeral, and the picketers complied with police instructions in staging their demonstration. The picketing took place within a 10- by 25-foot plot of public land adjacent to a public street, behind a temporary fence. That plot was approximately 1,000 feet from the church where the funeral was held. Several buildings separated the picket site from the church. The Westboro picketers displayed their signs for about 30 minutes before the funeral began and sang hymns and recited Bible verses. None of the picketers entered church property or went to the cemetery. They did not yell or use profanity, and there was no violence associated with the picketing.

The funeral procession passed within 200 to 300 feet of the picket site. Although Snyder testified that he could see the tops of the picket signs as he drove to the funeral, he did not see what was written on the signs until later that night, while watching a news broadcast covering the event.

B

Snyder filed suit against Phelps, Phelps's daughters, and the Westboro Baptist Church (collectively Westboro or the church) in the United States District Court for the District of Maryland under that court's diversity jurisdiction. Snyder alleged five state tort law claims: defamation, publicity given to private life, intentional infliction of emotional distress, intrusion upon seclusion, and civil conspiracy. Westboro moved for summary judgment contending, in part, that the church's speech was insulated from liability by the First Amendment.

The District Court awarded Westboro summary judgment on Snyder's claims for defamation and publicity given to private life, concluding that Snyder could not prove the necessary elements of those torts. A trial was held on the remaining claims. At trial, Snyder described the severity of his emotional injuries. He testified that he is unable to separate the thought of his dead son from his thoughts of Westboro's picketing, and that he often becomes tearful, angry, and physically ill when he thinks about it. Expert witnesses testified that Snyder's emotional anguish had resulted in severe depression and had exacerbated pre-existing health conditions.

A jury found for Snyder on the intentional infliction of emotional distress, intrusion upon seclusion, and civil conspiracy claims, and held Westboro liable for $2.9 million in compensatory damages and $8 million in punitive damages. Westboro filed several post-trial motions . . . . The District Court remitted the punitive damages award to $2.1 million, but left the jury verdict otherwise intact.

In the Court of Appeals, Westboro's primary argument was that the church was entitled to judgment as a matter of law because the First Amendment fully protected Westboro's speech. The Court of Appeals agreed. The court reviewed the picket signs and concluded that Westboro's statements were entitled to First Amendment protection because those statements were on matters of public concern, were not provably false, and were expressed solely through hyperbolic rhetoric. We granted certiorari.

II

To succeed on a claim for intentional infliction of emotional distress in Maryland, a plaintiff must demonstrate that the defendant intentionally or recklessly engaged in extreme and outrageous conduct that caused the plaintiff to suffer severe emotional distress. The Free Speech Clause of the First Amendment — "Congress shall make no law . . . abridging the freedom of speech" — can serve as a defense in state tort suits, including suits for intentional infliction of emotional distress. See, *e.g.*, *Hustler Magazine, Inc. v. Falwell* (1988).

Whether the First Amendment prohibits holding Westboro liable for its speech in this case turns largely on whether that speech is of public or private concern, as determined by all the circumstances of the case. "[S]peech on 'matters of public concern' . . . is 'at the heart of the First Amendment's protection.' " *Dun & Bradstreet, Inc. v. Greenmoss Builders, Inc.* (1985) (opinion of Powell, J.) (quoting *First Nat. Bank of Boston v. Bellotti* (1978) [Casebook p. 697]). The First Amendment reflects "a profound national commitment to the principle that debate on public issues should be uninhibited, robust, and wide-open." *New York Times Co. v. Sullivan* (1964). . . . Accordingly, "speech on public issues occupies the highest rung of the hierarchy of First Amendment values, and is entitled to special protection." *Connick v. Myers* (1983) [Casebook p. 725].

" '[N]ot all speech is of equal First Amendment importance,' " however, and where matters of purely private significance are at issue, First Amendment protections are often less rigorous. *Hustler* (quoting *Dun & Bradstreet*); see *Connick*. That is because restricting speech on purely private matters does not implicate the same constitutional concerns as limiting speech on matters of public interest: "[T]here is no threat to the free and robust debate of public issues; there is no potential interference with a meaningful dialogue of ideas"; and the "threat of liability" does not pose the risk of "a reaction of self-censorship" on matters of public import. *Dun & Bradstreet*.

We noted a short time ago, in considering whether public employee speech addressed a matter of public concern, that "the boundaries of the public concern test are not well defined." *San Diego v. Roe* (2004) [Casebook p. 733]. Although that remains true today, we have articulated some guiding principles, principles that accord broad protection to speech to ensure that courts themselves do not become inadvertent censors.

Speech deals with matters of public concern when it can "be fairly considered as relating to any matter of political, social, or other concern to the community," *Connick*, or when it "is a subject of legitimate news interest; that is, a subject of general interest and of value and concern to the public," *San Diego*. The arguably "inappropriate or controversial character of a statement is irrelevant to the question whether it deals with a matter of public concern." *Rankin v. McPherson* (1987) [Casebook p. 735].

Our opinion in *Dun & Bradstreet*, on the other hand, provides an example of speech of only private concern. In that case we held, as a general matter, that information about a particular individual's credit report "concerns no public issue." The content of the report, we explained, "was speech solely in the individual interest of the speaker and its specific business audience." That was confirmed by the fact that the particular report was sent to only five subscribers to the reporting service, who were bound not to disseminate it further. To cite another example, we concluded in *San Diego v. Roe* that, in the context of a government employer regulating the speech of its employees, videos of an employee engaging in sexually explicit acts did not address a public concern; the videos "did nothing to inform the public about any aspect of the [employing agency's] functioning or operation."

Deciding whether speech is of public or private concern requires us to examine the " 'content, form, and context' " of that speech, " 'as revealed by the whole record.' " *Dun & Bradstreet* (quoting *Connick*). As in other First Amendment cases, the court is obligated "to 'make an independent examination of the whole record' in order to make sure that 'the judgment does not constitute a forbidden intrusion on the field of free expression.' " *Bose Corp. v. Consumers Union of United States, Inc.*, 466 U.S. 485, 499 (1984). In considering content, form, and context, no factor is dispositive, and it is necessary to evaluate all the circumstances of the speech, including what was said, where it was said, and how it was said.

The "content" of Westboro's signs plainly relates to broad issues of interest to society at large, rather than matters of "purely private concern." *Dun & Bradstreet.* The placards read "God Hates the USA/Thank God for 9/11," "America is Doomed," "Don't Pray for the USA," "Thank God for IEDs," "Fag Troops," "Semper Fi Fags," "God Hates Fags," "Maryland Taliban," "Fags Doom Nations," "Not Blessed Just Cursed," "Thank God for Dead Soldiers," "Pope in Hell," "Priests Rape Boys," "You're Going to Hell," and "God Hates You." While these messages may fall short of refined social or political commentary, the issues they highlight — the political and moral conduct of the United States and its citizens, the fate of our Nation, homosexuality in the military, and scandals involving the Catholic clergy — are matters of public import. The signs certainly convey Westboro's position on those issues, in a manner designed, unlike the private speech in *Dun & Bradstreet*, to reach as broad a public audience as possible. And even if a few of the signs — such as "You're Going to Hell" and "God Hates You" — were viewed as containing messages related to Matthew Snyder or the Snyders specifically, that would not change the fact that the overall thrust and dominant theme of Westboro's demonstration spoke to broader public issues.

Apart from the content of Westboro's signs, Snyder contends that the "context" of the speech — its connection with his son's funeral — makes the speech a matter of private rather than public concern. The fact that Westboro spoke in connection with a funeral, however, cannot by itself transform the nature of Westboro's speech. Westboro's signs, displayed on public land next to a public street, reflect the fact that the church finds much to condemn in modern society. Its speech is "fairly characterized as constituting speech on a matter of public concern," *Connick*, and the funeral setting does not alter that conclusion.

Snyder argues that the church members in fact mounted a personal attack on Snyder and his family, and then attempted to "immunize their conduct by claiming that they were actually protesting the United States' tolerance of homosexuality or the supposed evils of the Catholic Church." We are not concerned in this case that Westboro's speech on public matters was in any way contrived to insulate speech on a private matter from liability. Westboro had been actively engaged in speaking on the subjects addressed in its picketing long before it became aware of Matthew Snyder, and there can be no serious claim that Westboro's picketing did not represent its "honestly believed" views on public issues. There was no pre-existing relationship or conflict between Westboro and Snyder that might suggest Westboro's speech on public matters was intended to mask an attack on Snyder over a private matter. Contrast *Connick* (finding public employee speech a matter of private concern when it was "no coincidence that [the speech] followed upon the heels of [a] transfer notice" affecting the employee).

Snyder goes on to argue that Westboro's speech should be afforded less than full First Amendment protection "not only because of the words" but also because the church members exploited the funeral "as a platform to bring their message to a broader audience." There is no doubt that Westboro chose to stage its picketing at the Naval Academy, the Maryland State House, and Matthew Snyder's funeral to increase publicity for its views and because of the relation between those sites and its views — in the case of the military funeral, because Westboro believes that God is killing American soldiers as punishment for the Nation's sinful policies.

Westboro's choice to convey its views in conjunction with Matthew Snyder's funeral made the expression of those views particularly hurtful to many, especially to Matthew's father. The record makes clear that the applicable legal term — "emotional distress" — fails to capture fully the anguish Westboro's choice added to Mr. Snyder's already incalculable grief. But Westboro conducted its picketing peacefully on matters of public concern at a public place adjacent to a public street. Such space occupies a "special position in terms of First Amendment protection." *United States v. Grace*, 461 U.S. 171, 180 (1983). "[W]e have repeatedly referred to public streets as the archetype of a traditional public forum," noting that " '[t]ime out of mind' public streets and sidewalks have been used for public assembly and debate." *Frisby v. Schultz* (1988) [Casebook p. 390].

That said, "[e]ven protected speech is not equally permissible in all places and at all times." *Id.* Westboro's choice of where and when to conduct its picketing is not beyond the Government's regulatory reach — it is "subject to reasonable time, place, or manner restrictions" that are consistent with the standards announced in this Court's precedents. Maryland now has a law imposing restrictions on funeral picketing, as do 43 other States and the Federal Government. To the extent these laws are content neutral, they raise very different questions from the tort verdict at issue in this case. Maryland's law, however, was not in effect at the time of the events at issue here, so we have no occasion to consider how it might apply to facts such as those before us, or whether it or other similar regulations are constitutional. . . .

Simply put, the church members had the right to be where they were. Westboro alerted local authorities to its funeral protest and fully complied with police guidance on where the picketing could be staged. The picketing was conducted under police supervision some 1,000 feet from the church, out of the sight of those at the church. The protest was not unruly; there was no shouting, profanity, or violence.

The record confirms that any distress occasioned by Westboro's picketing turned on the content and viewpoint of the message conveyed, rather than any interference with the funeral itself. A group of parishioners standing at the very spot where Westboro stood, holding signs that said "God Bless America" and "God Loves You," would not have been subjected to liability. It was what Westboro said that exposed it to tort damages.

Given that Westboro's speech was at a public place on a matter of public concern, that speech is entitled to "special protection" under the First Amendment. Such speech cannot be restricted simply because it is upsetting or arouses contempt. "If there is a bedrock principle underlying the First Amendment, it is that the government may not prohibit the expression of an idea simply because society finds the idea itself offensive or disagreeable." *Texas v. Johnson* (1989) [Casebook p. 459] . . . .

The jury here was instructed that it could hold Westboro liable for intentional infliction of emotional distress based on a finding that Westboro's picketing was "outrageous." "Outrageousness," however, is a highly malleable standard with "an inherent subjectiveness about it which would allow a jury to impose liability on the basis of the jurors' tastes or views, or perhaps on the basis of their dislike of a particular expression." *Hustler.* In a case such as this, a jury is "unlikely to be neutral with respect to the content of [the] speech," posing "a real danger of becoming an instrument for the suppression of . . . 'vehement, caustic, and sometimes unpleasan[t]' " expression. Such a risk is unacceptable; "in public debate [we] must tolerate insulting, and even outrageous, speech in order to provide adequate 'breathing space' to the freedoms protected by the First Amendment." *Boos v. Barry* (1988) [Casebook p. 475]. What Westboro said, in the whole context of how and where it chose to say it, is entitled to "special protection" under the First Amendment, and that protection cannot be overcome by a jury finding that the picketing was outrageous.

For all these reasons, the jury verdict imposing tort liability on Westboro for intentional infliction of emotional distress must be set aside. . . .

IV

Our holding today is narrow. We are required in First Amendment cases to carefully review the record, and the reach of our opinion here is limited by the particular facts before us. . . .

Westboro believes that America is morally flawed; many Americans might feel the same about Westboro. Westboro's funeral picketing is certainly hurtful and its contribution to public discourse may be negligible. But Westboro addressed matters of public import on public property, in a peaceful manner, in full compliance with the guidance of local officials. The speech was indeed planned to coincide with Matthew Snyder's funeral, but did not itself disrupt that funeral, and

Westboro's choice to conduct its picketing at that time and place did not alter the nature of its speech.

Speech is powerful. It can stir people to action, move them to tears of both joy and sorrow, and — as it did here — inflict great pain. On the facts before us, we cannot react to that pain by punishing the speaker. As a Nation we have chosen a different course — to protect even hurtful speech on public issues to ensure that we do not stifle public debate. That choice requires that we shield Westboro from tort liability for its picketing in this case.

The judgment of the United States Court of Appeals for the Fourth Circuit is affirmed.

JUSTICE BREYER, concurring.

. . . While I agree with the Court's conclusion that the picketing addressed matters of public concern, I do not believe that our First Amendment analysis can stop at that point. A State can sometimes regulate picketing, even picketing on matters of public concern. See *Frisby v. Schultz* (1988) [Casebook p. 390]. Moreover, suppose that A were physically to assault B, knowing that the assault (being newsworthy) would provide A with an opportunity to transmit to the public his views on a matter of public concern. The constitutionally protected nature of the end would not shield A's use of unlawful, unprotected means. And in some circumstances the use of certain words as means would be similarly unprotected. See *Chaplinsky v. New Hampshire* (1942) ("fighting words"). . . .

The dissent requires us to ask whether our holding unreasonably limits liability for intentional infliction of emotional distress — to the point where A (in order to draw attention to his views on a public matter) might launch a verbal assault upon B, a private person, publicly revealing the most intimate details of B's private life, while knowing that the revelation will cause B severe emotional harm. Does our decision leave the State powerless to protect the individual against invasions of, *e.g.*, personal privacy, even in the most horrendous of such circumstances?

As I understand the Court's opinion, it does not hold or imply that the State is always powerless to provide private individuals with necessary protection. Rather, the Court has reviewed the underlying facts in detail, as will sometimes prove necessary where First Amendment values and state-protected (say, privacy-related) interests seriously conflict. That review makes clear that Westboro's means of communicating its views consisted of picketing in a place where picketing was lawful and in compliance with all police directions. The picketing could not be seen or heard from the funeral ceremony itself. And Snyder testified that he saw no more than the tops of the picketers' signs as he drove to the funeral. To uphold the application of state law in these circumstances would punish Westboro for seeking to communicate its views on matters of public concern without proportionately advancing the State's interest in protecting its citizens against severe emotional harm. Consequently, the First Amendment protects Westboro. As I read the Court's opinion, it holds no more.

JUSTICE ALITO, dissenting.

Our profound national commitment to free and open debate is not a license for the vicious verbal assault that occurred in this case.

Petitioner Albert Snyder is not a public figure. He is simply a parent whose son, Marine Lance Corporal Matthew Snyder, was killed in Iraq. Mr. Snyder wanted what is surely the right of any parent who experiences such an incalculable loss: to bury his son in peace. But respondents, members of the Westboro Baptist Church, deprived him of that elementary right. They first issued a press release and thus turned Matthew's funeral into a tumultuous media event. They then appeared at the church, approached as closely as they could without trespassing, and launched a malevolent verbal attack on Matthew and his family at a time of acute emotional vulnerability. As a result, Albert Snyder suffered severe and lasting emotional injury. The Court now holds that the First Amendment protected respondents' right to brutalize Mr. Snyder. I cannot agree.

I

Respondents and other members of their church have strong opinions on certain moral, religious, and political issues, and the First Amendment ensures that they have almost limitless opportunities to express their views. . . . And they may express their views in terms that are "uninhibited," "vehement," and "caustic." *New York Times Co. v. Sullivan* (1964).

It does not follow, however, that they may intentionally inflict severe emotional injury on private persons at a time of intense emotional sensitivity by launching vicious verbal attacks that make no contribution to public debate. To protect against such injury, "most if not all jurisdictions" permit recovery in tort for the intentional infliction of emotional distress (or IIED). *Hustler Magazine, Inc. v. Falwell* (1988).

This is a very narrow tort with requirements that "are rigorous, and difficult to satisfy." . . . [But] respondents long ago abandoned any effort to show that those tough standards were not satisfied here. . . . They did not dispute that Mr. Snyder suffered " 'wounds that are truly severe and incapable of healing themselves.' " Nor did they dispute that their speech was " 'so outrageous in character, and so extreme in degree, as to go beyond all possible bounds of decency, and to be regarded as atrocious, and utterly intolerable in a civilized community.' " Instead, they maintained that the First Amendment gave them a license to engage in such conduct. They are wrong.

II

It is well established that a claim for the intentional infliction of emotional distress can be satisfied by speech. . . . And although this Court has not decided the question, I think it is clear that the First Amendment does not entirely preclude liability for the intentional infliction of emotional distress by means of speech.

This Court has recognized that words may "by their very utterance inflict injury" and that the First Amendment does not shield utterances that form "no essential part of any exposition of ideas, and are of such slight social value as a step to truth that any benefit that may be derived from them is clearly outweighed by the social interest in order and morality." *Chaplinsky v. New Hampshire* (1942). When grave injury is intentionally inflicted by means of an attack like the one at issue here, the First Amendment should not interfere with recovery.

III

In this case, respondents brutally attacked Matthew Snyder, and this attack, which was almost certain to inflict injury, was central to respondents' well-practiced strategy for attracting public attention.

On the morning of Matthew Snyder's funeral, respondents could have chosen to stage their protest at countless locations. . . . But of course, a small group picketing at [locations such as a public park or the White House] would have probably gone unnoticed.

The Westboro Baptist Church, however, has devised a strategy that remedies this problem. As the Court notes, church members have protested at nearly 600 military funerals. They have also picketed the funerals of police officers, firefighters, and the victims of natural disasters, accidents, and shocking crimes. And in advance of these protests, they issue press releases to ensure that their protests will attract public attention.

This strategy works because it is expected that respondents' verbal assaults will wound the family and friends of the deceased and because the media is irresistibly drawn to the sight of persons who are visibly in grief. The more outrageous the funeral protest, the more publicity the Westboro Baptist Church is able to obtain. Thus, when the church recently announced its intention to picket the funeral of a 9-year-old girl killed in the shooting spree in Tucson — proclaiming that she was "better off dead" — their announcement was national news, and the church was able to obtain free air time on the radio in exchange for canceling its protest. Similarly, in 2006, the church got air time on a talk radio show in exchange for canceling its threatened protest at the funeral of five Amish girls killed by a crazed gunman.

In this case, respondents implemented the Westboro Baptist Church's publicity-seeking strategy. Their press release stated that they were going "to picket the funeral of Lance Cpl. Matthew A. Snyder" because "God Almighty killed Lance Cpl. Snyder. He died in shame, not honor — for a fag nation cursed by God . . . . Now in Hell — sine die." This announcement guaranteed that Matthew's funeral would be transformed into a raucous media event and began the wounding process. It is well known that anticipation may heighten the effect of a painful event.

On the day of the funeral, respondents, true to their word, displayed placards that conveyed the message promised in their press release. . . .

. . . Since respondents chose to stage their protest at Matthew Snyder's funeral and not at any of the other countless available venues, a reasonable person would have assumed that there was a connection between the messages on the placards and the deceased. Moreover, since a church funeral is an event that naturally brings to mind thoughts about the afterlife, some of respondents' signs — *e.g.*, "God Hates You," "Not Blessed Just Cursed," and "You're Going to Hell" — would have likely been interpreted as referring to God's judgment of the deceased.

Other signs would most naturally have been understood as suggesting — falsely — that Matthew was gay. Homosexuality was the theme of many of the signs. There were signs reading "God Hates Fags," "Semper Fi Fags," "Fags Doom Nations," and "Fag Troops." Another placard depicted two men engaging in anal intercourse. A reasonable bystander seeing those signs would have likely concluded that they were meant to suggest that the deceased was a homosexual.

After the funeral, the Westboro picketers reaffirmed the meaning of their protest. They posted an online account entitled "The Burden of Marine Lance Cpl. Matthew A. Snyder. The Visit of Westboro Baptist Church to Help the Inhabitants of Maryland Connect the Dots!" [Albert Snyder discovered the posting, referred to by the parties as the "epic," during an Internet search for his son's name.] Belying any suggestion that they had simply made general comments about homosexuality, the Catholic Church, and the United States military, the "epic" addressed the Snyder family directly:

> God blessed you, Mr. and Mrs. Snyder, with a resource and his name was Matthew. He was an arrow in your quiver! In thanks to God for the comfort the child could bring you, you had a DUTY to prepare that child to serve the LORD his GOD — PERIOD! You did JUST THE OPPOSITE — you raised him for the devil.
>
> . . . .
>
> Albert and Julie RIPPED that body apart and taught Matthew to defy his Creator, to divorce, and to commit adultery. They taught him how to support the largest pedophile machine in the history of the entire world, the Roman Catholic monstrosity. Every dime they gave the Roman Catholic monster they condemned their own souls. They also, in supporting satanic Catholicism, taught Matthew to be an idolater.
>
> . . . .
>
> Then after all that they sent him to fight for the United States of Sodom, a filthy country that is in lock step with his evil, wicked, and sinful manner of life, putting him in the cross hairs of a God that is so mad He has smoke coming from his nostrils and fire from his mouth! How dumb was that?

In light of this evidence, it is abundantly clear that respondents, going far beyond commentary on matters of public concern, specifically attacked Matthew Snyder because (1) he was a Catholic and (2) he was a member of the United States military. Both Matthew and petitioner were private figures, and this attack was not speech on a matter of public concern. While commentary on the Catholic Church or the United States military constitutes speech on matters of public concern, speech regarding Matthew Snyder's purely private conduct does not.

Justice Breyer provides an apt analogy to a case in which the First Amendment would permit recovery in tort for a verbal attack:

> [S]uppose that A were physically to assault B, knowing that the assault (being newsworthy) would provide A with an opportunity to transmit to the public his views on a matter of public concern. The constitutionally protected nature of the end would not shield A's use of unlawful, unprotected means. And in some circumstances the use of certain words as means would be similarly unprotected.

This captures what respondents did in this case. Indeed, this is the strategy that they have routinely employed — and that they will now continue to employ — inflicting severe and lasting emotional injury on an ever growing list of innocent victims.

IV

The Court concludes that respondents' speech was protected by the First Amendment for essentially three reasons, but none is sound.

First — and most important — the Court finds that "the overall thrust and dominant theme of [their] demonstration spoke to" broad public issues. As I have attempted to show, this portrayal is quite inaccurate; respondents' attack on Matthew was of central importance. But in any event, I fail to see why actionable speech should be immunized simply because it is interspersed with speech that is protected. The First Amendment allows recovery for defamatory statements that are interspersed with nondefamatory statements on matters of public concern, and there is no good reason why respondents' attack on Matthew Snyder and his family should be treated differently.

Second, the Court suggests that respondents' personal attack on Matthew Snyder is entitled to First Amendment protection because it was not motivated by a private grudge, but I see no basis for the strange distinction that the Court appears to draw. Respondents' motivation — "to increase publicity for its views," — did not transform their statements attacking the character of a private figure into statements that made a contribution to debate on matters of public concern. Nor did their publicity-seeking motivation soften the sting of their attack. And as far as culpability is concerned, one might well think that wounding statements uttered in the heat of a private feud are less, not more, blameworthy than similar statements made as part of a cold and calculated strategy to slash a stranger as a means of attracting public attention.

Third, the Court finds it significant that respondents' protest occurred on a public street, but this fact alone should not be enough to preclude IIED liability. To be sure, statements made on a public street may be less likely to satisfy the elements of the IIED tort than statements made on private property, but there is no reason why a public street in close proximity to the scene of a funeral should be regarded as a free-fire zone in which otherwise actionable verbal attacks are shielded from liability. If the First Amendment permits the States to protect their residents from the harm inflicted by such attacks — and the Court does not hold otherwise — then the location of the tort should not be dispositive. A physical assault may occur without trespassing; it is no defense that the perpetrator had "the right to be where [he was]." And the same should be true with respect to unprotected speech. Neither classic "fighting words" nor defamatory statements are immunized when they occur in a public place, and there is no good reason to treat a verbal assault based on the conduct or character of a private figure like Matthew Snyder any differently. . . .

[Funerals] are unique events at which special protection against emotional assaults is in order. At funerals, the emotional well-being of bereaved relatives is particularly vulnerable. Exploitation of a funeral for the purpose of attracting public attention . . . may permanently stain [relatives'] memories of the final moments before a loved one is laid to rest. Allowing family members to have a few hours of peace without harassment does not undermine public debate. I would therefore hold that, in this setting, the First Amendment permits a private figure to recover for the intentional infliction of emotional distress caused by speech on a matter of private concern. . . .

VI

Respondents' outrageous conduct caused petitioner great injury, and the Court now compounds that injury by depriving petitioner of a judgment that acknowledges the wrong he suffered.

In order to have a society in which public issues can be openly and vigorously debated, it is not necessary to allow the brutalization of innocent victims like petitioner. I therefore respectfully dissent.

NOTE: INTENTIONAL INFLICTION OF EMOTIONAL DISTRESS AND THE FIRST AMENDMENT

1.   As Justice Alito notes, a few weeks after the funeral of Matthew Snyder, one of the picketers posted a message on the Westboro Baptist Church Web site entitled "The Burden of Marine Lance Cpl. Matthew A. Snyder. The Visit of Westboro Baptist Church to Help the Inhabitants of Maryland Connect the Dots!" The message (referred to as the "epic") addressed the Snyder family directly. (See the extracts in the dissenting opinion.)

The majority, in holding that the church members were shielded from tort liability by the First Amendment, refused to consider the "epic" because it was not discussed in Snyder's petition for certiorari. Justice Alito responded by saying that the "epic" was "not a distinct claim but a piece of evidence that the jury considered in imposing liability for the claims now before this Court. The protest and the epic are parts of a single course of conduct that the jury found to constitute intentional infliction of emotional distress."

Suppose that the jury handed down a verdict finding Westboro liable for intentional infliction of emotional distress (IIED) based on the "epic," and that the validity of the verdict was squarely presented to the Supreme Court. Would that verdict withstand scrutiny under the First Amendment?

2. As Justice Alito noted (in an omitted passage), the Fourth Circuit, in reversing the verdict in the actual case, "appears to have concluded that the First Amendment does not permit an IIED plaintiff to recover for speech that cannot reasonably be interpreted as stating actual facts about an individual." The Fourth Circuit relied in part on *Hustler*. Is that an accurate reading of the *Hustler* opinion?

3. Although *Hustler* was the Supreme Court's only prior decision on an IIED claim, the Court devotes surprisingly little attention to it. What is the relationship between the two decisions? Are there any IIED claims that would be barred by *Hustler* but not by *Snyder*?

PROBLEM: A "CYBERSTALKING" PROSECUTION

In recent years there has been much concern about "cyberbullying" and "cyberstalking." The State of Oceana has enacted a law that makes "cyberstalking" a gross misdemeanor. The offense is defined as follows:

(1) A person is guilty of cyberstalking if he or she, with intent to harass, intimidate, torment, or embarrass any other person, and under circumstances not constituting telephone harassment, makes an electronic communication, including e-mail, to such other person or a third party:

(a) Using any lewd, lascivious, indecent, or obscene words, images, or language, or suggesting the commission of any lewd or lascivious act;

(b) Anonymously or repeatedly whether or not conversation occurs; or

(c) Threatening to inflict injury on the person or property of the person called or any member of his or her family or household.

Steven Johnson has been prosecuted under this statute for sending two email messages to members of the city council of Bayport, a city in Oceana. The messages were sent shortly after the election of the first black member of the council, Ralph Smith. The emails were also sent to the local newspaper and to some city officials. The content of the first message was as follows:

As you know, there is a nigger on our city council named Ralph Smith. Our city government must be corrupt to have this porch monkey as an elected official. According to our year 2000 census, coons only make up .49% of our population, and I know I would never vote for one of those spooks. I don't see how a person who is different from 99.51% of our population can properly make decisions for us.

Sincerely,

Bayport Anonymous

Bayport Mayor Rita Harmon responded to the email with a posting on her Facebook page. The posting said: "Recently I received a hateful bigoted message from a cowardly ignorant individual. The message is too vile to quote, but the sender knows who he or she is. I will say only: messages like these have no place in Bayport, and the city will not tolerate this kind of message."

Johnson saw the Facebook posting and sent an email to the mayor, with a copy to everyone who had received the first message, including Smith. This second message said:

> You are a stupid nigger lover, and I never said I hate niggers, but I am just concerned that we would give them any sort of position in our government.

The mayor turned the matter over to the county Sheriff's Department, and the department traced "Bayport Anonymous" to Johnson. The District Attorney then filed the cyberstalking charges.

Johnson has admitted to sending both emails from his computer, but he has moved to dismiss the cyberstalking charges on the ground that the statute violates the First Amendment on its face and as applied to the messages he sent.

How should the court rule on the motion?

PROBLEM: AN OBSESSIVE BLOGGER

Alan Grogan is a graduate of the University of Illiana. Six months ago, he launched a blog centered on James Wilkins, who had just been elected as president of the student government association at the University.

"Welcome to 'James Wilkins Watch,' " Grogan wrote in his inaugural blog post. "This is a site for concerned University of Illiana alumni, students and others who oppose the recent election of James Wilkins — a RADICAL HOMOSEXUAL ACTIVIST, RACIST, ELITIST, & LIAR — as the new head of student government at our beloved University."

Subsequent blog posts — appearing two or three times each week over a period of months — contained numerous attacks, both verbal and pictorial, against Wilkins. These included the following:

- "Wilkins is an outright anti-Christian bigot who openly mocks God, the Bible, and the sanctity of unborn human life."

- Wilkins is "Satan's representative" and "a viciously militant homosexual activist."

- Wilkins suffers a "narcissistic personality," is an "elite pervert" and a "privileged pervert."

- Wilkins harbors a "severe contempt" for others' civil rights and has views "much like Nazi Germany's leaders."

- A picture of Wilkins with "Pervert" written over his face.

- A swastika superimposed over a gay pride flag, with an arrow pointing toward Wilkins.

(This is only a small sample of the posts.)

Wilkins has brought suit against Grogan asserting a variety of state-law tort claims including intentional infliction of emotional distress. The complaint recites a total of 85 particular statements similar to the examples above and asserts that

Grogan's conduct was "beyond all possible bounds of decency," "not for any proper purpose," and "of such a character as to be intolerable in a civilized society." Wilkins seeks compensatory and punitive damages and also an injunction requiring Grogan to cease and desist from posting similar content in the future.

Grogan has moved to dismiss the IIED count on the ground that it is barred by the First Amendment. How should the court rule?

Chapter 3

CONTENT REGULATION: NEW CANDIDATES FOR CATEGORIAL EXCLUSION OR LIMITED PROTECTION

Page 264: *add new section at the end of the chapter:*

D. OTHER CONTENT, OTHER HARMS

UNITED STATES v. STEVENS
130 S. Ct. 1577 (2010)

CHIEF JUSTICE ROBERTS delivered the opinion of the Court.

Congress enacted 18 U.S.C. § 48 to criminalize the commercial creation, sale, or possession of certain depictions of animal cruelty. The statute does not address underlying acts harmful to animals, but only portrayals of such conduct. The question presented is whether the prohibition in the statute is consistent with the freedom of speech guaranteed by the First Amendment.

I

Section 48 establishes a criminal penalty of up to five years in prison for anyone who knowingly "creates, sells, or possesses a depiction of animal cruelty," if done "for commercial gain" in interstate or foreign commerce. § 48(a). A depiction of "animal cruelty" is defined as one "in which a living animal is intentionally maimed, mutilated, tortured, wounded, or killed," if that conduct violates federal or state law where "the creation, sale, or possession takes place." § 48(c)(1). In what is referred to as the "exceptions clause," the law exempts from prohibition any depiction "that has serious religious, political, scientific, educational, journalistic, historical, or artistic value." § 48(b).

The legislative background of § 48 focused primarily on the interstate market for "crush videos." According to the House Committee Report on the bill, such videos feature the intentional torture and killing of helpless animals, including cats, dogs, monkeys, mice, and hamsters. Crush videos often depict women slowly crushing animals to death "with their bare feet or while wearing high heeled shoes," sometimes while "talking to the animals in a kind of dominatrix patter" over "[t]he cries and squeals of the animals, obviously in great pain." Apparently these depictions "appeal to persons with a very specific sexual fetish who find them sexually arousing or otherwise exciting." The acts depicted in crush videos are typically prohibited by the animal cruelty laws enacted by all 50 States and the District of Columbia. But crush videos rarely disclose the participants' identities, inhibiting prosecution of the underlying conduct.

This case, however, involves an application of § 48 to depictions of animal fighting. Dogfighting, for example, is unlawful in all 50 States and the District of Columbia, and has been restricted by federal law since 1976. Respondent Robert J. Stevens ran a business, "Dogs of Velvet and Steel," and an associated Web site, through which he sold videos of pit bulls engaging in dogfights and attacking other animals. Among these videos were Japan Pit Fights and Pick-A-Winna: A Pit Bull Documentary, which include contemporary footage of dogfights in Japan (where such conduct is allegedly legal) as well as footage of American dogfights from the 1960's and 1970's. A third video, Catch Dogs and Country Living, depicts the use of pit bulls to hunt wild boar, as well as a "gruesome" scene of a pit bull attacking a domestic farm pig. On the basis of these videos, Stevens was indicted on three counts of violating § 48.

Stevens moved to dismiss the indictment, arguing that § 48 is facially invalid under the First Amendment. The District Court denied the motion. It held that the depictions subject to § 48, like obscenity or child pornography, are categorically unprotected by the First Amendment. It went on to hold that § 48 is not substantially overbroad, because the exceptions clause sufficiently narrows the statute to constitutional applications. The jury convicted Stevens on all counts, and the District Court sentenced him to three concurrent sentences of 37 months' imprisonment, followed by three years of supervised release.

The en banc Third Circuit, over a three-judge dissent, declared § 48 facially unconstitutional and vacated Stevens's conviction. The Court of Appeals first held that § 48 regulates speech that is protected by the First Amendment. The Court declined to recognize a new category of unprotected speech for depictions of animal cruelty, and rejected the Government's analogy between animal cruelty depictions and child pornography.

The Court of Appeals then held that § 48 could not survive strict scrutiny as a content-based regulation of protected speech. It found that the statute lacked a compelling government interest and was neither narrowly tailored to preventing animal cruelty nor the least restrictive means of doing so. It therefore held § 48 facially invalid.

In an extended footnote, the Third Circuit noted that § 48 "might also be unconstitutionally overbroad," because it "potentially covers a great deal of constitutionally protected speech" and "sweeps [too] widely" to be limited only by prosecutorial discretion. But the Court of Appeals declined to rest its analysis on this ground.

We granted certiorari.

II

The Government's primary submission is that § 48 necessarily complies with the Constitution because the banned depictions of animal cruelty, as a class, are categorically unprotected by the First Amendment. We disagree.

The First Amendment provides that "Congress shall make no law . . . abridging the freedom of speech." "[A]s a general matter, the First Amendment means that government has no power to restrict expression because of its message, its ideas, its subject matter, or its content." *Ashcroft v. American Civil Liberties Union* (2002) [Casebook p. 624]. Section 48 explicitly regulates expression based on content: The statute restricts "visual [and] auditory depiction[s]," such as photographs, videos, or sound recordings, depending on whether they depict conduct in which a living animal is intentionally harmed. As such, § 48 is " 'presumptively invalid,' and the Government bears the burden to rebut that presumption." *United States v. Playboy Entertainment Group, Inc.*, 529 U.S. 803, 817 (2000) (quoting *R.A.V. v. St. Paul* (1992) [Casebook p. 630]).

"From 1791 to the present," however, the First Amendment has "permitted restrictions upon the content of speech in a few limited areas," and has never "include[d] a freedom to disregard these traditional limitations." *R.A.V.* These "historic and traditional categories long familiar to the bar," *Simon & Schuster, Inc. v. Members of N.Y. State Crime Victims Bd.* (1991) [Casebook p. 446] (Kennedy, J., concurring in judgment) — including obscenity, *Roth v. United States* (1957) [Casebook p. 141], defamation, *Beauharnais v. Illinois* (1952) [Casebook p. 83], fraud, *Virginia Bd. of Pharmacy v. Virginia Citizens Consumer Council, Inc.* (1976), incitement, *Brandenburg v. Ohio* (1969) [Casebook p. 52], and speech integral to criminal conduct, *Giboney v. Empire Storage & Ice Co.* (1949) [Casebook p. 194] — are "well-defined and narrowly limited classes of speech, the prevention and punishment of which have never been thought to raise any Constitutional problem." *Chaplinsky v. New Hampshire* (1942) [Casebook p. 69].

The Government argues that "depictions of animal cruelty" should be added to the list. It contends that depictions of "illegal acts of animal cruelty" that are "made, sold, or possessed for commercial gain" necessarily "lack expressive value," and may accordingly "be regulated as *unprotected* speech." Brief for United States 10 (emphasis added). The claim is not just that Congress may regulate depictions of animal cruelty subject to the First Amendment, but that these depictions are outside the reach of that Amendment altogether — that they fall into a "First Amendment Free Zone." *Board of Airport Comm'rs of Los Angeles v. Jews for Jesus, Inc.* (1987) [Casebook p. 311].

As the Government notes, the prohibition of animal cruelty itself has a long history in American law, starting with the early settlement of the Colonies. But we are unaware of any similar tradition excluding *depictions* of animal cruelty from "the freedom of speech" codified in the First Amendment, and the Government points us to none.

The Government contends that "historical evidence" about the reach of the First Amendment is not "a necessary prerequisite for regulation today," and that categories of speech may be exempted from the First Amendment's protection without any long-settled tradition of subjecting that speech to regulation. Instead, the Government points to Congress's "legislative judgment that . . . depictions of animals being intentionally tortured and killed [are] of such minimal redeeming value as to render [them] unworthy of First Amendment protection," and asks the Court to uphold the ban on the same basis. The Government thus proposes that a claim of categorical exclusion should be considered under a simple balancing test: "Whether a given category of speech enjoys First Amendment protection depends upon a categorical balancing of the value of the speech against its societal costs." Brief for United States 8.

As a free-floating test for First Amendment coverage, that sentence is startling and dangerous. The First Amendment's guarantee of free speech does not extend only to categories of speech that survive an ad hoc balancing of relative social costs and benefits. The First Amendment itself reflects a judgment by the American people that the benefits of its restrictions on the Government outweigh the costs. Our Constitution forecloses any attempt to revise that judgment simply on the basis that some speech is not worth it. The Constitution is not a document "prescribing limits, and declaring that those limits may be passed at pleasure." *Marbury v. Madison*, 1 Cranch 137, 178 (1803).

To be fair to the Government, its view did not emerge from a vacuum. As the Government correctly notes, this Court has often *described* historically unprotected categories of speech as being " 'of such slight social value as a step to truth that any benefit that may be derived from them is clearly outweighed by the social interest in order and morality.' " *R.A.V.* (quoting *Chaplinsky*). In *New York v. Ferber* (1982), we noted that within these categories of unprotected speech, "the evil to be restricted so overwhelmingly outweighs the expressive interests, if any, at stake, that no process of case-by-case adjudication is required," because "the balance of competing interests is clearly struck." The Government derives its proposed test from these descriptions in our precedents.

But such descriptions are just that — descriptive. They do not set forth a test that may be applied as a general matter to permit the Government to imprison any speaker so long as his speech is deemed valueless or unnecessary, or so long as an ad hoc calculus of costs and benefits tilts in a statute's favor.

When we have identified categories of speech as fully outside the protection of the First Amendment, it has not been on the basis of a simple cost-benefit analysis. In *Ferber*, for example, we classified child pornography as such a category. We noted that the State of New York had a compelling interest in protecting children from abuse, and that the value of using children in these works (as opposed to simulated conduct or adult actors) was *de minimis*. But our decision did not rest on this "balance of competing interests" alone. We made clear that *Ferber* presented a special case: The market for child pornography was "intrinsically related" to the underlying abuse, and was therefore "an integral part of the production of such materials, an activity illegal throughout the Nation." As we noted, " '[i]t rarely has been suggested that the constitutional freedom for speech and press extends its immunity to speech or writing used as an integral part of conduct in violation of a valid criminal statute.' " *Ferber* (quoting *Giboney*). *Ferber* thus grounded its analysis in a previously recognized, long-established category of unprotected speech, and our subsequent decisions have shared this understanding. See *Osborne v. Ohio* (1990) (describing *Ferber* as finding "persuasive" the argument that the advertising and sale of child pornography was "an integral part" of its unlawful production (internal quotation marks omitted)); *Ashcroft v. Free Speech Coalition* (2002) (noting that distribution and sale "were intrinsically related to the sexual abuse of children," giving the speech at issue "a proximate link to the crime from which it came").

Our decisions in *Ferber* and other cases cannot be taken as establishing a freewheeling authority to declare new categories of speech outside the scope of the First Amendment. Maybe there are some categories of speech that have been historically unprotected, but have not yet been specifically identified or discussed as such in our case law. But if so, there is no evidence that "depictions of animal cruelty" is among them. We need not foreclose the future recognition of such additional categories to reject the Government's highly manipulable balancing test as a means of identifying them.

III

Because we decline to carve out from the First Amendment any novel exception for § 48, we review Stevens's First Amendment challenge under our existing doctrine.

A

Stevens challenged § 48 on its face, arguing that any conviction secured under the statute would be unconstitutional. The court below decided the case on that basis, and we granted the Solicitor General's petition for certiorari to determine "whether 18 U.S.C. 48 is facially invalid under the Free Speech Clause of the First Amendment."

To succeed in a typical facial attack, Stevens would have to establish "that no set of circumstances exists under which [§ 48] would be valid," or that the statute lacks any "plainly legitimate sweep." . . . Here the Government asserts that Stevens cannot prevail because § 48 is plainly legitimate as applied to crush videos and animal fighting depictions. Deciding this case through a traditional facial analysis would require us to resolve whether these applications of § 48 are in fact consistent with the Constitution.

In the First Amendment context, however, this Court recognizes "a second type of facial challenge," whereby a law may be invalidated as overbroad if "a substantial number of its applications are unconstitutional, judged in relation to the statute's plainly legitimate sweep." *Washington State Grange v. Washington State Republican Party*, 552 U.S. 442 (2008). Stevens argues that § 48 applies to common depictions of ordinary and lawful activities, and that these depictions constitute the vast majority of materials subject to the statute. The Government makes no effort to defend such a broad ban as constitutional. Instead, the Government's entire defense of § 48 rests on interpreting the statute as narrowly limited to specific types of "extreme" material. As the parties have presented the issue, therefore, the constitutionality of § 48 hinges on how broadly it is construed. It is to that question that we now turn.

B

As we explained two Terms ago, "[t]he first step in overbreadth analysis is to construe the challenged statute; it is impossible to determine whether a statute reaches too far without first knowing what the statute covers." *United States v.*

Williams (2008). Because § 48 is a federal statute, there is no need to defer to a state court's authority to interpret its own law.

We read § 48 to create a criminal prohibition of alarming breadth. To begin with, the text of the statute's ban on a "depiction of animal cruelty" nowhere requires that the depicted conduct be cruel. That text applies to "any . . . depiction" in which "a living animal is intentionally maimed, mutilated, tortured, wounded, or killed." § 48(c)(1). "[M]aimed, mutilated, [and] tortured" convey cruelty, but "wounded" or "killed" do not suggest any such limitation.

The Government contends that the terms in the definition should be read to require the additional element of "accompanying acts of cruelty." (The dissent hinges on the same assumption.) The Government bases this argument on the definiendum, "depiction of animal cruelty," and on " 'the commonsense canon of *noscitur a sociis.'* " As that canon recognizes, an ambiguous term may be "given more precise content by the neighboring words with which it is associated." Likewise, an unclear definitional phrase may take meaning from the term to be defined.

But the phrase "wounded . . . or killed" at issue here contains little ambiguity. The Government's opening brief properly applies the ordinary meaning of these words, stating for example that to " 'kill' is 'to deprive of life.' " We agree that "wounded" and "killed" should be read according to their ordinary meaning. Nothing about that meaning requires cruelty.

While not requiring cruelty, § 48 does require that the depicted conduct be "illegal." But this requirement does not limit § 48 along the lines the Government suggests. There are myriad federal and state laws concerning the proper treatment of animals, but many of them are not designed to guard against animal cruelty. Protections of endangered species, for example, restrict even the humane "wound[ing] or kill[ing]" of "living animal[s]." § 48(c)(1). Livestock regulations are often designed to protect the health of human beings, and hunting and fishing rules (seasons, licensure, bag limits, weight requirements) can be designed to raise revenue, preserve animal populations, or prevent accidents. The text of § 48(c) draws no distinction based on the reason the intentional killing of an animal is made illegal, and includes, for example, the humane slaughter of a stolen cow.

What is more, the application of § 48 to depictions of illegal conduct extends to conduct that is illegal in only a single jurisdiction. Under subsection (c)(1), the depicted conduct need only be illegal in "the State in which the creation, sale, or possession takes place, regardless of whether the . . . wounding . . . or killing took place in [that] State." A depiction of entirely lawful conduct runs afoul of the ban if that depiction later finds its way into another State where the same conduct is unlawful. This provision greatly expands the scope of § 48, because although there may be "a broad societal consensus" against cruelty to animals, there is substantial disagreement on what types of conduct are properly regarded as cruel. Both views about cruelty to animals and regulations having no connection to cruelty vary widely from place to place.

In the District of Columbia, for example, all hunting is unlawful. Other jurisdictions permit or encourage hunting, and there is an enormous national market for hunting-related depictions in which a living animal is intentionally killed. Hunting periodicals have circulations in the hundreds of thousands or millions, and hunting television programs, videos, and Web sites are equally popular. The demand for hunting depictions exceeds the estimated demand for crush videos or animal fighting depictions by several orders of magnitude. Nonetheless, because the statute allows each jurisdiction to export its laws to the rest of the country, § 48(a) extends to *any* magazine or video depicting lawful hunting, so long as that depiction is sold within the Nation's Capital.

Those seeking to comply with the law thus face a bewildering maze of regulations from at least 56 separate jurisdictions. [For example, some] States permit hunting with crossbows, while others forbid it, or restrict it only to the disabled. . . .

The disagreements among the States — and the "commonwealth[s], territor[ies], or possession[s] of the United States" — extend well beyond hunting. State agricultural regulations permit different methods of livestock slaughter in different places or as applied to different animals. . . . Even cockfighting, long considered immoral in much of America, is legal in Puerto Rico and was legal in Louisiana until 2008. An otherwise-lawful image of any of these practices, if sold or possessed for commercial gain within a State that happens to forbid the practice, falls within the prohibition of § 48(a).

C

The only thing standing between defendants who sell such depictions and five years in federal prison — other than the mercy of a prosecutor — is the statute's exceptions clause. Subsection (b) exempts from prohibition "any depiction that has serious religious, political, scientific, educational, journalistic, historical, or artistic value." The Government argues that this clause substantially narrows the statute's reach: News reports about animal cruelty have "journalistic" value; pictures of bullfights in Spain have "historical" value; and instructional hunting videos have "educational" value. Thus, the Government argues, § 48 reaches only crush videos, depictions of animal fighting (other than Spanish bullfighting), and perhaps other depictions of "extreme acts of animal cruelty."

The Government's attempt to narrow the statutory ban, however, requires an unrealistically broad reading of the exceptions clause. As the Government reads the clause, any material with "redeeming societal value," " 'at least some minimal value,' " or anything more than "scant social value," is excluded under § 48(b). But the text says "serious" value, and "serious" should be taken seriously. We decline the Government's invitation — advanced for the first time in this Court — to regard as "serious" anything that is not "scant." (Or, as the dissent puts it, " 'trifling.' ") As the Government recognized below, "serious" ordinarily means a good bit more. The District Court's jury instructions required value that is "significant and of great import," and the Government defended these instructions as properly relying on "a commonly accepted meaning of the word 'serious.' "

Quite apart from the requirement of "serious" value in § 48(b), the excepted speech must also fall within one of the enumerated categories. Much speech does not. Most hunting videos, for example, are not obviously instructional in nature, except in the sense that all life is a lesson. According to Safari Club International and the Congressional Sportsmen's Foundation, many popular videos "have primarily entertainment value" and are designed to "entertai[n] the viewer, marke[t] hunting equipment, or increas[e] the hunting community." . . . The Government offers no principled explanation why these depictions of hunting or depictions of Spanish bullfights would be *inherently* valuable while those of Japanese dogfights are not. The dissent contends that hunting depictions must have serious value because hunting has serious value, in a way that dogfights presumably do not. But § 48(b) addresses the value of the *depictions*, not of the underlying activity. There is simply no adequate reading of the exceptions clause that results in the statute's banning only the depictions the Government would like to ban.

The Government explains that the language of § 48(b) was largely drawn from our opinion in *Miller v. California* (1973) [Casebook p. 155], which excepted from its definition of obscenity any material with "serious literary, artistic, political, or scientific value." According to the Government, this incorporation of the *Miller* standard into § 48 is therefore surely enough to answer any First Amendment objection.

In *Miller* we held that "serious" value shields depictions of sex from regulation as obscenity. Limiting *Miller*'s exception to "serious" value ensured that " '[a] quotation from Voltaire in the flyleaf of a book [would] not constitutionally redeem an otherwise obscene publication.' " We did not, however, determine that serious value could be used as a general precondition to protecting *other* types of speech in the first place. *Most* of what we say to one another lacks "religious, political, scientific, educational, journalistic, historical, or artistic value" (let alone serious value), but it is still sheltered from government regulation. Even "[w]holly neutral futilities . . . come under the protection of free speech as fully as do Keats' poems or Donne's sermons." *Winters v. New York* (1948) [Casebook p. 149] (Frankfurter, J., dissenting).

Thus, the protection of the First Amendment presumptively extends to many forms of speech that do not qualify for the serious-value exception of § 48(b), but nonetheless fall within the broad reach of § 48(c).

D

Not to worry, the Government says: The Executive Branch construes § 48 to reach only "extreme" cruelty, and it "neither has brought nor will bring a prosecution for anything less." The Government hits this theme hard, invoking its prosecutorial discretion several times. But the First Amendment protects against the Government; it does not leave us at the mercy of *noblesse oblige*. We would not uphold an unconstitutional statute merely because the Government promised to use it responsibly.

This prosecution is itself evidence of the danger in putting faith in government representations of prosecutorial restraint. When this legislation was enacted, the Executive Branch announced that it would interpret § 48 as covering only depictions "of wanton cruelty to animals designed to appeal to a prurient interest in sex." See Statement by President William J. Clinton upon Signing H.R. 1887 (Dec. 9, 1999). No one suggests that the videos in this case fit that description. The Government's assurance that it will apply § 48 far more restrictively than its language provides is pertinent only as an implicit acknowledgment of the potential constitutional problems with a more natural reading.

Nor can we rely upon the canon of construction that "ambiguous statutory language [should] be construed to avoid serious constitutional doubts." . . . To read § 48 as the Government desires requires rewriting, not just reinterpretation.

*   *   *

Our construction of § 48 decides the constitutional question; the Government makes no effort to defend the constitutionality of § 48 as applied beyond crush videos and depictions of animal fighting. It argues that those particular depictions are intrinsically related to criminal conduct or are analogous to obscenity (if not themselves obscene), and that the ban on such speech is narrowly tailored to reinforce restrictions on the underlying conduct, prevent additional crime arising from the depictions, or safeguard public mores. But the Government nowhere attempts to extend these arguments to depictions of any other activities — depictions that are presumptively protected by the First Amendment but that remain subject to the criminal sanctions of § 48.

Nor does the Government seriously contest that the presumptively impermissible applications of § 48 (properly construed) far outnumber any permissible ones. However "growing" and "lucrative" the markets for crush videos and dogfighting depictions might be, they are dwarfed by the market for other depictions, such as hunting magazines and videos, that we have determined to be within the scope of § 48. We therefore need not and do not decide whether a statute limited to crush videos or other depictions of extreme animal cruelty would be constitutional. We hold only that § 48 is not so limited but is instead substantially overbroad, and therefore invalid under the First Amendment.

The judgment of the United States Court of Appeals for the Third Circuit is affirmed.

JUSTICE ALITO, dissenting.

The Court strikes down in its entirety a valuable statute, 18 U.S.C. § 48, that was enacted not to suppress speech, but to prevent horrific acts of animal cruelty — in particular, the creation and commercial exploitation of "crush videos," a form of depraved entertainment that has no social value. The Court's approach, which has the practical effect of legalizing the sale of such videos and is thus likely to spur a resumption of their production, is unwarranted. Respondent was convicted under § 48 for selling videos depicting dogfights. On appeal, he argued, among other things, that § 48 is unconstitutional as applied to the facts of this case, and he highlighted features of those videos that might distinguish them from other dogfight videos brought to our attention. The Court of Appeals — incorrectly, in my view — declined to decide whether § 48 is unconstitutional as applied to respondent's videos and instead reached out to hold that the statute is facially invalid.

Today's decision does not endorse the Court of Appeals' reasoning, but it nevertheless strikes down § 48 using what has been aptly termed the "strong medicine" of the overbreadth doctrine.

Instead of applying the doctrine of overbreadth, I would vacate the decision below and instruct the Court of Appeals on remand to decide whether the videos that respondent sold are constitutionally protected. If the question of overbreadth is to be decided, however, I do not think the present record supports the Court's conclusion that § 48 bans a substantial quantity of protected speech.

I

. . . The "strong medicine" of overbreadth invalidation need not and generally should not be administered when the statute under attack is unconstitutional as applied to the challenger before the court. . . .

I see no reason to depart here from the generally preferred procedure of considering the question of overbreadth only as a last resort. Because the Court has addressed the overbreadth question, however, I will explain why I do not think that the record supports the conclusion that § 48, when properly interpreted, is overly broad. . . .

III

In holding that § 48 violates the overbreadth rule, the Court declines to decide whether, as the Government maintains, § 48 is constitutional as applied to two broad categories of depictions that exist in the real world: crush videos and depictions of deadly animal fights. Instead, the Court tacitly assumes for the sake of argument that § 48 is valid as applied to these depictions, but the Court concludes that § 48 reaches too much protected speech to survive. The Court relies primarily on depictions of hunters killing or wounding game and depictions of animals being slaughtered for food. I address the Court's examples below.

A

I turn first to depictions of hunting. . . . "When a federal court is dealing with a federal statute challenged as overbroad, it should, of course, construe the statute to avoid constitutional problems, if the statute is subject to such a limiting construction."

Applying this canon, I would hold that § 48 does not apply to depictions of hunting. First, because § 48 targets depictions of "animal cruelty," I would interpret that term to apply only to depictions involving acts of animal cruelty as defined by applicable state or federal law, not to depictions of acts that happen to be illegal for reasons having nothing to do with the prevention of animal cruelty. Virtually all state laws prohibiting animal cruelty either expressly define the term "animal" to exclude wildlife or else specifically exempt lawful hunting activities, so the statutory prohibition set forth in § 48(a) may reasonably be interpreted not to reach most if not all hunting depictions.

Second, even if the hunting of wild animals were otherwise covered by § 48(a), I would hold that hunting depictions fall within the exception in § 48(b) for depictions that have "serious" (i.e., not "trifling") "scientific," "educational," or "historical" value. . . . [It] is widely thought that hunting has "scientific" value in that it promotes conservation, "historical" value in that it provides a link to past times when hunting played a critical role in daily life, and "educational" value in that it furthers the understanding and appreciation of nature and our country's past and instills valuable character traits. And if hunting itself is widely thought to serve these values, then it takes but a small additional step to conclude that depictions of hunting make a non-trivial contribution to the exchange of ideas. Accordingly, I would hold that hunting depictions fall comfortably within the exception set out in § 48(b).

I do not have the slightest doubt that Congress, in enacting § 48, had no intention of restricting the creation, sale, or possession of depictions of hunting. . . .

For these reasons, I am convinced that § 48 has no application to depictions of hunting. But even if § 48 did impermissibly reach the sale or possession of depictions of hunting in a few unusual situations (for example, the sale in Oregon of a depiction of hunting with a crossbow in Virginia or the sale in Washington State of the hunting of a sharp-tailed grouse in Idaho), those isolated applications would hardly show that § 48 bans a substantial amount of protected speech.

B

Although the Court's overbreadth analysis rests primarily on the proposition that § 48 substantially restricts the sale and possession of hunting depictions, the Court cites a few additional examples, including depictions of methods of slaughter and the docking of the tails of dairy cows.

Such examples do not show that the statute is substantially overbroad, for two reasons. First, as explained above, § 48 can reasonably be construed to apply only to depictions involving acts of animal cruelty as defined by applicable state or federal law, and anti-cruelty laws do not ban the sorts of acts depicted in the Court's hypotheticals. . . .

Second, nothing in the record suggests that any one has ever created, sold, or possessed for sale a depiction of the slaughter of food animals or of the docking of the tails of dairy cows that would not easily qualify under the exception set out in § 48(b). . . .

The Court notes, finally, that cockfighting, which is illegal in all States, is still legal in Puerto Rico, and I take the Court's point to be that it would be impermissible to ban the creation, sale, or possession in Puerto Rico of a depiction of a cockfight that was legally staged in Puerto Rico. But assuming for the sake of argument that this is correct, this veritable sliver of unconstitutionality would not be enough to justify striking down § 48 *in toto*.

In sum, we have a duty to interpret § 48 so as to avoid serious constitutional concerns, and § 48 may reasonably be construed not to reach almost all, if not all, of the depictions that the Court finds constitutionally protected. Thus, § 48 does not appear to have a large number of unconstitutional applications. Invalidation for overbreadth is appropriate only if the challenged statute suffers from *substantial* overbreadth-judged not just in absolute terms, but in relation to the statute's "plainly legitimate sweep." *United States v. Williams* (2008). As I explain in the following Part, § 48 has a substantial core of constitutionally permissible applications.

IV

A

1

As the Court of Appeals recognized, "the primary conduct that Congress sought to address through its passage [of § 48] was the creation, sale, or possession of 'crush videos.' " A sample crush video, which has been lodged with the Clerk, records the following event:

> [A] kitten, secured to the ground, watches and shrieks in pain as a woman thrusts her high-heeled shoe into its body, slams her heel into the kitten's eye socket and mouth loudly fracturing its skull, and stomps repeatedly on the animal's head. The kitten hemorrhages blood, screams blindly in pain, and is ultimately left dead in a moist pile of blood-soaked hair and bone.

Brief for Humane Society of United States as *Amicus Curiae* 2 (hereinafter Humane Society Brief).

It is undisputed that the *conduct* depicted in crush videos may constitutionally be prohibited. All 50 States and the District of Columbia have enacted statutes prohibiting animal cruelty. But before the enactment of § 48, the underlying conduct depicted in crush videos was nearly impossible to prosecute. These videos, which "often appeal to persons with a very specific sexual fetish," were made in secret, generally without a live audience, and "the faces of the women inflicting the torture in the material often were not shown, nor could the location of the place where the cruelty was being inflicted or the date of the activity be ascertained from the depiction." Thus, law enforcement authorities often were not able to identify the parties responsible for the torture. In the rare instances in which it was possible to identify and find the perpetrators, they "often were able to successfully assert as a defense that the State could not prove its jurisdiction over the place where the act occurred or that the actions depicted took place within the time specified in the State statute of limitations."

In light of the practical problems thwarting the prosecution of the creators of crush videos under state animal cruelty laws, Congress concluded that the only effective way of stopping the underlying criminal conduct was to prohibit the commercial exploitation of the videos of that conduct. And Congress' strategy appears to have been vindicated. We are told that "[b]y 2007, sponsors of § 48 declared the crush video industry dead. Even overseas Websites shut down in the wake of § 48. Now, after the Third Circuit's decision [facially invalidating the statute], crush videos are already back online." Humane Society Brief 5.

2

The First Amendment protects freedom of speech, but it most certainly does not protect violent criminal conduct, even if engaged in for expressive purposes. Crush videos present a highly unusual free speech issue because they are so closely linked with violent criminal conduct. The videos record the commission of violent criminal acts, and it appears that these crimes are committed for the sole purpose of creating the videos. In addition, as noted above, Congress was presented with compelling evidence that the only way of preventing these crimes was to target the sale of the videos. Under these circumstances, I cannot believe that the First Amendment commands Congress to step aside and allow the underlying crimes to continue.

The most relevant of our prior decisions is *Ferber*, which concerned child pornography. The Court there held that child pornography is not protected speech, and I believe that *Ferber*'s reasoning dictates a similar conclusion here.

In *Ferber*, an important factor — I would say the most important factor — was that child pornography involves the commission of a crime that inflicts severe personal injury to the "children who are made to engage in sexual conduct for commercial purposes." The *Ferber* Court repeatedly described the production of child pornography as child "abuse," "molestation," or "exploitation." As later noted in *Ashcroft v. Free Speech Coalition* (2002), in *Ferber* "[t]he production of the work, not its content, was the target of the statute."

Second, *Ferber* emphasized the fact that these underlying crimes could not be effectively combated without targeting the distribution of child pornography. . . .

Third, the *Ferber* Court noted that the value of child pornography "is exceedingly modest, if not *de minimis*," and that any such value was "overwhelmingly outweigh[ed]" by "the evil to be restricted."

All three of these characteristics are shared by § 48, as applied to crush videos. First, the conduct depicted in crush videos is criminal in every State and the District of Columbia. Thus, any crush video made in this country records the actual commission of a criminal act that inflicts severe physical injury and excruciating pain and ultimately results in death. Those who record the underlying criminal acts are likely to be criminally culpable, either as aiders and abettors or conspirators. And in the tight and secretive market for these videos, some who sell the videos or possess them with the intent to make a profit may be similarly culpable. To the extent that § 48 reaches such persons, it surely does not violate the First Amendment.

Second, the criminal acts shown in crush videos cannot be prevented without targeting the conduct prohibited by § 48 — the creation, sale, and possession for sale of depictions of animal torture with the intention of realizing a commercial profit. The evidence presented to Congress posed a stark choice: Either ban the commercial exploitation of crush videos or tolerate a continuation of the criminal acts that they record. Faced with this evidence, Congress reasonably chose to target the lucrative crush video market.

Finally, the harm caused by the underlying crimes vastly outweighs any minimal value that the depictions might conceivably be thought to possess. Section 48 reaches only the actual recording of acts of animal torture; the statute does not apply to verbal descriptions or to simulations. And, unlike the child pornography statute in *Ferber* or its federal counterpart, 18 U.S.C. § 2252, § 48(b) provides an exception for depictions having any "serious religious, political, scientific, educational, journalistic, historical, or artistic value."

It must be acknowledged that § 48 differs from a child pornography law in an important respect: preventing the abuse of children is certainly much more important than preventing the torture of the animals used in crush videos. . . . But while protecting children is unquestionably *more* important than protecting animals, the Government also has a compelling interest in preventing the torture depicted in crush videos.

The animals used in crush videos are living creatures that experience excruciating pain. Our society has long banned such cruelty, which is illegal throughout the country. In *Ferber*, the Court noted that "virtually all of the States and the United States have passed legislation proscribing the production of or otherwise combating 'child pornography,'" and the Court declined to "second-guess [that] legislative judgment." Here, likewise, the Court of Appeals erred in second-guessing the legislative judgment about the importance of preventing cruelty to animals.

Section 48's ban on trafficking in crush videos also helps to enforce the criminal laws and to ensure that criminals do not profit from their crimes. . . . In short, *Ferber* is the case that sheds the most light on the constitutionality of Congress' effort to halt the production of crush videos. Applying the principles set forth in *Ferber*, I would hold that crush videos are not protected by the First Amendment.

B

Application of the *Ferber* framework also supports the constitutionality of § 48 as applied to depictions of brutal animal fights. (For convenience, I will focus on videos of dogfights, which appear to be the most common type of animal fight videos.)

First, such depictions, like crush videos, record the actual commission of a crime involving deadly violence. Dogfights are illegal in every State and the District of Columbia, and under federal law constitute a felony punishable by imprisonment for up to five years.

Second, Congress had an ample basis for concluding that the crimes depicted in these videos cannot be effectively controlled without targeting the videos. Like crush videos and child pornography, dogfight videos are very often produced as part of a "low-profile, clandestine industry," and "the need to market the resulting products requires a visible apparatus of distribution." *Ferber*. In such circumstances, Congress had reasonable grounds for concluding that it would be "difficult, if not impossible, to halt" the underlying exploitation of dogs by pursuing only those who stage the fights.

The commercial trade in videos of dogfights is "an integral part of the production of such materials," *Ferber.* . . . For one thing, some dogfighting videos are made "solely for the purpose of selling the video (and not for a live audience)." Moreover, "[v]ideo documentation is vital to the criminal enterprise because it provides *proof* of a dog's fighting prowess — proof demanded by potential buyers and critical to the underground market." Such recordings may also serve as "'training' videos for other fight organizers." In short, because videos depicting live dogfights are essential to the success of the criminal dogfighting subculture, the commercial sale of such videos helps to fuel the market for, and thus to perpetuate the perpetration of, the criminal conduct depicted in them.

Third, depictions of dogfights that fall within § 48's reach have by definition no appreciable social value. As noted, § 48(b) exempts depictions having any appreciable social value, and thus the mere inclusion of a depiction of a live fight in a larger work that aims at communicating an idea or a message with a modicum of social value would not run afoul of the statute.

Finally, the harm caused by the underlying criminal acts greatly outweighs any trifling value that the depictions might be thought to possess. As the Humane Society explains:

> The abused dogs used in fights endure physical torture and emotional manipulation throughout their lives to predispose them to violence; common tactics include feeding the animals hot peppers and gunpowder, prodding them with sticks, and electrocution. Dogs are conditioned never to give up a fight, even if they will be gravely hurt or killed. As a result, dogfights inflict horrific injuries on the participating animals, including lacerations, ripped ears, puncture wounds and broken bones. Losing dogs are routinely refused treatment, beaten further as "punishment" for the loss, and executed by drowning, hanging, or incineration.

For these dogs, unlike the animals killed in crush videos, the suffering lasts for years rather than minutes. As with crush videos, moreover, the statutory ban on commerce in dogfighting videos is also supported by compelling governmental interests in effectively enforcing the Nation's criminal laws and preventing criminals from profiting from their illegal activities.

In sum, § 48 may validly be applied to at least two broad real-world categories of expression covered by the statute: crush videos and dogfighting videos. Thus, the statute has a substantial core of constitutionally permissible applications. Moreover, for the reasons set forth above, the record does not show that § 48, properly interpreted, bans a substantial amount of protected speech in absolute terms. *A fortiori*, respondent has not met his burden of demonstrating that any impermissible applications of the statute are "substantial" in relation to its "plainly legitimate sweep." *Williams.* Accordingly, I would reject respondent's claim that § 48 is facially unconstitutional under the overbreadth doctrine.

*   *   *

For these reasons, I respectfully dissent.

NOTE: THE IMPLICATIONS OF *STEVENS*

1. The Third Circuit held that § 48 is "facially invalid" under the First Amendment. The Supreme Court affirms, but on the ground that § 48 is "substantially overbroad, and therefore invalid under the First Amendment." What is the difference between the two holdings? (Note that in Part III-A of the opinion the Court distinguishes between "a traditional facial analysis" and "a second type of facial challenge.")

2. In Part II of his opinion, Chief Justice Roberts lists the "historic and traditional" categories of speech where the First Amendment permits restrictions on content. (All of the cases that he cites as exemplifying the categories are set forth in this and the preceding chapters, either as principal cases or as the subject of a Note.) Are there any categories that you would expect to find on the list but that are not there? Are you surprised by any of the cases cited by the Chief Justice?

3. The Chief Justice says that *Chaplinsky*'s oft-quoted description of "historically unprotected categories of speech" is "just that" — a description. And the Court emphatically repudiates the Government's argument that *Chaplinsky* and its progeny provide "a test that may be applied as a general matter" to identify new categories of unprotected speech. Based on pre-*Stevens* precedents, is the Court persuasive in saying that the *Chaplinsky* language did no more than describe the Court's holdings?

4. The majority and the dissent offer sharply divergent readings of *Ferber*. Reread *Ferber*. Who has the better of the argument?

PROBLEM: WRITING A "CRUSH VIDEO" STATUTE

1. Only a few weeks after the decision in *United States v. Stevens*, Rep. Elton Gallegly — the sponsor of the legislation held unconstitutional by the Supreme Court — introduced a bill (H.R. 5092) to replace the existing version of 18 U.S.C. § 48. Under H.R. 5092, the new provision would read as follows:

(a) Prohibition — Whoever knowingly sells or offers to sell an animal crush video in interstate or foreign commerce for commercial gain shall be fined under this title or imprisoned not more than 5 years, or both.

(b) Rule of Construction — Nothing in subsection (a) shall be construed to prohibit the selling or offering to sell a video that depicts hunting.

(c) Definitions — In this section —

(1) the term "animal crush video" means any visual depiction, including any photograph, motion-picture film, video recording, or electronic image, which depicts animals being intentionally crushed, burned, drowned, or impaled, that —

(A) depicts actual conduct in which a living animal is tortured, maimed, or mutilated that violates any criminal prohibition on intentional cruelty under Federal law or the law of the State in which the depiction is sold; and

(B) taken as a whole, does not have religious, political, scientific, educational, journalistic, historical, or artistic value; and

(2) the term "State" means each of the several States, the District of Columbia, the Commonwealth of Puerto Rico, the Virgin Islands, Guam, American Samoa, the Commonwealth of the Northern Mariana Islands, and any other commonwealth, territory, or possession of the United States.

Note the limitations that respond to the decision in *Stevens*. Would the statute be constitutional under the First Amendment?

2. After H.R. 5092 was introduced, the House Judiciary Committee held a hearing on the *Stevens* decision. A few weeks later, Rep. Gallegly introduced a new bill, H.R. 5566. The new bill underwent considerable revision as it moved through the legislative process. Ultimately, an amended version was passed by both Houses and signed into law by the President (Pub. L. 111-394). Section 48 now reads in relevant part as follows:

(a) DEFINITION. — In this section the term "animal crush video" means any photograph, motion-picture film, video or digital recording, or electronic image that —

(1) depicts actual conduct in which 1 or more living non-human mammals, birds, reptiles, or amphibians is intentionally crushed, burned, drowned, suffocated, impaled, or otherwise subjected to serious bodily injury (as defined [elsewhere in Title 18]); and

(2) is obscene.

(b) PROHIBITIONS. —

(1) CREATION OF ANIMAL CRUSH VIDEOS. — It shall be unlawful for any person to knowingly create an animal crush video, if —

(A) the person intends or has reason to know that the animal crush video will be distributed in, or using a means or facility of, interstate or foreign commerce; or

(B) the animal crush video is distributed in, or using a means or facility of, interstate or foreign commerce.

(2) DISTRIBUTION OF ANIMAL CRUSH VIDEOS. — It shall be unlawful for any person to knowingly sell, market, advertise, exchange, or distribute an animal crush video in, or using a means or facility of, interstate or foreign commerce.

(c) EXTRATERRITORIAL APPLICATION. — Subsection (b) shall apply to the knowing sale, marketing, advertising, exchange, distribution, or creation of an animal crush video outside of the United States, if —

(1) the person engaging in such conduct intends or has reason to know that the animal crush video will be transported into the United States or its territories or possessions; or

(2) the animal crush video is transported into the United States or its territories or possessions.

Note the differences between the rewrite of section 48 in H.R. 5092 and in the law as enacted. Was it necessary for the legislation to include all of the limitations contained in P.L. 394?

3. Justice Alito, dissenting in *Stevens*, argued that the original version of § 48 could constitutionally be applied to depictions of brutal animal fights. Would H.R. 5092 have covered such material? Does the newly enacted § 48? Does the Court hold that the depictions described by Justice Alito *are* protected by the First Amendment?

BROWN v. ENTERTAINMENT MERCHANTS ASSOCIATION
2011 U.S. LEXIS 4802 (2011)

JUSTICE SCALIA delivered the opinion of the Court.

We consider whether a California law imposing restrictions on violent video games comports with the First Amendment.

I

California Assembly Bill 1179 (2005) (Act), prohibits the sale or rental of "violent video games" to minors, and requires their packaging to be labeled "18." The Act covers games "in which the range of options available to a player includes killing, maiming, dismembering, or sexually assaulting an image of a human being, if those acts are depicted" in a manner that "[a] reasonable person, considering the game as a whole, would find appeals to a deviant or morbid interest of minors," that is "patently offensive to prevailing standards in the community as to what is suitable for minors," and that "causes the game, as a whole, to lack serious literary, artistic, political, or scientific value for minors." Violation of the Act is punishable by a civil fine of up to $1,000.

Respondents, representing the video-game and software industries, brought a preenforcement challenge to the Act in the United States District Court for the Northern District of California. That court concluded that the Act violated the First Amendment and permanently enjoined its enforcement. The Court of Appeals affirmed, and we granted certiorari.

II

California correctly acknowledges that video games qualify for First Amendment protection. The Free Speech Clause exists principally to protect discourse on public matters, but we have long recognized that it is difficult to distinguish politics from entertainment, and dangerous to try. "Everyone is familiar with instances of propaganda through fiction. What is one man's amusement, teaches another's doctrine." *Winters v. New York* (1948) [Casebook p.

149]. Like the protected books, plays, and movies that preceded them, video games communicate ideas — and even social messages — through many familiar literary devices (such as characters, dialogue, plot, and music) and through features distinctive to the medium (such as the player's interaction with the virtual world). That suffices to confer First Amendment protection. Under our Constitution, "esthetic and moral judgments about art and literature . . . are for the individual to make, not for the Government to decree, even with the mandate or approval of a majority." *United States v. Playboy Entertainment Group, Inc.*, 529 U.S. 803 (2000). And whatever the challenges of applying the Constitution to ever-advancing technology, "the basic principles of freedom of speech and the press, like the First Amendment's command, do not vary" when a new and different medium for communication appears. *Joseph Burstyn, Inc. v. Wilson*, 343 U.S. 495 (1952).

The most basic of those principles is this: "[A]s a general matter, . . . government has no power to restrict expression because of its message, its ideas, its subject matter, or its content." *Ashcroft v. American Civil Liberties Union* (2002) [Casebook p. 171]. There are of course exceptions. " 'From 1791 to the present,' . . . the First Amendment has 'permitted restrictions upon the content of speech in a few limited areas,' and has never 'include[d] a freedom to disregard these traditional limitations.' " *United States v. Stevens* (2010). These limited areas — such as obscenity, *Roth v. United States* (1957) [Casebook p. 141], incitement, *Brandenburg v. Ohio* (1969) [Casebook p. 52], and fighting words, *Chaplinsky v. New Hampshire* (1942) [Casebook p. 69] — represent "well-defined and narrowly limited classes of speech, the prevention and punishment of which have never been thought to raise any Constitutional problem."

Last Term, in *Stevens*, we held that new categories of unprotected speech may not be added to the list by a legislature that concludes certain speech is too harmful to be tolerated. *Stevens* concerned a federal statute purporting to criminalize the creation, sale, or possession of certain depictions of animal cruelty. See 18 U.S.C. § 48 (amended 2010). The statute covered depictions "in which a living animal is intentionally maimed, mutilated, tortured, wounded, or killed" if that harm to the animal was illegal where the "the creation, sale, or possession t[ook] place." A saving clause largely borrowed from our obscenity jurisprudence, see *Miller v. California* (1973) [Casebook p. 155], exempted depictions with "serious religious, political, scientific, educational, journalistic, historical, or artistic value." We held that statute to be an impermissible content-based restriction on speech. There was no American tradition of forbidding the *depiction of* animal cruelty — though States have long had laws against *committing* it.

The Government argued in *Stevens* that lack of a historical warrant did not matter; that it could create new categories of unprotected speech by applying a "simple balancing test" that weighs the value of a particular category of speech against its social costs and then punishes that category of speech if it fails the test. We emphatically rejected that "startling and dangerous" proposition. . . .

That holding controls this case. As in *Stevens*, California has tried to make violent-speech regulation look like obscenity regulation by appending a saving clause required for the latter. That does not suffice. Our cases have been clear that the obscenity exception to the First Amendment does not cover whatever a legislature finds shocking, but only depictions of "sexual conduct," *Miller*. *See also Cohen v. California* (1971); *Roth*.

Stevens was not the first time we have encountered and rejected a State's attempt to shoehorn speech about violence into obscenity. In *Winters*, we considered a New York criminal statute "forbid[ding] the massing of stories of bloodshed and lust in such a way as to incite to crime against the person." The New York Court of Appeals upheld the provision as a law against obscenity. "[T]here can be no more precise test of written indecency or obscenity," it said, "than the continuing and changeable experience of the community as to what types of books are likely to bring about the corruption of public morals or other analogous injury to the public order." That is of course the same expansive view of governmental power to abridge the freedom of speech based on interest-balancing that we rejected in *Stevens*. Our opinion in *Winters*, which concluded that the New York statute failed a heightened vagueness standard applicable to restrictions upon speech entitled to First Amendment protection, made clear that violence is not part of the obscenity that the Constitution permits to be regulated. The speech reached by the statute contained "no indecency or obscenity in any sense heretofore known to the law."

Because speech about violence is not obscene, it is of no consequence that California's statute mimics the New York statute regulating obscenity-for-minors that we upheld in *Ginsberg v. New York* (1968) [Casebook p. 604]. That case approved a prohibition on the sale to minors of *sexual* material that would be obscene from the perspective of a child. We held that the legislature could "adjus[t] the definition of obscenity 'to social realities by permitting the appeal of this type of material to be assessed in terms of the sexual interests . . .' of . . . minors." And because "obscenity is not protected expression," the New York statute could be sustained so long as the legislature's judgment that the proscribed materials were harmful to children "was not irrational."

The California Act is something else entirely. It does not adjust the boundaries of an existing category of unprotected speech to ensure that a definition designed for adults is not uncritically applied to children. California does not argue that it is empowered to prohibit selling offensively violent works *to adults* — and it is wise not to, since that is but a hair's breadth from the argument rejected in *Stevens*. Instead, it wishes to create a wholly new category of content-based regulation that is permissible only for speech directed at children.

That is unprecedented and mistaken. "[M]inors are entitled to a significant measure of First Amendment protection, and only in relatively narrow and well-defined circumstances may government bar public dissemination of protected materials to them." *Erznoznik v. Jacksonville* (1975) [Casebook p. 185]. No doubt a State possesses legitimate power to protect children from harm, *Ginsberg*; *Prince v. Massachusetts*, 321 U.S. 158, 165 (1944), but that does not include a free-floating power to restrict the ideas to which children may be exposed. "Speech that is neither obscene as to youths nor subject to some other legitimate proscription cannot be suppressed solely to protect the young from ideas or images that a legislative body thinks unsuitable for them." *Erznoznik*.

California's argument would fare better if there were a longstanding tradition in this country of specially restricting children's access to depictions of violence, but there is none. Certainly the *books* we give children to read — or read to them when they are younger — contain no shortage of gore. Grimm's Fairy Tales, for example, are grim indeed. As her just deserts for trying to poison Snow White, the wicked queen is made to dance in red hot slippers "till she fell dead on the floor, a sad example of envy and jealousy." THE COMPLETE BROTHERS GRIMM FAIRY TALES (2006 ed.). Cinderella's evil stepsisters have their eyes pecked out by doves. And Hansel and Gretel (children!) kill their captor by baking her in an oven.

High-school reading lists are full of similar fare. Homer's Odysseus blinds Polyphemus the Cyclops by grinding out his eye with a heated stake. The ODYSSEY OF HOMER, Book IX, p. 125 (S. Butcher & A. Lang trans. 1909) ("Even so did we seize the fiery-pointed brand and whirled it round in his eye, and the blood flowed about the heated bar. And the breath of the flame singed his eyelids and brows all about, as the ball of the eye burnt away, and the roots thereof crackled in the flame"). In the *Inferno*, Dante and Virgil watch corrupt politicians struggle to stay submerged beneath a lake of boiling pitch, lest they be skewered by devils above the surface. And Golding's *Lord of the Flies* recounts how a schoolboy called Piggy is savagely murdered *by other children* while marooned on an island.[4]

This is not to say that minors' consumption of violent entertainment has never encountered resistance. In the 1800's, dime novels depicting crime and "penny dreadfuls" (named for their price and content) were blamed in some quarters for juvenile delinquency. When motion pictures came along, they became the villains instead. "The days when the police looked upon dime novels as the most dangerous of textbooks in the school for crime are drawing to a close . . . . They say that the moving picture machine . . . tends even more than did the dime novel to turn the thoughts of the easily influenced to paths which sometimes lead to prison." *Moving Pictures as Helps to Crime*, N.Y. TIMES, Feb. 21, 1909. For a time, our Court did permit broad censorship of movies because of their capacity to be "used for evil," see *Mutual Film Corp. v. Industrial Comm'n of Ohio*, 236 U.S. 230, 242 (1915), but we eventually reversed course, *Joseph Burstyn, Inc.*, 343 U.S. at 502; *see also Erznoznik* (invalidating a drive-in movies restriction designed to protect children). Radio dramas were next, and then came comic books. Many in the late 1940's and early 1950's blamed comic books for fostering a "preoccupation with violence and horror" among the young, leading to a rising juvenile crime rate. But efforts to convince Congress to restrict comic books failed.[5] And, of course, after comic books

---

[4] Justice Alito accuses us of pronouncing that playing violent video games "is not different in 'kind' " from reading violent literature. Well of course it is different in kind, but not in a way that causes the provision and viewing of violent video games, unlike the provision and reading of books, not to be expressive activity and hence not to enjoy First Amendment protection. Reading Dante is unquestionably more cultured and intellectually edifying than playing Mortal Kombat. But these cultural and intellectual differences are not *constitutional* ones. Crudely violent video games, tawdry TV shows, and cheap novels and magazines are no less forms of speech than *The Divine Comedy*, and restrictions upon them must survive strict scrutiny — a question to which we devote our attention in Part III, *infra*. Even if we can see in them "nothing of any possible value to society . . . , they are as much entitled to the protection of free speech as the best of literature." *Winters*.

[5] The crusade against comic books was led by a psychiatrist, Frederic Wertham, who told the Senate

came television and music lyrics.

California claims that video games present special problems because they are "interactive," in that the player participates in the violent action on screen and determines its outcome. The latter feature is nothing new: Since at least the publication of *The Adventures of You: Sugarcane Island* in 1969, young readers of choose-your-own-adventure stories have been able to make decisions that determine the plot by following instructions about which page to turn to. As for the argument that video games enable participation in the violent action, that seems to us more a matter of degree than of kind. As Judge Posner has observed, all literature is interactive. "[T]he better it is, the more interactive. Literature when it is successful draws the reader into the story, makes him identify with the characters, invites him to judge them and quarrel with them, to experience their joys and sufferings as the reader's own."

Justice Alito has done considerable independent research to identify video games in which "the violence is astounding." . . . Justice Alito recounts all these disgusting video games in order to disgust us — but disgust is not a valid basis for restricting expression. And the same is true of Justice Alito's description of those video games he has discovered that have a racial or ethnic motive for their violence — " 'ethnic cleansing' [of] . . . African Americans, Latinos, or Jews." To what end does he relate this? Does it somehow increase the "aggressiveness" that California wishes to suppress? Who knows? But it does arouse the reader's ire, and the reader's desire to put an end to this horrible message. Thus, ironically, Justice Alito's argument highlights the precise danger posed by the California Act: that the *ideas* expressed by speech — whether it be violence, or gore, or racism — and not its objective effects, may be the real reason for governmental proscription.

III

Because the Act imposes a restriction on the content of protected speech, it is invalid unless California can demonstrate that it passes strict scrutiny — that is, unless it is justified by a compelling government interest and is narrowly drawn to serve that interest. *R.A.V. v. St. Paul* (1992) [Casebook p. 630]. The State must specifically identify an "actual problem" in need of solving, *Playboy*, and the curtailment of free speech must be actually necessary to the solution, see *R.A.V.* That is a demanding standard. "It is rare that a regulation restricting speech because of its content will ever be permissible."

California cannot meet that standard. At the outset, it acknowledges that it cannot show a direct causal link between violent video games and harm to minors. Rather, relying upon our decision in *Turner Broadcasting System, Inc. v. FCC* (1994) [Casebook p. 593], the State claims that it need not produce such proof because the legislature can make a predictive judgment that such a link exists,

---

Judiciary Committee that "as long as the crime comic books industry exists in its present forms there are no secure homes." Wertham's objections extended even to Superman comics, which he described as "particularly injurious to the ethical development of children." Wertham's crusade did convince the New York Legislature to pass a ban on the sale of certain comic books to minors, but it was vetoed by Governor Thomas Dewey on the ground that it was unconstitutional given our opinion in *Winters*.

based on competing psychological studies. But reliance on *Turner Broadcasting* is misplaced. That decision applied *intermediate scrutiny* to a content-neutral regulation. California's burden is much higher, and because it bears the risk of uncertainty, ambiguous proof will not suffice.

The State's evidence is not compelling. California relies primarily on the research of Dr. Craig Anderson and a few other research psychologists whose studies purport to show a connection between exposure to violent video games and harmful effects on children. These studies have been rejected by every court to consider them, and with good reason: They do not prove that violent video games cause minors to act aggressively (which would at least be a beginning). Instead, "[n]early all of the research is based on correlation, not evidence of causation, and most of the studies suffer from significant, admitted flaws in methodology." They show at best some correlation between exposure to violent entertainment and minuscule real-world effects, such as children's feeling more aggressive or making louder noises in the few minutes after playing a violent game than after playing a non-violent game.[7]

Even taking for granted Dr. Anderson's conclusions that violent video games produce some effect on children's feelings of aggression, those effects are both small and indistinguishable from effects produced by other media. In his testimony in a similar lawsuit, Dr. Anderson admitted that the "effect sizes" of children's exposure to violent video games are "about the same" as that produced by their exposure to violence on television. And he admits that the same effects have been found when children watch cartoons starring Bugs Bunny or the Road Runner, or when they play video games like Sonic the Hedgehog that are rated "E" (appropriate for all ages), or even when they "vie[w] a picture of a gun."

Of course, California has (wisely) declined to restrict Saturday morning cartoons, the sale of games rated for young children, or the distribution of pictures of guns. The consequence is that its regulation is wildly underinclusive when judged against its asserted justification, which in our view is alone enough to defeat it. Underinclusiveness raises serious doubts about whether the government is in fact pursuing the interest it invokes, rather than disfavoring a particular speaker or viewpoint. See *City of Ladue v. Gilleo* (1994) [Casebook p. 400]. Here, California has singled out the purveyors of video games for disfavored treatment — at least when compared to booksellers, cartoonists, and movie producers — and has given no persuasive reason why.

The Act is also seriously underinclusive in another respect — and a respect that renders irrelevant the contentions of the concurrence and the dissents that video games are qualitatively different from other portrayals of violence. The California Legislature is perfectly willing to leave this dangerous, mind-altering material in the hands of children so long as one parent (or even an aunt or uncle) says it's OK. And there are not even any requirements as to how this parental or avuncular relationship is to be verified; apparently the child's or putative parent's, aunt's, or

---

[7] One study, for example, found that children who had just finished playing violent video games were more likely to fill in the blank letter in "explo_e" with a "d" (so that it reads "explode") than with an "r" ("explore"). The prevention of this phenomenon, which might have been anticipated with common sense, is not a compelling state interest.

uncle's say-so suffices. That is not how one addresses a serious social problem.

California claims that the Act is justified in aid of parental authority: By requiring that the purchase of violent video games can be made only by adults, the Act ensures that parents can decide what games are appropriate. At the outset, we note our doubts that punishing third parties for conveying protected speech to children *just in case* their parents disapprove of that speech is a proper governmental means of aiding parental authority. Accepting that position would largely vitiate the rule that "only in relatively narrow and well-defined circumstances may government bar public dissemination of protected materials to [minors]." *Erznoznik*.

But leaving that aside, California cannot show that the Act's restrictions meet a substantial need of parents who wish to restrict their children's access to violent video games but cannot do so. The video-game industry has in place a voluntary rating system designed to inform consumers about the content of games. The system, implemented by the Entertainment Software Rating Board (ESRB), assigns age-specific ratings to each video game submitted: EC (Early Childhood); E (Everyone); E10+ (Everyone 10 and older); T (Teens); M (17 and older); and AO (Adults Only — 18 and older). The Video Software Dealers Association encourages retailers to prominently display information about the ESRB system in their stores; to refrain from renting or selling adults-only games to minors; and to rent or sell "M" rated games to minors only with parental consent. In 2009, the Federal Trade Commission (FTC) found that, as a result of this system, "the video game industry outpaces the movie and music industries" in "(1) restricting target-marketing of mature-rated products to children; (2) clearly and prominently disclosing rating information; and (3) restricting children's access to mature-rated products at retail." This system does much to ensure that minors cannot purchase seriously violent games on their own, and that parents who care about the matter can readily evaluate the games their children bring home. Filling the remaining modest gap in concerned-parents' control can hardly be a compelling state interest.

And finally, the Act's purported aid to parental authority is vastly overinclusive. Not all of the children who are forbidden to purchase violent video games on their own have parents who care whether they purchase violent video games. While some of the legislation's effect may indeed be in support of what some parents of the restricted children actually want, its entire effect is only in support of what the State thinks parents *ought* to want. This is not the narrow tailoring to "assisting parents" that restriction of First Amendment rights requires.

* * *

California's effort to regulate violent video games is the latest episode in a long series of failed attempts to censor violent entertainment for minors. . . . We have no business passing judgment on the view of the California Legislature that violent video games (or, for that matter, any other forms of speech) corrupt the young or harm their moral development. Our task is only to say whether or not such works constitute a "well-defined and narrowly limited clas[s] of speech, the prevention and punishment of which have never been thought to raise any Constitutional problem," *Chaplinsky* (the answer plainly is no); and if not, whether the regulation of such works is justified by that high degree of necessity we have described as a compelling state interest (it is not). Even where the protection of children is the object, the constitutional limits on governmental action apply.

California's legislation straddles the fence between (1) addressing a serious social problem and (2) helping concerned parents control their children. Both ends are legitimate, but when they affect First Amendment rights they must be pursued by means that are neither seriously underinclusive nor seriously overinclusive. As a means of protecting children from portrayals of violence, the legislation is seriously underinclusive, not only because it excludes portrayals other than video games, but also because it permits a parental or avuncular veto. And as a means of assisting concerned parents it is seriously overinclusive because it abridges the First Amendment rights of young people whose parents (and aunts and uncles) think violent video games are a harmless pastime. And the overbreadth in achieving one goal is not cured by the underbreadth in achieving the other. Legislation such as this, which is neither fish nor fowl, cannot survive strict scrutiny.

We affirm the judgment below.

JUSTICE ALITO, with whom THE CHIEF JUSTICE joins, concurring in the judgment.

The California statute that is before us in this case represents a pioneering effort to address what the state legislature and others regard as a potentially serious social problem: the effect of exceptionally violent video games on impressionable minors, who often spend countless hours immersed in the alternative worlds that these games create. Although the California statute is well intentioned, its terms are not framed with the precision that the Constitution demands, and I therefore agree with the Court that this particular law cannot be sustained.

I disagree, however, with the approach taken in the Court's opinion. In considering the application of unchanging constitutional principles to new and rapidly evolving technology, this Court should proceed with caution. We should make every effort to understand the new technology. We should take into account the possibility that developing technology may have important societal implications that will become apparent only with time. We should not jump to the conclusion that new technology is fundamentally the same as some older thing with which we are familiar. And we should not hastily dismiss the judgment of legislators, who may be in a better position than we are to assess the implications of new technology. The opinion of the Court exhibits none of this caution. . . .

I

[Justice Alito agreed with the video game industry that the California law was impermissibly vague and did not provide the fair notice that the Constitution requires. He therefore saw "no need to reach the broader First Amendment issues addressed by the Court."]

II

Having outlined how I would decide this case, I will now briefly elaborate on my reasons for questioning the wisdom of the Court's approach. Some of these reasons are touched upon by the dissents, and while I am not prepared at this time to go as far as either Justice Thomas or Justice Breyer, they raise valid concerns.

A

The Court is wrong in saying that the holding in *United States v. Stevens* "controls this case." First, the statute in *Stevens* differed sharply from the statute at issue here. *Stevens* struck down a law that broadly prohibited *any person* from creating, selling, or possessing depictions of animal cruelty for commercial gain. The California law involved here, by contrast, is limited to the sale or rental of violent video games *to minors.* The California law imposes no restriction on the creation of violent video games, or on the possession of such games by anyone, whether above or below the age of 18. The California law does not regulate the sale or rental of violent games by adults. And the California law does not prevent parents and certain other close relatives from buying or renting violent games for their children or other young relatives if they see fit.

Second, *Stevens* does not support the proposition that a law like the one at issue must satisfy strict scrutiny. The portion of *Stevens* on which the Court relies rejected the Government's contention that depictions of animal cruelty were categorically outside the range of *any* First Amendment protection. Going well beyond *Stevens*, the Court now holds that any law that attempts to prevent minors from purchasing violent video games must satisfy strict scrutiny instead of the more lenient standard applied in *Ginsberg v. New York* (1968) [Casebook p. 604], our most closely related precedent. As a result of today's decision, a State may prohibit the sale to minors of what *Ginsberg* described as "girlie magazines," but a State must surmount a formidable (and perhaps insurmountable) obstacle if it wishes to prevent children from purchasing the most violent and depraved video games imaginable.

Third, *Stevens* expressly left open the possibility that a more narrowly drawn statute targeting depictions of animal cruelty might be compatible with the First Amendment. In this case, the Court's sweeping opinion will likely be read by many, both inside and outside the video-game industry, as suggesting that no regulation of minors' access to violent video games is allowed — at least without supporting evidence that may not be realistically obtainable given the nature of the phenomenon in question.

B

The Court's opinion distorts the effect of the California law. I certainly agree with the Court that the government has no "free-floating power to restrict the ideas to which children may be exposed," but the California law does not exercise such a power. If parents want their child to have a violent video game, the California law does not interfere with that parental prerogative. Instead, the California law reinforces parental decisionmaking in exactly the same way as the New York statute upheld in *Ginsberg.* Under both laws, minors are prevented from purchasing certain materials; and under both laws, parents are free to supply their children with these items if that is their wish. . . .

C

Finally, the Court is far too quick to dismiss the possibility that the experience of playing video games (and the effects on minors of playing violent video games) may be very different from anything that we have seen before. Any assessment of the experience of playing video games must take into account certain characteristics of the video games that are now on the market and those that are likely to be available in the near future.

Today's most advanced video games create realistic alternative worlds in which millions of players immerse themselves for hours on end. These games feature visual imagery and sounds that are strikingly realistic, and in the near future video-game graphics may be virtually indistinguishable from actual video footage. Many of the games already on the market can produce high definition images, and it is predicted that it will not be long before video-game images will be seen in three dimensions. It is also forecast that video games will soon provide sensory feedback. By wearing a special vest or other device, a player will be able to experience physical sensations supposedly felt by a character on the screen. Some *amici* who support respondents foresee the day when " 'virtual-reality shoot-'em-ups' " will allow children to " 'actually feel the splatting blood from the blown-off head' " of a victim.

Persons who play video games also have an unprecedented ability to participate in the events that take place in the virtual worlds that these games create. Players can create their own video-game characters and can use photos to produce characters that closely resemble actual people. A person playing a sophisticated game can make a multitude of choices and can thereby alter the course of the action in the game. In addition, the means by which players control the action in video games now bear a closer relationship to the means by which people control action in the real world. While the action in older games was often directed with buttons or a joystick, players dictate the action in newer games by engaging in the same motions that they desire a character in the game to perform. For example, a player who wants a video-game character to swing a baseball bat — either to hit a ball or smash a skull — could bring that about by simulating the motion of actually swinging a bat.

These present-day and emerging characteristics of video games must be considered together with characteristics of the violent games that have already been marketed.

In some of these games, the violence is astounding. Victims by the dozens are killed with every imaginable implement, including machine guns, shotguns, clubs, hammers, axes, swords, and chainsaws. Victims are dismembered, decapitated, disemboweled, set on fire, and chopped into little pieces. They cry out in agony and beg for mercy. Blood gushes, splatters, and pools. Severed body parts and gobs of human remains are graphically shown. In some games, points are awarded based, not only on the number of victims killed, but on the killing technique employed.

It also appears that there is no antisocial theme too base for some in the video-game industry to exploit. There are games in which a player can take on the identity and reenact the killings carried out by the perpetrators of the murders at

Columbine High School and Virginia Tech. The objective of one game is to rape a mother and her daughters; in another, the goal is to rape Native American women. There is a game in which players engage in "ethnic cleansing" and can choose to gun down African-Americans, Latinos, or Jews. In still another game, players attempt to fire a rifle shot into the head of President Kennedy as his motorcade passes by the Texas School Book Depository.

If the technological characteristics of the sophisticated games that are likely to be available in the near future are combined with the characteristics of the most violent games already marketed, the result will be games that allow troubled teens to experience in an extraordinarily personal and vivid way what it would be like to carry out unspeakable acts of violence.

The Court is untroubled by this possibility. According to the Court, the "interactive" nature of video games is "nothing new" because "all literature is interactive." Disagreeing with this assessment, the International Game Developers Association (IGDA) — a group that presumably understands the nature of video games and that supports respondents — tells us that video games are "far more concretely interactive." And on this point, the game developers are surely correct.

It is certainly true, as the Court notes, that " '[l]iterature, when it is successful draws the reader into the story, makes him identify with the characters, invites him to judge them and quarrel with them, to experience their joys and sufferings as the reader's own.' " But only an extraordinarily imaginative reader who reads a description of a killing in a literary work will experience that event as vividly as he might if he played the role of the killer in a video game. To take an example, think of a person who reads the passage in *Crime and Punishment* in which Raskolnikov kills the old pawn broker with an axe. See F. DOSTOYEVSKY, CRIME AND PUNISHMENT 78 (Modern Library ed. 1950). Compare that reader with a video-game player who creates an avatar that bears his own image; who sees a realistic image of the victim and the scene of the killing in high definition and in three dimensions; who is forced to decide whether or not to kill the victim and decides to do so; who then pretends to grasp an axe, to raise it above the head of the victim, and then to bring it down; who hears the thud of the axe hitting her head and her cry of pain; who sees her split skull and feels the sensation of blood on his face and hands. For most people, the two experiences will not be the same.

When all of the characteristics of video games are taken into account, there is certainly a reasonable basis for thinking that the experience of playing a video game may be quite different from the experience of reading a book, listening to a radio broadcast, or viewing a movie. And if this is so, then for at least some minors, the effects of playing violent video games may also be quite different. The Court acts prematurely in dismissing this possibility out of hand.

* * *

For all these reasons, I would hold only that the particular law at issue here fails to provide the clear notice that the Constitution requires. I would not squelch legislative efforts to deal with what is perceived by some to be a significant and developing social problem. If differently framed statutes are enacted by the States or by the Federal Government, we can consider the constitutionality of those laws when cases challenging them are presented to us.

JUSTICE THOMAS, dissenting.

The Court's decision today does not comport with the original public understanding of the First Amendment. . . . The practices and beliefs of the founding generation establish that "the freedom of speech," as originally understood, does not include a right to speak to minors (or a right of minors to access speech) without going through the minors' parents or guardians. I would hold that the law at issue is not facially unconstitutional under the First Amendment, and reverse and remand for further proceedings.

I

In my view, the "practices and beliefs held by the Founders" reveal another category of excluded speech: speech to minor children bypassing their parents. The historical evidence shows that the founding generation believed parents had absolute authority over their minor children and expected parents to use that authority to direct the proper development of their children. . . . The founding generation would not have considered it an abridgment of "the freedom of speech" to support parental authority by restricting speech that bypasses minors' parents. . . .

[Justice Thomas went on to support his conclusion with a detailed historical analysis.]

JUSTICE BREYER, dissenting.

. . . Applying traditional First Amendment analysis, I would uphold the [California] statute as constitutional on its face and would consequently reject the industries' facial challenge. . . .

I

B

A facial challenge to this statute based on the First Amendment can succeed only if "a substantial number of its applications are unconstitutional, judged in relation to the statute's plainly legitimate sweep." *United States v. Stevens* (2010). Moreover, it is more difficult to mount a facial First Amendment attack on a statute that seeks to regulate activity that involves action as well as speech. See *Broadrick v. Oklahoma*, 413 U.S. 601 (1973). Hence, I shall focus here upon an area within which I believe the State can legitimately apply its statute, namely sales to minors under the age of 17 (the age cutoff used by the industry's own ratings system), of highly realistic violent video games, which a reasonable game maker would know meet the Act's criteria. That area lies at the heart of the statute. I shall assume that the number of instances in which the State will enforce the statute within that area is comparatively large, and that the number outside that area (for example, sales to

17-year-olds) is comparatively small. And the activity the statute regulates combines speech with action (a virtual form of target practice).

C

In determining whether the statute is unconstitutional, I would apply both this Court's "vagueness" precedents and a strict form of First Amendment scrutiny. In doing so, the special First Amendment category I find relevant is not (as the Court claims) the category of "depictions of violence," but rather the category of "protection of children." This Court has held that the "power of the state to control the conduct of children reaches beyond the scope of its authority over adults." *Prince v. Massachusetts*, 321 U.S. 158, 170 (1944). And the " 'regulatio[n] of communication addressed to [children] need not conform to the requirements of the [F]irst [A]mendment in the same way as those applicable to adults.' " *Ginsberg v. New York* (1968) [Casebook p. 604].

The majority's claim that the California statute, if upheld, would create a "new categor[y] of unprotected speech" is overstated. No one here argues that depictions of violence, even extreme violence, *automatically* fall outside the First Amendment's protective scope as, for example, do obscenity and depictions of child pornography. We properly speak of *categories* of expression that lack protection when, like "child pornography," the category is broad, when it applies automatically, and when the State can prohibit everyone, including adults, from obtaining access to the material within it. But where, as here, careful analysis must precede a narrower judicial conclusion (say, denying protection to a shout of "fire" in a crowded theater, or to an effort to teach a terrorist group how to peacefully petition the United Nations), we do not normally describe the result as creating a "new category of unprotected speech." See *Schenck v. United States* (1919) [Casebook p. 3]; *Holder v. Humanitarian Law Project* [this Supp. Chapter 8].

Thus, in *Stevens*, after rejecting the claim that *all* depictions of animal cruelty (a category) fall outside the First Amendment's protective scope, we went on to decide whether the particular statute at issue violates the First Amendment under traditional standards; and we held that, because the statute was overly broad, it was invalid. Similarly, here the issue is whether, applying traditional First Amendment standards, this statute does, or does not, pass muster.

II

In my view, California's statute provides "fair notice of what is prohibited," and consequently it is not impermissibly vague. [Discussion omitted.]

III

Video games combine physical action with expression. Were physical activity to predominate in a game, government could appropriately intervene, say by requiring parents to accompany children when playing a game involving actual target practice, or restricting the sale of toys presenting physical dangers to children. But because video games also embody important expressive and artistic elements, I agree with the Court that the First Amendment significantly limits the State's power to regulate. And I would determine whether the State has exceeded those limits by applying a strict standard of review.

Like the majority, I believe that the California law must be "narrowly tailored" to further a "compelling interest," without there being a "less restrictive" alternative that would be "at least as effective." I would not apply this strict tandard "mechanically." Rather, in applying it, I would evaluate the degree to which the statute injures speech-related interests, the nature of the potentially-justifying "compelling interests," the degree to which the statute furthers that interest, the nature and effectiveness of possible alternatives, and, in light of this evaluation, whether, overall, "the statute works speech-related harm . . . out of proportion to the benefits that the statute seeks to provide."

First Amendment standards applied in this way are difficult but not impossible to satisfy. Applying "strict scrutiny" the Court has upheld restrictions on speech that, for example, ban the teaching of peaceful dispute resolution to a group on the State Department's list of terrorist organizations, *Holder*, and limit speech near polling places, *Burson v. Freeman* (1992) [Casebook p. 449] (plurality opinion). And applying less clearly defined but still rigorous standards, the Court has allowed States to require disclosure of petition signers, *Doe v. Reed* (2010) [this Supp. Chapter 11], and to impose campaign contribution limits that were " 'closely drawn' to match a 'sufficiently important interest,' " *Nixon v. Shrink Missouri Government PAC*, 528 U.S. 377 (2000).

Moreover, although the Court did not specify the "level of scrutiny" it applied in *Ginsberg*, we have subsequently described that case as finding a "compelling interest" in protecting children from harm sufficient to justify limitations on speech. See *Sable Communications of Cal., Inc. v. FCC* (1989) [Casebook p. 614]. Since the Court in *Ginsberg* specified that the statute's prohibition applied to material that was not obscene, I cannot dismiss *Ginsberg* on the ground that it concerned obscenity. Nor need I depend upon the fact that the Court in *Ginsberg* insisted only that the legislature have a "rational" basis for finding the depictions there at issue harmful to children. For in this case, California has substantiated its claim of harm with considerably stronger evidence.

A

California's law imposes no more than a modest restriction on expression. The statute prevents no one from playing a video game, it prevents no adult from buying a video game, and it prevents no child or adolescent from obtaining a game provided a parent is willing to help. All it prevents is a child or adolescent from buying, without a parent's assistance, a gruesomely violent video game of a kind that the industry *itself* tells us it wants to keep out of the hands of those under the age of 17. . . .

B

The interest that California advances in support of the statute is compelling. As this Court has previously described that interest, it consists of both (1) the "basic" parental claim "to authority in their own household to direct the rearing of their children," which makes it proper to enact "laws designed to aid discharge of [parental] responsibility," and (2) the State's "independent interest in the well-being of its youth." And where these interests work in tandem, it is not fatally "underinclusive" for a State to advance its interests in protecting children against the special harms present in an interactive video game medium through a default rule that still allows parents to provide their children with what their parents wish.

Both interests are present here. As to the need to help parents guide their children, the Court noted in 1968 that " 'parental control or guidance cannot always be provided.' " Today, 5.3 million grade-school-age children of working parents are routinely home alone. Thus, it has, if anything, become more important to supplement parents' authority to guide their children's development.

As to the State's independent interest, we have pointed out that juveniles are more likely to show a " 'lack of maturity' " and are "more vulnerable or susceptible to negative influences and outside pressures," and that their "character . . . is not as well formed as that of an adult." *Roper v. Simmons*, 543 U.S. 551 (2005). And we have therefore recognized "a compelling interest in protecting the physical and psychological well-being of minors."

At the same time, there is considerable evidence that California's statute significantly furthers this compelling interest. That is, in part, because video games are excellent teaching tools. . . . Video games can help develop habits, accustom the player to performance of the task, and reward the player for performing that task well. Why else would the Armed Forces incorporate video games into its training?

When the military uses video games to help soldiers train for missions, it is using this medium for a beneficial purpose. But California argues that when the teaching features of video games are put to less desirable ends, harm can ensue. In particular, extremely violent games can harm children by rewarding them for being violently aggressive in play, and thereby often teaching them to be violently aggressive in life. And video games can cause more harm in this respect than can typically passive media, such as books or films or television programs.

There are many scientific studies that support California's views. Social scientists, for example, have found *causal* evidence that playing these games results in harm. Longitudinal studies, which measure changes over time, have found that increased exposure to violent video games causes an increase in aggression over the same period. . . .

Some of these studies take care to explain in a commonsense way why video games are potentially more harmful than, say, films or books or television. In essence, they say that the closer a child's behavior comes, not to watching, but to acting out horrific violence, the greater the potential psychological harm. . . .

Experts debate the conclusions of all these studies. . . . I, like most judges, lack the social science expertise to say definitively who is right. But associations of public health professionals who do possess that expertise have reviewed many of these studies and found a significant risk that violent video games, when compared with more passive media, are particularly likely to cause children harm. . . .

Unlike the majority, I would find sufficient grounds in these studies and expert opinions for this Court to defer to an elected legislature's conclusion that the video games in question are particularly likely to harm children. This Court has always thought it owed an elected legislature some degree of deference in respect to legislative facts of this kind, particularly when they involve technical matters that are beyond our competence, and even in First Amendment cases. . . . The majority, in reaching its own, opposite conclusion about the validity of the relevant studies, grants the legislature no deference at all.

C

I can find no "less restrictive" alternative to California's law that would be "at least as effective." See *Reno v. American Civil Liberties Union* (1997) [Casebook p. 615]. The majority points to a voluntary alternative: The industry tries to prevent those under 17 from buying extremely violent games by labeling those games with an "M" (Mature) and encouraging retailers to restrict their sales to those 17 and older. But this voluntary system has serious enforcement gaps. . . . [According to a recent Federal Trade Commission (FTC) report submitted to Congress,] 20% of those under 17 are still able to buy M-rated video games, and, breaking down sales by store, one finds that this number rises to nearly 50% in the case of one large national chain. And the industry could easily revert back to the substantial noncompliance that existed in 2004, particularly after today's broad ruling reduces the industry's incentive to police itself. . . .

IV

The upshot is that California's statute, as applied to its heartland of applications (i.e., buyers under 17; extremely violent, realistic video games), imposes a restriction on speech that is modest at most. That restriction is justified by a compelling interest (supplementing parents' efforts to prevent their children from purchasing potentially harmful violent, interactive material). And there is no equally effective, less restrictive alternative. California's statute is consequently constitutional on its face — though litigants remain free to challenge the statute as applied in particular instances, including any effort by the State to apply it to minors aged 17.

I add that the majority's different conclusion creates a serious anomaly in First Amendment law. *Ginsberg* makes clear that a State can prohibit the sale to minors of depictions of nudity; today the Court makes clear that a State cannot prohibit the sale to minors of the most violent interactive video games. But what sense does it make to forbid selling to a 13-year-old boy a magazine with an image of a nude woman, while protecting a sale to that 13-year-old of an interactive video game in which he actively, but virtually, binds and gags the woman, then tortures and kills her? What kind of First Amendment would permit the government to protect children by restricting sales of that extremely violent video game *only* when the woman — bound, gagged, tortured, and killed — is also topless?

This anomaly is not compelled by the First Amendment. It disappears once one recognizes that extreme violence, where interactive, and *without literary, artistic, or similar justification,* can prove at least as, if not more, harmful to children as photographs of nudity. And the record here is more than adequate to support such a view. That is why I believe that *Ginsberg* controls the outcome here *a fortiori*. And it is why I believe California's law is constitutional on its face. . . .

For these reasons, I respectfully dissent.

[Justice Breyer supplemented his opinion with two extensive appendices "listing peer-reviewed academic journal articles on the topic of psychological harm resulting from playing violent video games." The appendices fill more than 14 pages in the U.S. Reports.]

NOTE: VIOLENCE, INTERACTIVITY, AND THE PROTECTION OF CHILDREN

1.   Knowledgeable observers were surprised when the Supreme Court granted certiorari in *Brown* (under the name *Schwarzenegger v. Video Software Dealers Ass'n*), because every court to have considered a law like California's had held it unconstitutional. Although the outcome is as expected, the Justices divide four ways on the appropriate analysis, and only a bare majority joins the Court opinion.

2.   The Court says that *United States v. Stevens* — decided in 2010 — "controls this case." Justice Alito, who concurs in the judgment only on vagueness grounds, says the Court "is wrong." First, he says that the California law at issue in *Brown* "is limited to the sale or rental of violent video games to minors," while the prohibition in *Stevens* applied to "any person." Is that enough to take the case out of the realm of the *Stevens* holding? Consider, in this regard, the two opinions' treatment of the 1968 decision in *Ginsberg v. New York*.

Justice Alito also says that "*Stevens* does not support the proposition that a law like the one at issue must satisfy strict scrutiny." Reread *Stevens*. Does the opinion apply "strict scrutiny"?

3.   The Court places heavy reliance on the largely forgotten 1948 decision in *Winters v. New York* (Casebook p. 149). The Court cites *Winters* for the proposition that although the Free Speech Clause "exists primarily to protect discourse on public matters, . . . it is difficult to distinguish politics from entertainment, and dangerous to try." Consider the rationales for protecting speech articulated by Holmes, Brandeis, Hand, and Brennan. How strongly do they support the protection of "entertainment"? Does the Court in *Brown* give up too easily on the possibility of drawing the distinction?

4.   The Court and Justice Alito debate the significance of the "interactive" nature of video games. The majority, quoting Judge Richard Posner, says that "all literature is interactive." Justice Alito responds by comparing the experience of role-playing in a video game with that of a reader who reads Dostoyevsky's description of Raskolnikov's murder of the old pawnbroker. "For most people," he says, "the two experiences will not be the same." Who has the better of this argument?

5.   Justice Breyer, in dissent, argues that the Court opinion "creates a serious anomaly in First Amendment law." Under *Ginsberg*, "a State can prohibit the sale

to minors of depictions of nudity," but after *Brown*, "a State cannot prohibit the sale to minors of the most violent interactive video games." Does the Court adequately justify the different treatment of sexual content and violent content, especially in the context of distribution to minors?

6.　Justice Breyer finds a "compelling" state interest in helping parents to carry out their responsibilities and also in fostering "the well-being of its youth." He argues that the California law does no more than prevent "a child or adolescent from buying, without a parent's assistance, a gruesomely violent video game of a kind that the industry itself tells us it wants to keep out of the hands of those under the age of 17." Does the majority opinion adequately respond to this argument?

Chapter 4

TRANS-SUBSTANTIVE DOCTRINES

B. OVERBREADTH AND VAGUENESS

Page 321: *add at end of the chapter:*

NOTE: CLARIFYING THE VAGUENESS DOCTRINE

In *Holder v. Humanitarian Law Project (HLP)*, 130 S. Ct. 2705 (2010) (set forth as a principal case in Chapter 8 of this Supplement), the Court clarified several aspects of the vagueness doctrine. Plaintiffs in *HLP* challenged a federal statute which makes it a federal crime to "knowingly provid[e] material support or resources to a foreign terrorist organization." The statute defines "material support or resources" to include, *inter alia*, "training, "expert advice or assistance (when derived from "other specialized knowledge"), and "service." The Ninth Circuit Court of Appeals held that the statute, as applied to the plaintiffs, was impermissibly vague. The Supreme Court reversed. Although three Justices dissented on other aspects of the case, the Court was unanimous in rejecting the vagueness challenge.

The Court began by explaining how the Ninth Circuit departed from the governing principles:

> The Court of Appeals . . . merged plaintiffs' vagueness challenge with their First Amendment claims, holding that portions of the material-support statute were unconstitutionally vague because they applied to protected speech — regardless of whether those applications were clear. The court stated that, even if persons of ordinary intelligence understood the scope of the term "training," that term would "remai[n] impermissibly vague" because it could "be read to encompass speech and advocacy protected by the First Amendment." It also found "service" and a portion of "expert advice or assistance" to be vague because those terms covered protected speech.

> Further, in spite of its own statement that it was not addressing a "facial vagueness challenge," the Court of Appeals considered the statute's application to facts not before it. Specifically, the Ninth Circuit relied on the Government's statement that § 2339B would bar filing an amicus brief in support of a foreign terrorist organization — which plaintiffs have not told us they wish to do, and which the Ninth Circuit did not say plaintiffs wished to do — to conclude that the statute barred protected advocacy and was therefore vague. By deciding how the statute applied in hypothetical circumstances, the Court of Appeals' discussion of vagueness seemed to incorporate elements of First Amendment overbreadth doctrine.

In both of these respects, the Court of Appeals contravened the rule that "[a] plaintiff who engages in some conduct that is clearly proscribed cannot complain of the vagueness of the law as applied to the conduct of others." That rule makes no exception for conduct in the form of speech. Thus, even to the extent a heightened vagueness standard applies, a plaintiff whose speech is clearly proscribed cannot raise a successful vagueness claim under the Due Process Clause of the Fifth Amendment for lack of notice. And he certainly cannot do so based on the speech of others. Such a plaintiff may have a valid overbreadth claim under the First Amendment, but our precedents make clear that a Fifth Amendment vagueness challenge does not turn on whether a law applies to a substantial amount of protected expression. Otherwise the doctrines would be substantially redundant.

The plaintiffs did not argue that that material-support statute gives too much enforcement discretion to the Government, so "a proper analysis" required the Court to address only a single question: did the statute "provide a person of ordinary intelligence fair notice of what is prohibited"? See *United States v. Williams* (2008) (Casebook p. 216). The Court found that the material-support statute met this standard:

As a general matter, the statutory terms at issue here are quite different from the sorts of terms that we have previously declared to be vague. We have in the past "struck down statutes that tied criminal culpability to whether the defendant's conduct was 'annoying' or 'indecent' — wholly subjective judgments without statutory definitions, narrowing context, or settled legal meanings." *Williams*. Applying the statutory terms in this action — "training," "expert advice or assistance," "service," and "personnel" — does not require similarly untethered, subjective judgments.

Congress also took care to add narrowing definitions to the material-support statute over time. These definitions increased the clarity of the statute's terms. See § 2339A(b)(2) (" 'training' means instruction or teaching designed to impart a specific skill, as opposed to general knowledge"); § 2339A(b)(3) (" 'expert advice or assistance' means advice or assistance derived from scientific, technical or other specialized knowledge"); § 2339B(h) (clarifying the scope of "personnel"). And the knowledge requirement of the statute further reduces any potential for vagueness, as we have held with respect to other statutes containing a similar requirement.

Of course, the scope of the material-support statute may not be clear in every application. But the dispositive point here is that the statutory terms are clear in their application to plaintiffs' proposed conduct, which means that plaintiffs' vagueness challenge must fail. Even assuming that a heightened standard applies because the material-support statute potentially implicates speech, the statutory terms are not vague as applied to plaintiffs.

Most of the activities in which plaintiffs seek to engage readily fall within the scope of the terms "training" and "expert advice or assistance." . . . A person of ordinary intelligence would understand that instruction on resolving disputes through international law falls within the statute's definition of "training" because it imparts a "specific skill," not "general knowledge." Plaintiffs' activities also fall comfortably within the scope of "expert advice or assistance": A reasonable person would recognize that teaching [an organization] how to petition for humanitarian relief before the United Nations involves advice derived from, as the statute puts it, "specialized knowledge." § 2339A(b)(3). . . .

Consider the municipal ordinance discussed in Note 3 on page 320 of the Casebook. Does *HLP* preclude a vagueness challenge to that ordinance?

Chapter 5
COMPELLED EXPRESSION

B. COMPELLED SUBSIDY

Page 346: *add before the Note:*

PROBLEM: UNION CAMP AND RATIFICATION MONDAYS

Professors in the State University of Jefferson system are covered by a collective bargaining agreement between the State of Jefferson and the American Union of Education Professionals (AUEP, or Union). The agreement makes the university an "agency shop" — that is, all employees (in this case, all faculty) must either belong to the Union or pay representation ("agency") fees to it. Such agency shop agreements are permitted by Jefferson law.

Freda Hayek is a professor of history at Monticello State University (part of the State University system) who opposes the Union and unionism generally. As a non-member of the Union, she is required to pay agency fees. She visits the Union's website and discovers that the Union uses her agency fees for, among other things, the following activities:

(1) *Union Camp.* This is an annual convention of representatives from every AUEP local affiliate in the United States. At the convention, every local gets a chance to explain problems it encountered in its collective bargaining process over the past year and to solicit advice. In addition, representatives from the national union describe the resources they have available and how they can help the local affiliates. Over the last several years, the convention has also passed resolutions (official position statements) dealing with academic freedom, immigration restrictions on foreign professors wishing to visit American universities, and affirmative action in student admissions. Hayek's local uses her agency fees to defray the travel and registration costs for the local's representatives to Union Camp.

(2) *Ratification Mondays.* This is the term used by the Monticello State U. local for its campaign to win the state legislature's ratification of the contract between the local and the University. Traditionally, the contract is signed at the end of March. Every Monday in April the local stages a series of public events on the state capitol grounds in Jefferson City to publicize the contract and to pressure the legislature to ratify it. Each event is different: last year it included folk music concerts, speeches, and presentations about the history of teachers' unions and unions more generally.

After discovering this information, Hayek sues the local, alleging that its use of her agency fees for these activities violates her First Amendment rights. You are the law clerk to the judge assigned the case. How would you advise him?

Chapter 6

FREEDOM OF ASSOCIATION

Page 378: *add before the Problem:*

PROBLEM: ACCESS TO A GAY PRIDE FESTIVAL

Every year for the last 20 years the City of Freeport has issued a permit to Freeport Pride, a local group that operates a gay pride festival in Lakeside Park, a city-owned park. Freeport Pride rents out booths to social and political groups catering to gays and lesbians and to businesses that seek access to the gay and lesbian market. Any person or institution seeking to rent a booth must sign a pledge that it "respects all types of diversity" and does not discriminate on the basis of race, sex, religion or sexual orientation. Each booth is marked by a large sign that includes the sponsor's name attached to the phrase "Is Out and Proud!" (e.g., First National Bank of Freeport's sign reads "First National Bank of Freeport Is Out and Proud!").

Freeport Pride describes the goal of the festival as "presenting a positive vision for gays and lesbians and a safe and welcoming experience for men and women struggling with their sexual orientation." In theory, any person may attend the festival upon payment of the $10 entry fee (which goes toward litter removal, park restoration, and security).

Ted Thompson is a fundamentalist Christian minister who believes that gays and lesbians are going to hell. He wants gays and lesbians to "repent" and adopt his views, which Thompson believes are the only ones that ensure access to heaven.

Thompson applies to rent a booth, which is available because an economic downturn has meant that there is a surplus of booth space. Freeport Pride refuses to rent to him because he will not sign the diversity pledge. After that refusal, Thompson applies to purchase an advance-admission ticket to the festival for his adult son. When queried about his plans, he states that his son wants to walk through the festival grounds carrying a sign that says "Fags Go To Hell — Repent Now!" and distributing literature to any willing recipient. (Advance-sale tickets are normally sold without any questions asked.) Upon receiving his answer, Freeport Pride again refuses his request, this time without citing a reason.

Thompson and his son sue Freeport Pride in state court under the state's public accommodations law, which bans discrimination in public facilities on the basis of religion. They ask the court to issue an order requiring Freeport Pride to rent Thompson a booth and to sell an advance ticket to his son. Freeport Pride argues that such an order would violate its First Amendment rights. Should the argument prevail?

Page 379: *add at the end of the page:*

PROBLEM: EXCLUSION FROM A GAY SOFTBALL LEAGUE

Over the last thirty years amateur sports organizations have become a fixture in the gay and lesbian community. In particular, gay softball leagues have sprung up all over the country. Many of them have had to face the question whether to allow heterosexuals to participate.

The Elm City Gay Softball Association ("Association") is one such organization. The relevant parts of its by-laws read as follow:

Preamble

. . . The Association exists to promote a sense of pride and self-worth among members of the Elm City LGBT community. Too often, LGBT people associate sports with childhood experiences of ridicule, humiliation and exclusion. The Association seeks to provide opportunities for LGBT people to experience the camaraderie and confidence-building provided by participation in sports, in an environment that is welcoming, non-judgmental and non-threatening. It also believes that the example of LGBT people excelling in sports provides positive role models for the rest of the LGBT community, breaks down stereotypes about LGBT people in the broader Elm City community, and promotes social and civil equality. . . .

Non-Discrimination

. . . The Association does not wish to discriminate based on sexual orientation or any other invidious basis. However, in order to accomplish the goals set forth in the Preamble, the Association must ensure that every team in the league is predominantly comprised of LGBT players. For this reason, no team in the Association may have more than two players on the roster who self-identify as heterosexual. The Association reserves the right to conduct a discrete, respectful inquiry whenever it obtains probable cause to believe that a team is violating this rule. . . .

Last April the managers of each team in the league submitted their rosters for the summer season, as they do every April. Upon reviewing the rosters of the other teams, the manager of the Rangers, a photographer, asserted that he had been the wedding photographer at the opposite-sex weddings of three male members of another team, the Bruins, and challenged the Bruins' line-up. Upon investigating, the league upheld the challenge, and ordered the Bruins to drop one of the three men. The Bruins manager asked if any of the men would voluntarily resign from the team. When none of them did, the Bruins manager dropped one of them, Sam Sidley, based on a random selection.

The State of Nutmeg, where Elm City is located, has a law prohibiting any "public accommodation" from discriminating "on the basis of race, national origin, sex, religion, or sexual orientation." Sidley sues the Association under that law, alleging that he was discriminated against because he is heterosexual. Assume that the Association is a "public accommodation" under the state law. Does it nonetheless have a good First Amendment defense?

Chapter 8

CONTENT NEUTRALITY: THE PRINCIPLE AND ITS PROGENY

B. *O'BRIEN* AND THE TWO-TRACK ANALYSIS

Page 469: *insert before Section C:*

HOLDER v. HUMANITARIAN LAW PROJECT
130 S. Ct. 2705 (2010)

CHIEF JUSTICE ROBERTS delivered the opinion of the Court.

Congress has prohibited the provision of "material support or resources" to certain foreign organizations that engage in terrorist activity. That prohibition is based on a finding that the specified organizations "are so tainted by their criminal conduct that any contribution to such an organization facilitates that conduct." Antiterrorism and Effective Death Penalty Act of 1996 (AEDPA), § 301(a)(7). The plaintiffs in this litigation seek to provide support to two such organizations. Plaintiffs claim that they seek to facilitate only the lawful, nonviolent purposes of those groups, and that applying the material-support law to prevent them from doing so violates the Constitution. In particular, they claim that the statute is too vague, in violation of the Fifth Amendment, and that it infringes their rights to freedom of speech and association, in violation of the First Amendment. We conclude that the material-support statute is constitutional as applied to the particular activities plaintiffs have told us they wish to pursue. We do not, however, address the resolution of more difficult cases that may arise under the statute in the future.

I

This litigation concerns 18 U.S.C. § 2339B, which makes it a federal crime to "knowingly provid[e] material support or resources to a foreign terrorist organization." Congress has amended the definition of "material support or resources" periodically, but at present it is defined as follows:

> [T]he term "material support or resources" means any property, tangible or intangible, or service, including currency or monetary instruments or financial securities, financial services, lodging, training, expert advice or assistance, safehouses, false documentation or identification, communications equipment, facilities, weapons, lethal substances, explosives, personnel (1 or more individuals who may be or include oneself), and transportation, except medicine or religious materials.

The authority to designate an entity a "foreign terrorist organization" rests with the Secretary of State. She may, in consultation with the Secretary of the Treasury and the Attorney General, so designate an organization upon finding that it is foreign, engages in "terrorist activity" or "terrorism," and thereby "threatens the security of United States nationals or the national security of the United States." " '[N]ational security' means the national defense, foreign relations, or economic interests of the United States." An entity designated a foreign terrorist organization may seek review of that designation before the D.C. Circuit within 30 days of that designation.

In 1997, the Secretary of State designated 30 groups as foreign terrorist organizations. Two of those groups are the Kurdistan Workers' Party (also known as the Partiya Karkeran Kurdistan, or PKK) and the Liberation Tigers of Tamil Eelam (LTTE). The PKK is an organization founded in 1974 with the aim of establishing an independent Kurdish state in southeastern Turkey. The LTTE is an organization founded in 1976 for the purpose of creating an independent Tamil state in Sri Lanka [formerly Ceylon]. The District Court in this action found that the PKK and the LTTE engage in political and humanitarian activities. The Government has presented evidence that both groups have also committed numerous terrorist attacks, some of which have harmed American citizens. The LTTE sought judicial review of its designation as a foreign terrorist organization; the D.C. Circuit upheld that designation. The PKK did not challenge its designation.

Plaintiffs in this litigation are two U.S. citizens and six domestic organizations. [They include] the Humanitarian Law Project (HLP) (a human rights organization with consultative status to the United Nations) [and] Ralph Fertig (the HLP's president, and a retired administrative law judge). . . . In 1998, plaintiffs filed suit in federal court challenging the constitutionality of the material-support statute. Plaintiffs claimed that they wished to provide support for the humanitarian and political activities of the PKK and the LTTE in the form of monetary contributions, other tangible aid, legal training, and political advocacy, but that they could not do so for fear of prosecution under § 2339B.

As relevant here, plaintiffs claimed that the material-support statute was unconstitutional on two grounds: First, it violated their freedom of speech and freedom of association under the First Amendment, because it criminalized their provision of material support to the PKK and the LTTE, without requiring the Government to prove that plaintiffs had a specific intent to further the unlawful ends of those organizations. Second, plaintiffs argued that the statute was unconstitutionally vague.

[Over the course of more than a decade, the case bounced back and forth between the district court and the Ninth Circuit, and Congress amended the statute twice. Ultimately the Ninth Circuit rejected most of the plaintiffs' constitutional challenges, but it] held that, as applied to plaintiffs, the terms "training," "expert advice or assistance" (when derived from "other specialized knowledge"), and "service" were vague because they "continue[d] to cover constitutionally protected advocacy," but the term "personnel" was not vague because it "no longer criminalize[d] pure speech protected by the First Amendment."

The Government petitioned for certiorari, and plaintiffs filed a conditional cross-petition. We granted both petitions.

II

Given the complicated 12-year history of this litigation, we pause to clarify the questions before us. Plaintiffs challenge § 2339B's prohibition on four types of material support — "training," "expert advice or assistance," "service," and "personnel." They raise three constitutional claims. First, plaintiffs claim that § 2339B violates the Due Process Clause of the Fifth Amendment because these four statutory terms are impermissibly vague. Second, plaintiffs claim that § 2339B violates their freedom of speech under the First Amendment. Third, plaintiffs claim that § 2339B violates their First Amendment freedom of association.

Plaintiffs do not challenge the above statutory terms in all their applications. Rather, plaintiffs claim that § 2339B is invalid to the extent it prohibits them from engaging in certain specified activities. With respect to the HLP and Judge Fertig, those activities are: (1) "train[ing] members of [the] PKK on how to use humanitarian and international law to peacefully resolve disputes"; (2) "engag[ing] in political advocacy on behalf of Kurds who live in Turkey"; and (3) "teach[ing] PKK members how to petition various representative bodies such as the United Nations for relief." . . .

III

Plaintiffs claim, as a threshold matter, that we should affirm the Court of Appeals without reaching any issues of constitutional law. They contend that we should interpret the material-support statute, when applied to speech, to require proof that a defendant intended to further a foreign terrorist organization's illegal activities. That interpretation, they say, would end the litigation because plaintiffs' proposed activities consist of speech, but plaintiffs do not intend to further unlawful conduct by the PKK or the LTTE.

We reject plaintiffs' interpretation of § 2339B because it is inconsistent with the text of the statute. Section 2339B(a)(1) prohibits "knowingly" providing material support. It then specifically describes the type of knowledge that is required: "To violate this paragraph, a person must have knowledge that the organization is a designated terrorist organization . . . , that the organization has engaged or engages in terrorist activity . . . , or that the organization has engaged or engages in terrorism. . . ." Congress plainly spoke to the necessary mental state for a violation of § 2339B, and it chose knowledge about the organization's connection to terrorism, not specific intent to further the organization's terrorist activities. . . .

Scales v. United States (1961) [Casebook p. 49] is the case on which plaintiffs most heavily rely, but it is readily distinguishable. That case involved the Smith Act, which prohibited membership in a group advocating the violent overthrow of the government. The Court held that a person could not be convicted under the statute unless he had knowledge of the group's illegal advocacy and a specific intent to bring about violent overthrow. This action is different: Section 2339B does not criminalize mere membership in a designated foreign terrorist organization. It instead prohibits providing "material support" to such a group. Nothing about *Scales* suggests the need for a specific intent requirement in such a case. . . .

IV

[The Court first considered the question "whether the material-support statute, as applied to plaintiffs, is impermissibly vague under the Due Process Clause of the Fifth Amendment." The Court unanimously held that the plaintiffs' vagueness claim lacked merit. For this part of the opinion, see Chapter 4 of this Supplement.]

V

A

We next consider whether the material-support statute, as applied to plaintiffs, violates the freedom of speech guaranteed by the First Amendment. Both plaintiffs and the Government take extreme positions on this question. Plaintiffs claim that Congress has banned their "pure political speech." It has not. Under the material-support statute, plaintiffs may say anything they wish on any topic. They may speak and write freely about the PKK and LTTE, the governments of Turkey and Sri Lanka, human rights, and international law. They may advocate before the United Nations. As the Government states: "The statute does not prohibit independent advocacy or expression of any kind." Section 2339B also "does not prevent [plaintiffs] from becoming members of the PKK and LTTE or impose any sanction on them for doing so." Congress has not, therefore, sought to suppress ideas or opinions in the form of "pure political speech." Rather, Congress has prohibited "material support," which most often does not take the form of speech at all. And when it does, the statute is carefully drawn to cover only a narrow category of speech to, under the direction of, or in coordination with foreign groups that the speaker knows to be terrorist organizations.[4]

For its part, the Government takes the foregoing too far, claiming that the only thing truly at issue in this litigation is conduct, not speech. Section 2339B is directed at the fact of plaintiffs' interaction with the PKK and LTTE, the Government contends, and only incidentally burdens their expression. The Government argues that the proper standard of review is therefore the one set out in *United States v. O'Brien* (1968) [Casebook p. 450]. In that case, the Court rejected a First Amendment challenge to a conviction under a generally applicable prohibition on destroying draft cards, even though O'Brien had burned his card in protest against the draft. In so doing, we applied what we have since called "intermediate scrutiny," under which a "content-neutral regulation will be sustained under the First Amendment if it advances important governmental interests unrelated to the suppression of free speech and does not burden

---

[4] The dissent also analyzes the statute as if it prohibited "[p]eaceful political advocacy" or "pure speech and association," without more. Section 2339B does not do that, and we do not address the constitutionality of any such prohibitions. The dissent's claim that our decision is inconsistent with this Court's cases analyzing those sorts of restrictions is accordingly unfounded.

substantially more speech than necessary to further those interests."

The Government is wrong that the only thing actually at issue in this litigation is conduct, and therefore wrong to argue that *O'Brien* provides the correct standard of review. *O'Brien* does not provide the applicable standard for reviewing a content-based regulation of speech, see *R.A.V. v. St. Paul* (1992) [Casebook p. 630]; *Texas v. Johnson* (1989) [Casebook p. 459], and § 2339B regulates speech on the basis of its content. Plaintiffs want to speak to the PKK and the LTTE, and whether they may do so under § 2339B depends on what they say. If plaintiffs' speech to those groups imparts a "specific skill" or communicates advice derived from "specialized knowledge" — for example, training on the use of international law or advice on petitioning the United Nations — then it is barred. On the other hand, plaintiffs' speech is not barred if it imparts only general or unspecialized knowledge.

The Government argues that § 2339B should nonetheless receive intermediate scrutiny because it *generally* functions as a regulation of conduct. That argument runs headlong into a number of our precedents, most prominently *Cohen v. California* (1971) [Casebook p. 177]. *Cohen* also involved a generally applicable regulation of conduct, barring breaches of the peace. But when Cohen was convicted for wearing a jacket bearing an epithet, we did not apply *O'Brien*. Instead, we recognized that the generally applicable law was directed at Cohen because of what his speech communicated — he violated the breach of the peace statute because of the offensive content of his particular message. We accordingly applied more rigorous scrutiny and reversed his conviction.

This suit falls into the same category. The law here may be described as directed at conduct, as the law in *Cohen* was directed at breaches of the peace, but as applied to plaintiffs the conduct triggering coverage under the statute consists of communicating a message. As we explained in *Texas v. Johnson*: "If the [Government's] regulation is not related to expression, then the less stringent standard we announced in *United States v. O'Brien* for regulations of noncommunicative conduct controls. If it is, then we are outside of *O'Brien*'s test, and we must [apply] a more demanding standard."

B

The First Amendment issue before us is more refined than either plaintiffs or the Government would have it. It is not whether the Government may prohibit pure political speech, or may prohibit material support in the form of conduct. It is instead whether the Government may prohibit what plaintiffs want to do — provide material support to the PKK and LTTE in the form of speech.

Everyone agrees that the Government's interest in combating terrorism is an urgent objective of the highest order. Plaintiffs' complaint is that the ban on material support, applied to what they wish to do, is not "necessary to further that interest." The objective of combating terrorism does not justify prohibiting their speech, plaintiffs argue, because their support will advance only the legitimate activities of the designated terrorist organizations, not their terrorism.

Whether foreign terrorist organizations meaningfully segregate support of their legitimate activities from support of terrorism is an empirical question. When it enacted § 2339B in 1996, Congress made specific findings regarding the serious threat posed by international terrorism. One of those findings explicitly rejects plaintiffs' contention that their support would not further the terrorist activities of the PKK and LTTE: "[F]oreign organizations that engage in terrorist activity are so tainted by their criminal conduct that *any contribution to such an organization* facilitates that conduct." § 301(a)(7) (emphasis added). . . .

We are convinced that Congress was justified in rejecting [the view that ostensibly peaceful aid would have no harmful effects]. The PKK and the LTTE are deadly groups. "The PKK's insurgency has claimed more than 22,000 lives." [Here and elsewhere in this section of the opinion, the Court cited and quoted from the affidavit submitted by Kenneth R. McKune, the Associate Director of the State Department Counter Terrorism Office and a principal adviser to the Secretary of State on terrorism matters.] The LTTE has engaged in extensive suicide bombings and political assassinations, including killings of the Sri Lankan President, Security Minister, and Deputy Defense Minister. "On January 31, 1996, the LTTE exploded a truck bomb filled with an estimated 1,000 pounds of explosives at the Central Bank in Colombo, killing 100 people and injuring more than 1,400. This bombing was the most deadly terrorist incident in the world in 1996." It is not difficult to conclude as Congress did that the "tain[t]" of such violent activities is so great that working in coordination with or at the command of the PKK and LTTE serves to legitimize and further their terrorist means.

Material support meant to "promot[e] peaceable, lawful conduct" can further terrorism by foreign groups in multiple ways. "Material support" is a valuable resource by definition. Such support frees up other resources within the organization that may be put to violent ends. It also importantly helps lend legitimacy to foreign terrorist groups — legitimacy that makes it easier for those groups to persist, to recruit members, and to raise funds — all of which facilitate more terrorist attacks. "Terrorist organizations do not maintain *organizational* 'firewalls' that would prevent or deter . . . sharing and commingling of support and benefits." "[I]nvestigators have revealed how terrorist groups systematically conceal their activities behind charitable, social, and political fronts." M. LEVITT, HAMAS: POLITICS, CHARITY, AND TERRORISM IN THE SERVICE OF JIHAD 2-3 (2006). . . . [As stated by Levitt,] "Muddying the waters between its political activism, good works, and terrorist attacks, Hamas is able to use its overt political and charitable organizations as a financial and logistical support network for its terrorist operations."

Money is fungible, and "[w]hen foreign terrorist organizations that have a dual structure raise funds, they highlight the civilian and humanitarian ends to which such moneys could be put." But "there is reason to believe that foreign terrorist organizations do not maintain legitimate *financial* firewalls between those funds raised for civil, nonviolent activities, and those ultimately used to support violent, terrorist operations." Thus, "[f]unds raised ostensibly for charitable purposes have in the past been redirected by some terrorist groups to fund the purchase of arms and explosives." There is evidence that the PKK and the LTTE, in particular, have not "respected the line between humanitarian and violent activities."

The dissent argues that there is "no natural stopping place" for the proposition that aiding a foreign terrorist organization's lawful activity promotes the terrorist organization as a whole. But Congress has settled on just such a natural stopping place: The statute reaches only material support coordinated with or under the direction of a designated foreign terrorist organization. Independent advocacy that might be viewed as promoting the group's legitimacy is not covered.[6]

Providing foreign terrorist groups with material support in any form also furthers terrorism by straining the United States' relationships with its allies and undermining cooperative efforts between nations to prevent terrorist attacks. We see no reason to question Congress's finding that "international cooperation is required for an effective response to terrorism, as demonstrated by the numerous multilateral conventions in force providing universal prosecutive jurisdiction over persons involved in a variety of terrorist acts, including hostage taking, murder of an internationally protected person, and aircraft piracy and sabotage." The material-support statute furthers this international effort by prohibiting aid for foreign terrorist groups that harm the United States' partners abroad: "A number of designated foreign terrorist organizations have attacked moderate governments with which the United States has vigorously endeavored to maintain close and friendly relations," and those attacks "threaten [the] social, economic and political stability" of such governments. "[O]ther foreign terrorist organizations attack our NATO allies, thereby implicating important and sensitive multilateral security arrangements."

For example, the Republic of Turkey — a fellow member of NATO — is defending itself against a violent insurgency waged by the PKK. That nation and our other allies would react sharply to Americans furnishing material support to foreign groups like the PKK, and would hardly be mollified by the explanation that the support was meant only to further those groups' "legitimate" activities. From Turkey's perspective, there likely are no such activities.

C

[1]

In analyzing whether it is possible in practice to distinguish material support for a foreign terrorist group's violent activities and its nonviolent activities, we do not rely exclusively on our own inferences drawn from the record evidence. We have before us an affidavit [by Associate Director McKune] stating the Executive Branch's conclusion on that question. The State Department informs us that "[t]he experience and analysis of the U.S. government agencies charged with combating terrorism strongly suppor[t]" Congress's finding that all contributions to foreign terrorist organizations further their terrorism. In the Executive's view: "Given the

---

[6] The dissent also contends that the particular sort of material support plaintiffs seek to provide cannot be diverted to terrorist activities, in the same direct way as funds or goods. This contention misses the point. Both common sense and the evidence submitted by the Government make clear that material support of a terrorist group's lawful activities facilitates the group's ability to attract "funds," "financing," and "goods" that will further its terrorist acts.

purposes, organizational structure, and clandestine nature of foreign terrorist organizations, it is highly likely that any material support to these organizations will ultimately inure to the benefit of their criminal, terrorist functions — regardless of whether such support was ostensibly intended to support non-violent, non-terrorist activities."

That evaluation of the facts by the Executive, like Congress's assessment, is entitled to deference. This litigation implicates sensitive and weighty interests of national security and foreign affairs. The PKK and the LTTE have committed terrorist acts against American citizens abroad, and the material-support statute addresses acute foreign policy concerns involving relationships with our Nation's allies. We have noted that "neither the Members of this Court nor most federal judges begin the day with briefings that may describe new and serious threats to our Nation and its people." It is vital in this context "not to substitute . . . our own evaluation of evidence for a reasonable evaluation by the Legislative Branch."

Our precedents, old and new, make clear that concerns of national security and foreign relations do not warrant abdication of the judicial role. We do not defer to the Government's reading of the First Amendment, even when such interests are at stake. We are one with the dissent that the Government's "authority and expertise in these matters do not automatically trump the Court's own obligation to secure the protection that the Constitution grants to individuals." But when it comes to collecting evidence and drawing factual inferences in this area, "the lack of competence on the part of the courts is marked," and respect for the Government's conclusions is appropriate.

One reason for that respect is that national security and foreign policy concerns arise in connection with efforts to confront evolving threats in an area where information can be difficult to obtain and the impact of certain conduct difficult to assess. The dissent slights these real constraints in demanding hard proof — with "detail," "specific facts," and "specific evidence" — that plaintiffs' proposed activities will support terrorist attacks. That would be a dangerous requirement. In this context, conclusions must often be based on informed judgment rather than concrete evidence, and that reality affects what we may reasonably insist on from the Government. The material-support statute is, on its face, a preventive measure — it criminalizes not terrorist attacks themselves, but aid that makes the attacks more likely to occur. The Government, when seeking to prevent imminent harms in the context of international affairs and national security, is not required to conclusively link all the pieces in the puzzle before we grant weight to its empirical conclusions.

This context is different from that in decisions like *Cohen*. In that case, the application of the statute turned on the offensiveness of the speech at issue. Observing that "one man's vulgarity is another's lyric," we invalidated Cohen's conviction in part because we concluded that "governmental officials cannot make principled distinctions in this area." In this litigation, by contrast, Congress and the Executive are uniquely positioned to make principled distinctions between activities that will further terrorist conduct and undermine United States foreign policy, and those that will not.

We also find it significant that Congress has been conscious of its own responsibility to consider how its actions may implicate constitutional concerns. [For example,] § 2339B only applies to designated foreign terrorist organizations. There is, and always has been, a limited number of those organizations designated by the Executive Branch, and any groups so designated may seek judicial review of the designation. . . . [Most] importantly, Congress has avoided any restriction on independent advocacy, or indeed any activities not directed to, coordinated with, or controlled by foreign terrorist groups.

At bottom, plaintiffs simply disagree with the considered judgment of Congress and the Executive that providing material support to a designated foreign terrorist organization — even seemingly benign support — bolsters the terrorist activities of that organization. That judgment, however, is entitled to significant weight, and we have persuasive evidence before us to sustain it. Given the sensitive interests in national security and foreign affairs at stake, the political branches have adequately substantiated their determination that, to serve the Government's interest in preventing terrorism, it was necessary to prohibit providing material support in the form of training, expert advice, personnel, and services to foreign terrorist groups, even if the supporters meant to promote only the groups' nonviolent ends.

[2]

We turn to the particular speech plaintiffs propose to undertake. First, plaintiffs propose to "train members of [the] PKK on how to use humanitarian and international law to peacefully resolve disputes." Congress can, consistent with the First Amendment, prohibit this direct training. It is wholly foreseeable that the PKK could use the "specific skill[s]" that plaintiffs propose to impart as part of a broader strategy to promote terrorism. The PKK could, for example, pursue peaceful negotiation as a means of buying time to recover from short-term setbacks, lulling opponents into complacency, and ultimately preparing for renewed attacks. A foreign terrorist organization introduced to the structures of the international legal system might use the information to threaten, manipulate, and disrupt. This possibility is real, not remote.

Second, plaintiffs propose to "teach PKK members how to petition various representative bodies such as the United Nations for relief." The Government acts within First Amendment strictures in banning this proposed speech because it teaches the organization how to acquire "relief," which plaintiffs never define with any specificity, and which could readily include monetary aid. Indeed, earlier in this litigation, plaintiffs sought to teach the LTTE "to present claims for tsunami-related aid to mediators and international bodies," which naturally included monetary relief. Money is fungible, and Congress logically concluded that money a terrorist group such as the PKK obtains using the techniques plaintiffs propose to teach could be redirected to funding the group's violent activities.

Finally, plaintiffs propose to "engage in political advocacy on behalf of Kurds who live in Turkey," and "engage in political advocacy on behalf of Tamils who live in Sri Lanka." As explained above, plaintiffs do not specify their expected level of coordination with the PKK or LTTE or suggest what exactly their "advocacy" would consist of. Plaintiffs' proposals are phrased at such a high level of generality that they cannot prevail in this preenforcement challenge.

In responding to the foregoing, the dissent fails to address the real dangers at stake. It instead considers only the possible benefits of plaintiffs' proposed activities in the abstract. The dissent seems unwilling to entertain the prospect that training and advising a designated foreign terrorist organization on how to take advantage of international entities might benefit that organization in a way that facilitates its terrorist activities. In the dissent's world, such training is all to the good. Congress and the Executive, however, have concluded that we live in a different world: one in which the designated foreign terrorist organizations "are so tainted by their criminal conduct that any contribution to such an organization facilitates that conduct." AEDPA § 301(a)(7). One in which, for example, "the United Nations High Commissioner for Refugees was forced to close a Kurdish refugee camp in northern Iraq because the camp had come under the control of the PKK, and the PKK had failed to respect its 'neutral and humanitarian nature.' " Training and advice on how to work with the United Nations could readily have helped the PKK in its efforts to use the United Nations camp as a base for terrorist activities.

If only good can come from training our adversaries in international dispute resolution, presumably it would have been unconstitutional to prevent American citizens from training the Japanese Government on using international organizations and mechanisms to resolve disputes during World War II. It would, under the dissent's reasoning, have been contrary to our commitment to resolving disputes through "deliberative forces" for Congress to conclude that assisting Japan on that front might facilitate its war effort more generally. That view is not one the First Amendment requires us to embrace.

All this is not to say that any future applications of the material-support statute to speech or advocacy will survive First Amendment scrutiny. It is also not to say that any other statute relating to speech and terrorism would satisfy the First Amendment. In particular, we in no way suggest that a regulation of independent speech would pass constitutional muster, even if the Government were to show that such speech benefits foreign terrorist organizations. We also do not suggest that Congress could extend the same prohibition on material support at issue here to domestic organizations. We simply hold that, in prohibiting the particular forms of support that plaintiffs seek to provide to foreign terrorist groups, § 2339B does not violate the freedom of speech.

VI

Plaintiffs' final claim is that the material-support statute violates their freedom of association under the First Amendment. Plaintiffs argue that the statute criminalizes the mere fact of their associating with the PKK and the LTTE, thereby running afoul of decisions like *De Jonge v. Oregon* (1937) [Casebook p. 32], and cases in which we have overturned sanctions for joining the Communist Party.

The Court of Appeals correctly rejected this claim because the statute does not penalize mere association with a foreign terrorist organization. As the Ninth

Circuit put it: "The statute does not prohibit being a member of one of the designated groups or vigorously promoting and supporting the political goals of the group. . . . What [§ 2339B] prohibits is the act of giving material support. . . ." Plaintiffs want to do the latter. Our decisions scrutinizing penalties on simple association or assembly are therefore inapposite. *See, e.g., De Jonge.* . . .

The judgment of the United States Court of Appeals for the Ninth Circuit is affirmed in part and reversed in part, and the cases are remanded for further proceedings consistent with this opinion.

It is so ordered.

JUSTICE BREYER, with whom JUSTICES GINSBURG and SOTOMAYOR join, dissenting.

. . . I cannot agree with the Court's conclusion that the Constitution permits the Government to prosecute the plaintiffs criminally for engaging in coordinated teaching and advocacy furthering the designated organizations' lawful political objectives. In my view, the Government has not met its burden of showing that an interpretation of the statute that would prohibit this speech- and association-related activity serves the Government's compelling interest in combating terrorism. And I would interpret the statute as normally placing activity of this kind outside its scope.

I

. . . In my view, the Government has not made the strong showing necessary to justify under the First Amendment the criminal prosecution of those who engage in [the activities the plaintiffs wish to engage in]. All the activities involve the communication and advocacy of political ideas and lawful means of achieving political ends. Even the subjects the plaintiffs wish to teach — using international law to resolve disputes peacefully or petitioning the United Nations, for instance — concern political speech. We cannot avoid the constitutional significance of these facts on the basis that some of this speech takes place outside the United States and is directed at foreign governments, for the activities also involve advocacy in *this* country directed to our government and *its* policies. The plaintiffs, for example, wish to write and distribute publications and to speak before the United States Congress.

That this speech and association for political purposes is the *kind* of activity to which the First Amendment ordinarily offers its strongest protection is elementary. *See New York Times Co. v. Sullivan* (1964) [Casebook p. 89]; *Lovell v. City of Griffin* (1938) [Casebook p. 266].

Although in the Court's view the statute applies only where the PKK helps to coordinate a defendant's activities, the simple fact of "coordination" alone cannot readily remove protection that the First Amendment would otherwise grant. That amendment, after all, also protects the freedom of association. *See NAACP v. Claiborne Hardware Co.* (1982) [Casebook p. 58]; *De Jonge v. Oregon* (1937) [Casebook p. 32]. . . .

"Coordination" with a group that engages in unlawful activity also does not deprive the plaintiffs of the First Amendment's protection under any traditional "categorical" exception to its protection. The plaintiffs do not propose to solicit a crime. They will not engage in fraud or defamation or circulate obscenity. And the First Amendment protects advocacy even of unlawful action so long as that advocacy is not "directed to inciting or producing imminent lawless action and . . . *likely to incite or produce* such action." *Brandenburg v. Ohio* (1969) [Casebook p. 52] (emphasis added). Here the plaintiffs seek to advocate peaceful, lawful action to secure *political* ends; and they seek to teach others how to do the same. No one contends that the plaintiffs' speech to these organizations can be prohibited as incitement under *Brandenburg*.

Moreover, the Court has previously held that a person who associates with a group that uses unlawful means to achieve its ends does not thereby necessarily forfeit the First Amendment's protection for freedom of association. *See Scales v. United States* (1961) [Casebook p. 49] ("[Q]uasi-political parties or other groups that may embrace both legal and illegal aims differ from a technical conspiracy, which is defined by its criminal purpose"); *see also Claiborne Hardware* ("The right to associate does not lose all constitutional protection merely because some members of the group may have participated in conduct or advocated doctrine that itself is not protected"). Rather, the Court has pointed out in respect to associating with a group advocating overthrow of the Government through force and violence: "If the persons assembling have committed crimes elsewhere . . . , they may be prosecuted for their . . . violation of valid laws. But it is a different matter when the State, instead of prosecuting them for such offenses, seizes upon mere participation in a peaceable assembly and a lawful public discussion as the basis for a criminal charge." *De Jonge* (striking down conviction for attending and assisting at Communist Party meeting because "[n]otwithstanding [the party's] objectives, the defendant still enjoyed his personal right of free speech and to take part in peaceable assembly having a lawful purpose").

Not even the "serious and deadly problem" of international terrorism can require *automatic* forfeiture of First Amendment rights. . . . Thus, there is no general First Amendment exception that applies here. If the statute is constitutional in this context, it would have to come with a strong justification attached.

It is not surprising that the majority, in determining the constitutionality of criminally prohibiting the plaintiffs' proposed activities, would apply, not the kind of intermediate First Amendment standard that applies to conduct, but " 'a more demanding standard.' " *Ante* (quoting *Texas v. Johnson* (1989) [Casebook p. 459]). Indeed, where, as here, a statute applies criminal penalties and at least arguably does so on the basis of content-based distinctions, I should think we would scrutinize the statute and justifications "strictly" — to determine whether the prohibition is justified by a "compelling" need that cannot be "less restrictively" accommodated. *See*, [*e.g.*,] *Houston v. Hill* (1987) [Casebook p. 76].

But, even if we assume for argument's sake that "strict scrutiny" does not apply, no one can deny that we must at the very least "measure the validity of the means adopted by Congress against both the goal it has sought to achieve and the specific prohibitions of the First Amendment." And here I need go no further, for I doubt that the statute, as the Government would interpret it, can survive any reasonably applicable First Amendment standard.

The Government does identify a compelling countervailing interest, namely, the interest in protecting the security of the United States and its nationals from the threats that foreign terrorist organizations pose by denying those organizations financial and other fungible resources. I do not dispute the importance of this interest. But I do dispute whether the interest can justify the statute's criminal prohibition. To put the matter more specifically, precisely how does application of the statute to the protected activities before us help achieve that important security-related end?

The Government makes two efforts to answer this question. *First*, the Government says that the plaintiffs' support for these organizations is "fungible" in the same sense as other forms of banned support. Being fungible, the plaintiffs' support could, for example, free up other resources, which the organization might put to terrorist ends.

The proposition that the two very different kinds of "support" are "fungible," however, is not *obviously* true. There is no *obvious* way in which undertaking advocacy for political change through peaceful means or teaching the PKK and LTTE, say, how to petition the United Nations for political change is fungible with other resources that might be put to more sinister ends in the way that donations of money, food, or computer training are fungible. It is far from obvious that these advocacy activities can themselves be redirected, or will free other resources that can be directed, towards terrorist ends. Thus, we must determine whether the Government has come forward with evidence to support its claim.

The Government has provided us with no empirical information that might convincingly support this claim. Instead, the Government cites only to evidence that Congress was concerned about the "fungible" nature in general of resources, predominately money and material goods. . . .

The most one can say in the Government's favor about these [Congressional findings and the State Department affidavit] is that they *might* be read as offering highly general support for its argument. The statements do not, however, explain in any detail how the plaintiffs' political-advocacy-related activities might actually be "fungible" and therefore capable of being diverted to terrorist use. Nor do they indicate that Congress itself was concerned with "support" of this kind. The affidavit refers to "funds," "financing," and "goods" — none of which encompasses the plaintiffs' activities. The statutory statement and [a] House Report use broad terms like "contributions" and "services" that might be construed as encompassing the plaintiffs' activities. But in context, those terms are more naturally understood as referring to contributions of goods, money, or training and other services (say, computer programming) that could be diverted to, or free funding for, terrorist ends. Peaceful political advocacy does not obviously fall into these categories. . . .

Second, the Government says that the plaintiffs' proposed activities will "bolste[r] a terrorist organization's efficacy and strength in a community" and "undermin[e] this nation's efforts to *delegitimize and weaken* those groups." In the

Court's view, too, the Constitution permits application of the statute to activities of the kind at issue in part because those activities could provide a group that engages in terrorism with "legitimacy." The Court suggests that, armed with this greater "legitimacy," these organizations will more readily be able to obtain material support of the kinds Congress plainly intended to ban — money, arms, lodging, and the like.

Yet the Government does not claim that the statute forbids any speech "legitimating" a terrorist group. Rather, it reads the statute as permitting (1) membership in terrorist organizations, (2) "peaceably assembling with members of the PKK and LTTE for lawful discussion," or (3) "independent advocacy" on behalf of these organizations. The Court, too, emphasizes that activities not "*coordinated with*" the terrorist groups are not banned. And it argues that speaking, writing, and teaching aimed at furthering a terrorist organization's peaceful political ends could "mak[e] it easier for those groups to persist, to recruit members, and to raise funds."

But this "legitimacy" justification cannot by itself warrant suppression of political speech, advocacy, and association. Speech, association, and related activities on behalf of a group will often, perhaps always, help to legitimate that group. Thus, were the law to accept a "legitimating" effect, in and of itself and without qualification, as providing sufficient grounds for imposing such a ban, the First Amendment battle would be lost in untold instances where it should be won. Once one accepts this argument, there is no natural stopping place. The argument applies as strongly to "independent" as to "coordinated" advocacy. That fact is reflected in part in the Government's claim that the ban here, so supported, prohibits a lawyer hired by a designated group from filing on behalf of that group an amicus brief before the United Nations or even before this Court.

That fact is also reflected in the difficulty of drawing a line designed to accept the legitimacy argument in some instances but not in others. It is inordinately difficult to distinguish when speech activity will and when it will not initiate the chain of causation the Court suggests — a chain that leads from peaceful advocacy to "legitimacy" to increased support for the group to an increased supply of material goods that support its terrorist activities. Even were we to find some such line of distinction, its application would seem so inherently uncertain that it would often, perhaps always, "chill" protected speech beyond its boundary. In short, the justification, put forward simply in abstract terms and without limitation, must *always*, or it will *never*, be sufficient. Given the nature of the plaintiffs' activities, "always" cannot possibly be the First Amendment's answer.

Regardless, the "legitimacy" justification itself is inconsistent with critically important First Amendment case law. Consider the cases involving the protection the First Amendment offered those who joined the Communist Party intending only to further its peaceful activities. In those cases, this Court took account of congressional findings that the Communist Party not only advocated theoretically but also sought to put into practice the overthrow of our Government through force and violence. The Court had previously accepted Congress' determinations that the American Communist Party was a "Communist action organization" which (1) acted under the "control, direction, and discipline" of the world Communist movement, a movement that sought to employ "espionage, sabotage, terrorism, and any other means deemed necessary, to establish a Communist totalitarian dictatorship," and (2) "endeavor[ed]" to bring about "the overthrow of existing governments by . . . force if necessary."

Nonetheless, the Court held that the First Amendment protected an American's right to belong to that party — despite whatever "legitimating" effect membership might have had — as long as the person did not share the party's unlawful purposes. *See, e.g., De Jonge; Scales.* As I have pointed out, those cases draw further support from other cases permitting pure advocacy of even the most unlawful activity — as long as that advocacy is not "directed to inciting or producing imminent lawless action and . . . likely to incite or produce such action." *Brandenburg.* The Government's "legitimating" theory would seem to apply to these cases with equal justifying force; and, if recognized, it would have led this Court to conclusions other than those it reached.

Nor can the Government overcome these considerations simply by narrowing the covered activities to those that involve *coordinated*, rather than *independent*, advocacy. Conversations, discussions, or logistical arrangements might well prove necessary to carry out the speech-related activities here at issue (just as conversations and discussions are a necessary part of *membership* in any organization). The Government does not distinguish this kind of "coordination" from any other. I am not aware of any form of words that might be used to describe "coordination" that would not, at a minimum, seriously chill not only the kind of activities the plaintiffs raise before us, but also the "independent advocacy" the Government purports to permit. And, as for the Government's willingness to distinguish *independent* advocacy from *coordinated* advocacy, the former is more likely, not less likely, to confer legitimacy than the latter. Thus, other things being equal, the distinction "coordination" makes is arbitrary in respect to furthering the statute's purposes. And a rule of law that finds the "legitimacy" argument adequate in respect to the latter would have a hard time distinguishing a statute that sought to attack the former.

Consider the majority's development of the Government's themes. First, the majority discusses the plaintiffs' proposal to "train members of [the] PKK on how to use humanitarian and international law to peacefully resolve disputes." The majority justifies the criminalization of this activity in significant part on the ground that "peaceful negotiation[s]" might just "bu[y] time . . . , lulling opponents into complacency." And the PKK might use its new information about "the structures of the international legal system . . . to threaten, manipulate, and disrupt."

What is one to say about these arguments — arguments that would deny First Amendment protection to the peaceful teaching of international human rights law on the ground that a little knowledge about "the international legal system" is too dangerous a thing; that an opponent's subsequent willingness to negotiate might be faked, so let's not teach him how to try? What might be said of these claims by those who live, as we do, in a Nation committed to the resolution of disputes through "deliberative forces"? *Whitney v. California* (1927) [Casebook p. 26] (Brandeis, J., concurring).

In my own view, the majority's arguments stretch the concept of "fungibility" beyond constitutional limits. Neither Congress nor the Government advanced these particular hypothetical claims. I am not aware of any case in this Court — not *Gitlow v. New York* (1925) [Casebook p. 21], not *Schenck v. United States* (1919) [Casebook p. 3], not *Abrams v. United States* (1919) [Casebook p. 11], not the later Communist Party cases decided during the heat of the Cold War — in which the Court accepted anything like a claim that speech or teaching might be criminalized lest it, e.g., buy negotiating time for an opponent who would put that time to bad use.

Moreover, the risk that those who are taught will put otherwise innocent speech or knowledge to bad use is omnipresent, at least where that risk rests on little more than (even informed) speculation. Hence to accept this kind of argument without more and to apply it to the teaching of a subject such as international human rights law is to adopt a rule of law that, contrary to the Constitution's text and First Amendment precedent, would automatically forbid the teaching of any subject in a case where national security interests conflict with the First Amendment. The Constitution does not allow all such conflicts to be decided in the Government's favor.

The majority, as I have said, cannot limit the scope of its arguments through its claim that the plaintiffs remain free to engage in the protected activity *as long as it is not "coordinated."* That is because there is no practical way to organize classes for a group (say, wishing to learn about human rights law) without *"coordination."* Nor can the majority limit the scope of its argument by pointing to some special limiting circumstance present here. That is because the only evidence the majority offers to support its general claim consists of a single reference to a book about terrorism, which the Government did not mention, and which apparently says no more than that at one time the PKK suspended its armed struggle and then returned to it.

Second, the majority discusses the plaintiffs' proposal to "teach PKK members how to petition various representative bodies such as the United Nations *for relief.*" The majority's only argument with respect to this proposal is that the relief obtained "could readily include monetary aid," which the PKK might use to buy guns. The majority misunderstands the word "relief." In *this* context, as the record makes clear, the word "relief" does not refer to "money." It refers to recognition under the Geneva Conventions.

Throughout, the majority emphasizes that it would defer strongly to Congress' "informed judgment." But here, there is no evidence that Congress has made such a judgment regarding the specific activities at issue in these cases. In any event, "whenever the fundamental rights of free speech and assembly are alleged to have been invaded, it must remain open [for judicial determination] whether there actually did exist at the time a clear danger; whether the danger, if any, was imminent; and whether the evil apprehended was one so substantial as to justify the stringent restriction interposed by the legislature." *Whitney* (Brandeis, J., concurring). . . .

I concede that the Government's expertise in foreign affairs may warrant deference in respect to many matters, *e.g.,* our relations with Turkey. But it remains for this Court to decide whether the Government has shown that such an interest justifies criminalizing speech activity otherwise protected by the First Amendment. And the fact that other nations may like us less for granting that protection cannot in and of itself carry the day.

Finally, I would reemphasize that neither the Government nor the majority points to any specific facts that show that the speech-related activities before us are fungible in some *special way* or confer some *special* legitimacy upon the PKK. Rather, their arguments in this respect are general and speculative. Those arguments would apply to virtually all speech-related support for a dual-purpose group's peaceful activities (irrespective of whether the speech-related activity is coordinated). Both First Amendment logic and First Amendment case law prevent us from "sacrific[ing] First Amendment protections for so speculative a gain."

II

For the reasons I have set forth, I believe application of the statute as the Government interprets it would gravely and without adequate justification injure interests of the kind the First Amendment protects. Thus, there is "a serious doubt" as to the statute's constitutionality. And where that is so, we must "ascertain whether a construction of the statute is fairly possible by which the question may be avoided."

I believe that a construction that would avoid the constitutional problem is "fairly possible." In particular, I would read the statute as criminalizing First-Amendment-protected pure speech and association only when the defendant knows or intends that those activities will assist the organization's unlawful terrorist actions. Under this reading, the Government would have to show, at a minimum, that such defendants provided support that they knew was significantly likely to help the organization pursue its unlawful terrorist aims. . . .

. . . [The] majority's statutory claim that Congress did not use the word "knowingly" as I would use it is beside the point. Our consequent reading is consistent with the statute's text; it is consistent with Congress' basic intent; it interprets but does not significantly add to what the statute otherwise contains. We should adopt it.

III

Having interpreted the statute to impose the *mens rea* requirement just described, I would remand the cases so that the lower courts could consider more specifically the precise activities in which the plaintiffs still wish to engage and determine whether and to what extent a grant of declaratory and injunctive relief were warranted. I do not see why the majority does not also remand the cases for consideration of the plaintiffs' activities relating to "advocating" for the organizations' peaceful causes. . . .

IV

In sum, these cases require us to consider how to apply the First Amendment where national security interests are at stake. When deciding such cases, courts are aware and must respect the fact that the Constitution entrusts to the Executive and Legislative Branches the power to provide for the national defense, and that it grants particular authority to the President in matters of foreign affairs. Nonetheless, this Court has also made clear that authority and expertise in these matters do not automatically trump the Court's own obligation to secure the protection that the Constitution grants to individuals. In these cases, for the reasons I have stated, I believe the Court has failed to examine the Government's justifications with sufficient care. It has failed to insist upon specific evidence, rather than general assertion. It has failed to require tailoring of means to fit compelling ends. And ultimately it deprives the individuals before us of the protection that the First Amendment demands.

That is why, with respect, I dissent.

NOTE: SPEECH ACTIVITY AS "MATERIAL SUPPORT"

1. After rejecting the Government's attempt to invoke *United States v. O'Brien*, the Court puts precedent to the side in analyzing the First Amendment claim. In contrast, the dissent quotes from several cases, including *Scales*, *DeJonge*, and *Claiborne Hardware*. How strongly do these cases support the dissent's position?

2. The Court finds that Congress could prohibit material support directed to "a foreign terrorist organization's lawful activity" in part because "[m]oney is fungible." The dissent responds that "the majority's arguments stretch the concept of 'fungibility' beyond constitutional limits," particularly when the support involves "[p]eaceful political advocacy." Does the majority adequately explain how non-monetary support "frees up other resources" that terrorist groups "may put to violent ends"?

3. The Court also says that material support meant to promote "peaceable, lawful conduct" can be criminalized because such support "helps lend *legitimacy* to foreign terrorist groups," and that this legitimacy ultimately "facilitate[s] more terrorist attacks." The dissent strongly challenges the Court on this point, saying that the "legitimacy justification" has "no natural stopping place" and that it is "inconsistent with critically important First Amendment case law."

Consider particularly the subversive advocacy cases in Chapter One. Do any of them rely on a "legitimacy justification"? If not, does that mean that the argument should fail?

4. Consider the "street gang" Problem in Chapter 1 (Casebook p. 62). Does *HLP* foreclose a facial attack on the Oceana criminal syndicalism statute? On the facts presented, should the conviction be upheld?

Chapter 11

TESTING THE BOUNDARIES OF DOCTRINE

C. CAMPAIGN FINANCE

Page 724: *add at end of the page:*

CITIZENS UNITED v. FEDERAL ELECTION COMMISSION
130 S. Ct. 876 (2010)

Justice Kennedy delivered the opinion of the Court.

Federal law prohibits corporations and unions from using their general treasury funds to make independent expenditures for speech defined as an "electioneering communication" or for speech expressly advocating the election or defeat of a candidate. 2 U.S.C. § 441b. Limits on electioneering communications were upheld in *McConnell v. Federal Election Comm'n* (2003). The holding of *McConnell* rested to a large extent on an earlier case, *Austin v. Michigan Chamber of Commerce* (1990). *Austin* had held that political speech may be banned based on the speaker's corporate identity.

In this case we are asked to reconsider *Austin* and, in effect, *McConnell*. It has been noted that "*Austin* was a significant departure from ancient First Amendment principles," *Federal Election Comm'n v. Wisconsin Right to Life, Inc.* (2007) (*WRTL II*) (Scalia, J., concurring in part and concurring in judgment). We agree with that conclusion and hold that *stare decisis* does not compel the continued acceptance of *Austin*. The Government may regulate corporate political speech through disclaimer and disclosure requirements, but it may not suppress that speech altogether. We turn to the case now before us.

I

A

Citizens United is a nonprofit corporation. It brought this action in the United States District Court for the District of Columbia. A three-judge court later convened to hear the cause. The resulting judgment gives rise to this appeal.

Citizens United has an annual budget of about $12 million. Most of its funds are from donations by individuals; but, in addition, it accepts a small portion of its funds from for-profit corporations.

In January 2008, Citizens United released a film entitled *Hillary: The Movie*. We refer to the film as *Hillary*. It is a 90-minute documentary about then-Senator Hillary Clinton, who was a candidate in the Democratic Party's 2008 Presidential primary elections. *Hillary* mentions Senator Clinton by name and depicts interviews with political commentators and other persons, most of them quite critical of Senator Clinton. *Hillary* was released in theaters and on DVD, but Citizens United wanted to increase distribution by making it available through video-on-demand. . . .

To implement the proposal, Citizens United was prepared to pay for the video-on-demand; and to promote the film, it produced two 10-second ads and one 30-second ad for *Hillary*. Each ad includes a short (and, in our view, pejorative) statement about Senator Clinton, followed by the name of the movie and the movie's Website address. Citizens United desired to promote the video-on-demand offering by running advertisements on broadcast and cable television.

B

Before the Bipartisan Campaign Reform Act of 2002 (BCRA), federal law prohibited — and still does prohibit — corporations and unions from using general treasury funds to make direct contributions to candidates or independent expenditures that expressly advocate the election or defeat of a candidate, through any form of media, in connection with certain qualified federal elections. 2 U.S.C. § 441b (2000 ed.); see *McConnell*; *Federal Election Comm'n v. Massachusetts Citizens for Life, Inc. (MCFL)* (1986). BCRA § 203 amended § 441b to prohibit any "electioneering communication" as well. An electioneering communication is defined as "any broadcast, cable, or satellite communication" that "refers to a clearly identified candidate for Federal office" and is made within 30 days of a primary or 60 days of a general election. . . . Corporations and unions are barred from using their general treasury funds for express advocacy or electioneering communications. They may establish, however, a "separate segregated fund" (known as a political action committee, or PAC) for these purposes. The moneys received by the segregated fund are limited to donations from stockholders and employees of the corporation or, in the case of unions, members of the union.

C

Citizens United wanted to make *Hillary* available through video-on-demand within 30 days of the 2008 primary elections. It feared, however, that both the film and the ads would be covered by § 441b's ban on corporate-funded independent expenditures, thus subjecting the corporation to civil and criminal penalties under § 437g. In December 2007, Citizens United sought declaratory and injunctive relief against the FEC. It argued that (1) § 441b is unconstitutional as applied to *Hillary*; and (2) BCRA's disclaimer and disclosure requirements, BCRA §§ 201 and 311, are unconstitutional as applied to *Hillary* and to the three ads for the movie.

The District Court denied Citizens United's motion for a preliminary injunction, and then granted the FEC's motion for summary judgment . . . .

We noted probable jurisdiction. The case was reargued in this Court after the Court asked the parties to file supplemental briefs addressing whether we should overrule either or both *Austin* and the part of *McConnell* which addresses the facial validity of 2 U.S.C. § 441b.

II

Before considering whether *Austin* should be overruled, we first address whether Citizens United's claim that § 441b cannot be applied to *Hillary* may be resolved on other, narrower grounds. [The Court considered, and rejected, the possibility that it rule for Citizens United on a narrower ground. First, the Court ruled that *Hillary* was an "electioneering communication" as that term is used in BCRA, rejecting Citizens United's argument that video-on-demand distribution did not count as the public distribution of communications regulated by BCRA. It next held that, under *WRTL II*, *Hillary* had to be understood as express advocacy, and thus subject to BCRA's limits on corporate speech. The Court then rejected Citizens United's invitation to invalidate the relevant section of BCRA as applied to video-on-demand distribution. Citizens United argued that such distribution presents less potential for distorting the political process than the television ads that were at the center of Congress's concern when it enacted BCRA. The Court rejected this argument, observing that "any effort by the Judiciary to decide which means of communications are to be preferred . . . would raise questions as to the courts' own lawful authority." Finally, the Court rejected Citizens United's suggestion that the *MCFL* exception for advocacy groups be expanded to protect speech made by nonprofit corporations "funded overwhelmingly by individuals." The Court concluded that this approach would do too much damage to the text of BCRA, and would contradict *Austin* in the course of declining to reconsider that precedent.

[The Court concluded its preliminary analysis by rejecting the argument that Citizens United's voluntary dismissal of its facial challenge to BCRA amounted to a waiver of its attack on *Austin*. The Court concluded that the lower court had considered the facial challenge, which made the argument available for Supreme Court consideration. It also stated that a narrower decision would chill free speech by maintaining the uncertainty about groups' ability to engage in political speech.]

III

. . . The law before us is an outright ban, backed by criminal sanctions. Section 441b makes it a felony for all corporations — including nonprofit advocacy corporations — either to expressly advocate the election or defeat of candidates or to broadcast electioneering communications within 30 days of a primary election and 60 days of a general election. Thus, the following acts would all be felonies under § 441b: The Sierra Club runs an ad, within the crucial phase of 60 days before the general election, that exhorts the public to disapprove of a Congressman who favors logging in national forests; the National Rifle Association publishes a book urging the public to vote for the challenger because the incumbent U.S. Senator supports a handgun ban; and the American Civil Liberties Union creates a Web site telling the public to vote for a Presidential candidate in light of that candidate's defense of free speech. These prohibitions are classic examples of censorship.

Section 441b is a ban on corporate speech notwithstanding the fact that a PAC created by a corporation can still speak. A PAC is a separate association from the corporation. So the PAC exemption from § 441b's expenditure ban does not allow corporations to speak. . . .

Section 441b's prohibition on corporate independent expenditures is thus a ban on speech. As a "restriction on the amount of money a person or group can spend on political communication during a campaign," that statute "necessarily reduces the quantity of expression by restricting the number of issues discussed, the depth of their exploration, and the size of the audience reached." *Buckley v. Valeo* (1976) (*per curiam*). Were the Court to uphold these restrictions, the Government could repress speech by silencing certain voices at any of the various points in the speech process. If § 441b applied to individuals, no one would believe that it is merely a time, place, or manner restriction on speech. Its purpose and effect are to silence entities whose voices the Government deems to be suspect.

Speech is an essential mechanism of democracy, for it is the means to hold officials accountable to the people. . . . The First Amendment " 'has its fullest and most urgent application' to speech uttered during a campaign for political office."

For these reasons, political speech must prevail against laws that would suppress it, whether by design or inadvertence. Laws that burden political speech are "subject to strict scrutiny," which requires the Government to prove that the restriction "furthers a compelling interest and is narrowly tailored to achieve that interest." . . .

Premised on mistrust of governmental power, the First Amendment stands against attempts to disfavor certain subjects or viewpoints. Prohibited, too, are restrictions distinguishing among different speakers, allowing speech by some but not others. See *First Nat. Bank of Boston v. Bellotti* (1978). As instruments to censor, these categories are interrelated: Speech restrictions based on the identity of the speaker are all too often simply a means to control content.

Quite apart from the purpose or effect of regulating content, moreover, the Government may commit a constitutional wrong when by law it identifies certain preferred speakers. By taking the right to speak from some and giving it to others, the Government deprives the disadvantaged person or class of the right to use speech to strive to establish worth, standing, and respect for the speaker's voice. The Government may not by these means deprive the public of the right and privilege to determine for itself what speech and speakers are worthy of consideration. The First Amendment protects speech and speaker, and the ideas that flow from each.

The Court has upheld a narrow class of speech restrictions that operate to the disadvantage of certain persons, but these rulings were based on an interest in allowing governmental entities to perform their functions. *See, e.g., Bethel School Dist. No. 403 v. Fraser* (1986) [Casebook p. 760] (protecting the "function of public school education"); *Jones v. North Carolina Prisoners' Labor Union, Inc.*, 433 U.S. 119 (1977) (furthering "the legitimate penological objectives of the corrections system"); *Parker v. Levy*, 417 U.S. 733 (1974) (ensuring "the capacity of the Government to discharge its [military] responsibilities"); *Civil Service Comm'n v. Letter Carriers*, 413 U.S. 548 (1973) ("[F]ederal service should depend upon meritorious performance rather than political service"). The corporate independent expenditures at issue in this case, however, would not interfere with governmental functions, so these cases are inapposite. These precedents stand only for the proposition that there are certain governmental functions that cannot operate without some restrictions on particular kinds of speech. By contrast, it is inherent in the nature of the political process that voters must be free to obtain information from diverse sources in order to determine how to cast their votes. At least before *Austin*, the Court had not allowed the exclusion of a class of speakers from the general public dialogue.

We find no basis for the proposition that, in the context of political speech, the Government may impose restrictions on certain disfavored speakers. Both history and logic lead us to this conclusion.

A

1

The Court has recognized that First Amendment protection extends to corporations. *Bellotti* (citing *Linmark Associates, Inc. v. Willingboro*, 431 U.S. 85 (1977); *Time, Inc. v. Firestone*, 424 U.S. 448 (1976); *Doran v. Salem Inn, Inc.*, 422 U.S. 922 (1975); *Southeastern Promotions, Ltd. v. Conrad*, 420 U.S. 546 (1975); *Cox Broadcasting Corp. v. Cohn*, 420 U.S. 469 (1975); *Miami Herald Publishing Co. v. Tornillo*, 418 U.S. 241 (1974); *New York Times Co. v. United States* (1971) [Casebook p. 294] (*per curiam*); *Time, Inc. v. Hill*, 385 U.S. 374 (1967); *New York Times Co. v. Sullivan* (1964) [Casebook p. 89]; *Kingsley Int'l Pictures Corp. v. Regents of Univ. of N.Y.*, 360 U.S. 684 (1959); *Joseph Burstyn, Inc. v. Wilson*, 343 U.S. 495 (1952)); *see, e.g., Turner Broadcasting System, Inc. v. FCC*, 520 U.S. 180 (1997); *Denver Area Ed. Telecommunications Consortium, Inc. v. FCC*, 518 U.S. 727 (1996); *Turner Broadcasting System v. FCC* (1994) [Casebook p. 593]; *Simon & Schuster, Inc. v. Members of New York State Crime Victims Board*, 502 U.S. 105 (1991); *Sable Communications of Cal., Inc. v. FCC*, 492 U.S. 115 (1989); *Florida Star v. B.J.F.*, 491 U.S. 524 (1989); *Philadelphia Newspapers, Inc. v. Hepps*, 475 U.S. 767 (1986); *Landmark Communications, Inc. v. Virginia*, 435 U.S. 829 (1978); *Young v. American Mini Theatres, Inc.*, 427 U.S. 50 (1976); *Gertz v. Robert Welch, Inc.* (1974) [Casebook p. 106]; *Greenbelt Cooperative Publishing Assn., Inc. v. Bresler*, 398 U.S. 6 (1970).

This protection has been extended by explicit holdings to the context of political speech. *See, e.g., Grosjean v. American Press Co.* (1936) [Casebook p. 815]. Under the rationale of these precedents, political speech does not lose First Amendment protection "simply because its source is a corporation." *Bellotti*; see *Pacific Gas & Elec. Co. v. Public Util. Comm'n of Cal.*, 475 U.S. 1 (1986) (plurality opinion) ("The identity of the speaker is not decisive in determining whether speech is protected. Corporations and other associations, like individuals, contribute to the 'discussion, debate, and the dissemination of information and ideas' that the First Amendment seeks to foster."). The Court has thus rejected the argument that political speech of corporations or other associations should be treated differently under the First Amendment simply because such associations are not "natural persons."

At least since the latter part of the 19th century, the laws of some States and of the United States imposed a ban on corporate direct contributions to candidates. Yet not until 1947 did Congress first prohibit independent expenditures by corporations and labor unions . . . . In passing this Act Congress overrode the veto of President Truman, who warned that the expenditure ban was a "dangerous intrusion on free speech."

For almost three decades thereafter, the Court did not reach the question whether restrictions on corporate and union expenditures are constitutional. The question was in the background of *United States v. CIO*, 335 U.S. 106 (1948). There, a labor union endorsed a congressional candidate in its weekly periodical. The Court stated that "the gravest doubt would arise in our minds as to [the federal expenditure prohibition's] constitutionality" if it were construed to suppress that writing. The Court engaged in statutory interpretation and found the statute did not cover the publication. Four Justices, however, said they would reach the constitutional question and invalidate the Labor Management Relations Act's expenditure ban. *CIO* (Rutledge, J., joined by Black, Douglas, and Murphy, JJ., concurring in result). The concurrence explained that any " 'undue influence' " generated by a speaker's "large expenditures" was outweighed "by the loss for democratic processes resulting from the restrictions upon free and full public discussion."

In *United States v. Automobile Workers*, 352 U.S. 567 (1957), the Court again encountered the independent expenditure ban. After holding only that a union television broadcast that endorsed candidates was covered by the statute, the Court "[r]efus[ed] to anticipate constitutional questions" and remanded for the trial to proceed. Three Justices dissented, arguing that the Court should have reached the constitutional question and that the ban on independent expenditures was unconstitutional. . . . The dissent concluded that deeming a particular group "too powerful" was not a "justificatio[n]" for withholding First Amendment rights from any group-labor or corporate." . . .

Later, in *Pipefitters v. United States*, 407 U.S. 385 (1972), the Court reversed a conviction for expenditure of union funds for political speech-again without reaching the constitutional question. The Court would not resolve that question for another four years.

2

In *Buckley*, the Court addressed various challenges to the Federal Election Campaign Act of 1971 (FECA) as amended in 1974. These amendments created 18 U.S.C. § 608(e), an independent expenditure ban separate from § 610 that applied to individuals as well as corporations and labor unions.

Before addressing the constitutionality of § 608(e)'s independent expenditure ban, *Buckley* first upheld § 608(b), FECA's limits on direct contributions to candidates. . . . This followed from the Court's concern that large contributions could be given "to secure a political *quid pro quo*."

The *Buckley* Court explained that the potential for *quid pro quo* corruption distinguished direct contributions to candidates from independent expenditures.

The Court emphasized that "the independent expenditure ceiling . . . fails to serve any substantial governmental interest in stemming the reality or appearance of corruption in the electoral process," because "[t]he absence of prearrangement and coordination . . . alleviates the danger that expenditures will be given as a *quid pro quo* for improper commitments from the candidate." *Buckley* invalidated § 608(e)'s restrictions on independent expenditures, with only one Justice dissenting.

Buckley did not consider § 610's separate ban on corporate and union independent expenditures, the prohibition that had also been in the background in *CIO, Automobile Workers*, and *Pipefitters*. Had § 610 been challenged in the wake of *Buckley*, however, it could not have been squared with the reasoning and analysis of that precedent. The expenditure ban invalidated in *Buckley*, § 608(e), applied to corporations and unions, and some of the prevailing plaintiffs in *Buckley* were corporations. The *Buckley* Court did not invoke the First Amendment's overbreadth doctrine to suggest that § 608(e)'s expenditure ban would have been constitutional if it had applied only to corporations and not to individuals. *Buckley* cited with approval the *Automobile Workers* dissent, which argued that § 610 was unconstitutional.

Notwithstanding this precedent, Congress recodified § 610's corporate and union expenditure ban at 2 U.S.C. § 441b four months after *Buckley* was decided. Section 441b is the independent expenditure restriction challenged here.

Less than two years after *Buckley*, *Bellotti* reaffirmed the First Amendment principle that the Government cannot restrict political speech based on the speaker's corporate identity. *Bellotti* could not have been clearer when it struck down a state-law prohibition on corporate independent expenditures related to referenda issues:

> We thus find no support in the First . . . Amendment, or in the decisions of this Court, for the proposition that speech that otherwise would be within the protection of the First Amendment loses that protection simply because its source is a corporation that cannot prove, to the satisfaction of a court, a material effect on its business or property. . . . [That proposition] amounts to an impermissible legislative prohibition of speech based on the identity of the interests that spokesmen may represent in public debate over controversial issues and a requirement that the speaker have a sufficiently great interest in the subject to justify communication.

*   *   *

> In the realm of protected speech, the legislature is constitutionally disqualified from dictating the subjects about which persons may speak and the speakers who may address a public issue.

It is important to note that the reasoning and holding of *Bellotti* did not rest on the existence of a viewpoint-discriminatory statute. It rested on the principle that the Government lacks the power to ban corporations from speaking.

Bellotti did not address the constitutionality of the State's ban on corporate independent expenditures to support candidates. In our view, however, that restriction would have been unconstitutional under *Bellotti*'s central principle: that the First Amendment does not allow political speech restrictions based on a speaker's corporate identity.

3

Thus the law stood until *Austin*. . . . There, the Michigan Chamber of Commerce sought to use general treasury funds to run a newspaper ad supporting a specific candidate. Michigan law, however, prohibited corporate independent expenditures that supported or opposed any candidate for state office. A violation of the law was punishable as a felony. The Court sustained the speech prohibition.

To bypass *Buckley* and *Bellotti*, the *Austin* Court identified a new governmental interest in limiting political speech: an antidistortion interest. *Austin* found a compelling governmental interest in preventing "the corrosive and distorting effects of immense aggregations of wealth that are accumulated with the help of the corporate form and that have little or no correlation to the public's support for the corporation's political ideas."

B

The Court is thus confronted with conflicting lines of precedent: a pre-*Austin* line that forbids restrictions on political speech based on the speaker's corporate identity and a post-*Austin* line that permits them. No case before *Austin* had held that Congress could prohibit independent expenditures for political speech based on the speaker's corporate identity. . . .

In its defense of the corporate-speech restrictions in § 441b, the Government notes the antidistortion rationale on which *Austin* and its progeny rest in part, yet it all but abandons reliance upon it. It argues instead that two other compelling interests support *Austin*'s holding that corporate expenditure restrictions are constitutional: an anticorruption interest, see *Austin* (Stevens, J., concurring), and a shareholder-protection interest, see *Austin* (Brennan, J., concurring). We consider the three points in turn.

1

As for *Austin*'s antidistortion rationale, the Government does little to defend it. And with good reason, for the rationale cannot support § 441b. . . .

Austin interferes with the "open marketplace" of ideas protected by the First Amendment. It permits the Government to ban the political speech of millions of associations of citizens. Most of these are small corporations without large amounts of wealth. This fact belies the Government's argument that the statute is justified on the ground that it prevents the "distorting effects of immense aggregations of wealth." It is not even aimed at amassed wealth. . . .

2

. . . For the most part relinquishing the antidistortion rationale, the Government falls back on the argument that corporate political speech can be banned in order to prevent corruption or its appearance. In *Buckley*, the Court found this interest "sufficiently important" to allow limits on contributions but did not extend that reasoning to expenditure limits. . . .

A single footnote in *Bellotti* purported to leave open the possibility that corporate independent expenditures could be shown to cause corruption. *Bellotti* n.26 [Casebook p. 700]. . . . [We] now conclude that independent expenditures, including those made by corporations, do not give rise to corruption or the appearance of corruption. Dicta in *Bellotti*'s footnote suggested that "a corporation's right to speak on issues of general public interest implies no comparable right in the quite different context of participation in a political campaign for election to public office." Citing the portion of *Buckley* that invalidated the federal independent expenditure ban, and a law review student comment, *Bellotti* surmised that "Congress might well be able to demonstrate the existence of a danger of real or apparent corruption in independent expenditures by corporations to influence candidate elections." *Bellotti* n.26. *Buckley*, however, struck down a ban on independent expenditures to support candidates that covered corporations, and explained that "the distinction between discussion of issues and candidates and advocacy of election or defeat of candidates may often dissolve in practical application." *Bellotti*'s dictum is thus supported only by a law review student comment, which misinterpreted *Buckley*.

Seizing on this aside in *Bellotti*'s footnote, the Court in *NRWC* did say there is a "sufficient" governmental interest in "ensur[ing] that substantial aggregations of wealth amassed" by corporations would not "be used to incur political debts from legislators who are aided by the contributions." *NRWC* (citing *Automobile Workers*). *NRWC* decided no more than that a restriction on a corporation's ability to solicit funds for its segregated PAC, which made direct contributions to candidates, did not violate the First Amendment. *NRWC* thus involved contribution limits, which, unlike limits on independent expenditures, have been an accepted means to prevent *quid pro quo* corruption. Citizens United has not made direct contributions to candidates, and it has not suggested that the Court should reconsider whether contribution limits should be subjected to rigorous First Amendment scrutiny.

When *Buckley* identified a sufficiently important governmental interest in preventing corruption or the appearance of corruption, that interest was limited to *quid pro quo* corruption. The fact that speakers may have influence over or access to elected officials does not mean that these officials are corrupt:

> Favoritism and influence are not . . . avoidable in representative politics. It is in the nature of an elected representative to favor certain policies, and, by necessary corollary, to favor the voters and contributors who support those policies. It is well understood that a substantial and legitimate reason, if not the only reason, to cast a vote for, or to make a contribution to, one candidate over another is that the candidate will respond by producing those political outcomes the supporter favors.

Democracy is premised on responsiveness.

McConnell (opinion of Kennedy, J.)

Reliance on a "generic favoritism or influence theory . . . is at odds with standard First Amendment analyses because it is unbounded and susceptible to no limiting principle."

The appearance of influence or access, furthermore, will not cause the electorate to lose faith in our democracy. . . . The fact that a corporation, or any other speaker, is willing to spend money to try to persuade voters presupposes that the people have the ultimate influence over elected officials. This is inconsistent with any suggestion that the electorate will refuse " 'to take part in democratic governance' " because of additional political speech made by a corporation or any other speaker. *McConnell* (quoting *Nixon v. Shrink Missouri Government PAC* (2000)).

Caperton v. A.T. Massey Coal Co., 129 S. Ct. 2252 (2009), is not to the contrary. *Caperton* held that a judge was required to recuse himself "when a person with a personal stake in a particular case had a significant and disproportionate influence in placing the judge on the case by raising funds or directing the judge's election campaign when the case was pending or imminent." The remedy of recusal was based on a litigant's due process right to a fair trial before an unbiased judge. *Caperton*'s holding was limited to the rule that the judge must be recused, not that the litigant's political speech could be banned.

The *McConnell* record was "over 100,000 pages" long, yet it "does not have any direct examples of votes being exchanged for . . . expenditures." This confirms *Buckley*'s reasoning that independent expenditures do not lead to, or create the appearance of, *quid pro quo* corruption. In fact, there is only scant evidence that independent expenditures even ingratiate. Ingratiation and access, in any event, are not corruption. The BCRA record establishes that certain donations to political parties, called "soft money," were made to gain access to elected officials. This case, however, is about independent expenditures, not soft money. When Congress finds that a problem exists, we must give that finding due deference; but Congress may not choose an unconstitutional remedy. If elected officials succumb to improper influences from independent expenditures; if they surrender their best judgment; and if they put expediency before principle, then surely there is cause for concern. We must give weight to attempts by Congress to seek to dispel either the appearance or the reality of these influences. The remedies enacted by law, however, must comply with the First Amendment; and, it is our law and our tradition that more speech, not less, is the governing rule. . . .

3

The Government contends further that corporate independent expenditures can be limited because of its interest in protecting dissenting shareholders from being compelled to fund corporate political speech. This asserted interest, like *Austin*'s antidistortion rationale, would allow the Government to ban the political speech even of media corporations. . . . The First Amendment does not allow that power. There is, furthermore, little evidence of abuse that cannot be corrected by shareholders "through the procedures of corporate democracy." *Bellotti.* . . .

4

We need not reach the question whether the Government has a compelling interest in preventing foreign individuals or associations from influencing our Nation's political process. Section 441b is not limited to corporations or associations that were created in foreign countries or funded predominately by foreign shareholders. Section 441b therefore would be overbroad even if we assumed, *arguendo*, that the Government has a compelling interest in limiting foreign influence over our political process. . . .

D

Austin is overruled, so it provides no basis for allowing the Government to limit corporate independent expenditures. As the Government appears to concede, overruling *Austin* "effectively invalidate[s] not only BCRA Section 203, but also 2 U.S.C. 441b's prohibition on the use of corporate treasury funds for express advocacy." Section 441b's restrictions on corporate independent expenditures are therefore invalid and cannot be applied to *Hillary*.

Given our conclusion we are further required to overrule the part of *McConnell* that upheld BCRA § 203's extension of § 441b's restrictions on corporate independent expenditures. The *McConnell* Court relied on the antidistortion interest recognized in *Austin* to uphold a greater restriction on speech than the restriction upheld in *Austin*, and we have found this interest unconvincing and insufficient. This part of *McConnell* is now overruled. . . .

IV

[In part IV of the opinion the Court, now joined by the four partial dissenters but not by Justice Thomas, upheld BCRA's disclosure provisions. This part of the opinion is discussed in a Note, *infra*.]

V

When word concerning the plot of the movie *Mr. Smith Goes to Washington* reached the circles of Government, some officials sought, by persuasion, to discourage its distribution. Under *Austin*, though, officials could have done more than discourage its distribution — they could have banned the film. After all, it, like *Hillary*, was speech funded by a corporation that was critical of Members of Congress. *Mr. Smith Goes to Washington* may be fiction and caricature; but fiction and caricature can be a powerful force. . . .

Some members of the public might consider *Hillary* to be insightful and instructive; some might find it to be neither high art nor a fair discussion on how to set the Nation's course; still others simply might suspend judgment on these points but decide to think more about issues and candidates. Those choices and assessments, however, are not for the Government to make. "The First Amendment underwrites the freedom to experiment and to create in the realm of thought and speech. Citizens must be free to use new forms, and new forums, for the expression of ideas. The civic discourse belongs to the people, and the Government may not prescribe the means used to conduct it."

The judgment of the District Court is reversed with respect to the constitutionality of 2 U.S.C. § 441b's restrictions on corporate independent expenditures. The judgment is affirmed with respect to BCRA's disclaimer and disclosure requirements. The case is remanded for further proceedings consistent with this opinion. . . .

CHIEF JUSTICE ROBERTS, with whom JUSTICE ALITO joins, concurring. [Chief Justice Roberts joined Justice Kennedy's opinion, but also wrote separately to discuss the principles of judicial restraint and *stare decisis* implicated by the case.]

JUSTICE SCALIA, with whom JUSTICE ALITO joins, and with whom JUSTICE THOMAS joins in part, concurring.

I join the opinion of the Court.[1]

I write separately to address Justice Stevens' discussion of *"Original Understandings"* (opinion concurring in part and dissenting in part) (hereinafter referred to as the dissent). This section of the dissent purports to show that today's decision is not supported by the original understanding of the First Amendment. The dissent attempts this demonstration, however, in splendid isolation from the text of the First Amendment. It never shows why "the freedom of speech" that was the right of Englishmen did not include the freedom to speak in association with other individuals, including association in the corporate form. . . .

JUSTICE STEVENS, with whom JUSTICE GINSBURG, JUSTICE BREYER, and JUSTICE SOTOMAYOR join, concurring in part and dissenting in part.

The real issue in this case concerns how, not if, the appellant may finance its electioneering. Citizens United is a wealthy nonprofit corporation that runs a political action committee (PAC) with millions of dollars in assets. Under the Bipartisan Campaign Reform Act of 2002 (BCRA), it could have used those assets to televise and promote *Hillary: The Movie* wherever and whenever it wanted to. It also could have spent unrestricted sums to broadcast *Hillary* at any time other than the 30 days before the last primary election. Neither Citizens United's nor any other corporation's speech has been "banned." All that the parties dispute is whether Citizens United had a right to use the funds in its general treasury to pay for broadcasts during the 30-day period. The notion that the First Amendment dictates an affirmative answer to that question is, in my judgment, profoundly misguided. Even more misguided is the notion that the Court must rewrite the law relating to campaign expenditures by *for-profit* corporations and unions to decide this case.

---

[1] Justice Thomas does not join Part IV of the Court's opinion.

The basic premise underlying the Court's ruling is its iteration, and constant reiteration, of the proposition that the First Amendment bars regulatory distinctions based on a speaker's identity, including its "identity" as a corporation. While that glittering generality has rhetorical appeal, it is not a correct statement of the law. . . .

The majority's approach to corporate electioneering marks a dramatic break from our past. Congress has placed special limitations on campaign spending by corporations ever since the passage of the Tillman Act in 1907. We have unanimously concluded that this "reflects a permissible assessment of the dangers posed by those entities to the electoral process," *FEC v. National Right to Work Comm.* (1982) (*NRWC*), and have accepted the "legislative judgment that the special characteristics of the corporate structure require particularly careful regulation." The Court today rejects a century of history when it treats the distinction between corporate and individual campaign spending as an invidious novelty born of *Austin v. Michigan Chamber of Commerce* (1990). Relying largely on individual dissenting opinions, the majority blazes through our precedents . . . .

. . . Although I concur in the Court's decision to sustain BCRA's disclosure provisions and join Part IV of its opinion, I emphatically dissent from its principal holding.

I

The Court's ruling threatens to undermine the integrity of elected institutions across the Nation. The path it has taken to reach its outcome will, I fear, do damage to this institution. Before turning to the question whether to overrule *Austin* and part of *McConnell v. Federal Election Comm'n* (2003), it is important to explain why the Court should not be deciding that question.

Scope of the Case

[Justice Stevens criticized the Court for considering a facial challenge to the statutes at issue, arguing that it violated normal rules of judicial restraint and forced the Court to make empirical judgments about the statutes in the absence of a factual record that would have been developed had Citizens United not abandoned its facial challenge earlier in the litigation. In particular, he criticized the majority's argument that that a narrower ruling would have chilled would-be speakers. Justice Stevens argued that this argument was "particularly hard to square with the legal landscape following *WRTL II*, which held [in Chief Justice Roberts' controlling opinion] that a corporate communication could be regulated under § 203 only if it was 'susceptible of no reasonable interpretation other than as an appeal to vote for or against a specific candidate.' " In essence, he wondered how this interpretation of § 203 could be so vague as to chill speech, given that Chief Justice Roberts designed it "to make § 203 as simple and speech-protective as possible." He said that "[t]he Court does not explain how, in the span of a single election cycle [*i.e.*, since *WRTL II*] it has determined the Chief Justice's project to be a failure."

[Justice Stevens also argued that the Court could have ruled for Citizens United on narrower grounds. Finally, he criticized the Court's approach to *stare decisis*.]

III

The novelty of the Court's procedural dereliction and its approach to *stare decisis* is matched by the novelty of its ruling on the merits. The ruling rests on several premises. First, the Court claims that *Austin* and *McConnell* have "banned" corporate speech. Second, it claims that the First Amendment precludes regulatory distinctions based on speaker identity, including the speaker's identity as a corporation. Third, it claims that *Austin* and *McConnell* were radical outliers in our First Amendment tradition and our campaign finance jurisprudence. Each of these claims is wrong.

The So-Called "Ban"

Pervading the Court's analysis is the ominous image of a "categorical ba[n]" on corporate speech. . . . This characterization is highly misleading, and needs to be corrected.

In fact it already has been. Our cases have repeatedly pointed out that, "[c]ontrary to the [majority's] critical assumptions," the statutes upheld in *Austin* and *McConnell* do "not impose an *absolute* ban on all forms of corporate political spending." For starters, both statutes provide exemptions for PACs, separate segregated funds established by a corporation for political purposes. "The ability to form and administer separate segregated funds," we observed in *McConnell*, "has provided corporations and unions with a constitutionally sufficient opportunity to engage in express advocacy. That has been this Court's unanimous view." . . .

The laws upheld in *Austin* and *McConnell* leave open many additional avenues for corporations' political speech. . . .

At the time Citizens United brought this lawsuit, the only types of speech that could be regulated under § 203 were: (1) broadcast, cable, or satellite communications; (2) capable of reaching at least 50,000 persons in the relevant electorate; (3) made within 30 days of a primary or 60 days of a general federal election; (4) by a labor union or a non-*MCFL*, nonmedia corporation; (5) paid for with general treasury funds; and (6) "susceptible of no reasonable interpretation other than as an appeal to vote for or against a specific candidate." The category of communications meeting all of these criteria is not trivial, but the notion that corporate political speech has been "suppress[ed] . . . altogether," that corporations have been "exclu[ded] . . . from the general public dialogue," or that a work of fiction such as *Mr. Smith Goes to Washington* might be covered is nonsense. . . .

Identity-Based Distinctions

The second pillar of the Court's opinion is its assertion that "the Government cannot restrict political speech based on the speaker's . . . identity." . . . Like its paeans to unfettered discourse, the Court's denunciation of identity-based distinctions may have rhetorical appeal but it obscures reality.

. . . The First Amendment provides that "Congress shall make no law . . . abridging the freedom of speech, or of the press." Apart perhaps from measures designed to protect the press, that text might seem to permit no distinctions of any kind. Yet in a variety of contexts, we have held that speech can be regulated differentially on account of the speaker's identity, when identity is understood in categorical or institutional terms. The Government routinely places special restrictions on the speech rights of students, prisoners, members of the Armed Forces, foreigners, and its own employees. When such restrictions are justified by a legitimate governmental interest, they do not necessarily raise constitutional problems.[46] . . .

. . . It is fair to say that our First Amendment doctrine has "frowned on" certain identity-based distinctions, particularly those that may reflect invidious discrimination or preferential treatment of a politically powerful group. But it is simply incorrect to suggest that we have prohibited all legislative distinctions based on identity or content. Not even close.

The election context is distinctive in many ways, and the Court, of course, is right that the First Amendment closely guards political speech. But in this context, too, the authority of legislatures to enact viewpoint-neutral regulations based on content and identity is well settled. We have, for example, . . . consistently approved laws that bar Government employees, but not others, from contributing to or participating in political activities. These statutes burden the political expression of one class of speakers, namely, civil servants. Yet we have sustained them on the basis of longstanding practice and Congress' reasoned judgment that certain regulations which leave "untouched full participation . . . in political decisions at the ballot box," help ensure that public officials are "sufficiently free from improper influences," and that "confidence in the system of representative Government is not . . . eroded to a disastrous extent."

The same logic applies to this case with additional force because it is the identity of corporations, rather than individuals, that the Legislature has taken into account. As we have unanimously observed, legislatures are entitled to decide "that the special characteristics of the corporate structure require particularly careful regulation" in an electoral context. . . .

In short, the Court dramatically overstates its critique of identity-based distinctions, without ever explaining why corporate identity demands the same treatment as individual identity. Only the most wooden approach to the First Amendment could justify the unprecedented line it seeks to draw.

Our First Amendment Tradition

A third fulcrum of the Court's opinion is the idea that *Austin* and *McConnell* are radical outliers, "aberration[s]" in our First Amendment tradition. The Court has it exactly backwards. It is today's holding that is the radical departure from what had

---

[46] The majority states that the cases just cited are "inapposite" because they "stand only for the proposition that there are certain governmental functions that cannot operate without some restrictions on particular kinds of speech." The majority's creative suggestion that these cases stand only for that one proposition is quite implausible. In any event, the proposition lies at the heart of this case, as Congress and half the state legislatures have concluded, over many decades, that their core functions of administering elections and passing legislation cannot operate effectively without some narrow restrictions on corporate electioneering paid for by general treasury funds.

been settled First Amendment law. To see why, it is useful to take a long view.

1. *Original Understandings*

Let us start from the beginning. The Court invokes "ancient First Amendment principles" and original understandings to defend today's ruling, yet it makes only a perfunctory attempt to ground its analysis in the principles or understandings of those who drafted and ratified the Amendment. Perhaps this is because there is not a scintilla of evidence to support the notion that anyone believed it would preclude regulatory distinctions based on the corporate form. To the extent that the Framers' views are discernible and relevant to the disposition of this case, they would appear to cut strongly against the majority's position.

This is not only because the Framers and their contemporaries conceived of speech more narrowly than we now think of it, but also because they held very different views about the nature of the First Amendment right and the role of corporations in society. . . .

2. *Legislative and Judicial Interpretation*

A century of more recent history puts to rest any notion that today's ruling is faithful to our First Amendment tradition. At the federal level, the express distinction between corporate and individual political spending on elections stretches back to 1907, when Congress passed the Tillman Act, banning all corporate contributions to candidates. . . .

Over the years, the limitations on corporate political spending have been modified in a number of ways, as Congress responded to changes in the American economy and political practices that threatened to displace the commonweal. . . . The Taft-Hartley Act of 1947 is of special significance for this case. In that Act passed more than 60 years ago, Congress extended the prohibition on corporate support of candidates to cover not only direct contributions, but independent expenditures as well. The bar on contributions "was being so narrowly construed" that corporations were easily able to defeat the purposes of the Act by supporting candidates through other means.

Our colleagues emphasize that in two cases from the middle of the 20th century, several Justices wrote separately to criticize the expenditure restriction as applied to unions, even though the Court declined to pass on its constitutionality. Two features of these cases are of far greater relevance. First, those Justices were writing separately; which is to say, their position failed to command a majority. Prior to today, this was a fact we found significant in evaluating precedents. Second, each case in this line expressed support for the principle that corporate and union political speech financed with PAC funds, collected voluntarily from the organization's stockholders or members, receives greater protection than speech financed with general treasury funds.

This principle was carried forward when Congress enacted comprehensive campaign finance reform in the Federal Election Campaign Act of 1971 (FECA), which retained the restriction on using general treasury funds for contributions and expenditures. . . .

By the time Congress passed FECA in 1971, the bar on corporate contributions and expenditures had become such an accepted part of federal campaign finance regulation that when a large number of plaintiffs, including several nonprofit corporations, challenged virtually every aspect of the Act in *Buckley v. Valeo* (1976), no one even bothered to argue that the bar as such was unconstitutional. *Buckley* famously (or infamously) distinguished direct contributions from independent expenditures, but its silence on corporations only reinforced the understanding that corporate expenditures could be treated differently from individual expenditures. "Since our decision in *Buckley*, Congress' power to prohibit corporations and unions from using funds in their treasuries to finance advertisements expressly advocating the election or defeat of candidates in federal elections has been firmly embedded in our law." *McConnell.* . . .

The corporate/individual distinction was not questioned by the Court's disposition, in 1986, of a challenge to the expenditure restriction as applied to a distinctive type of nonprofit corporation. In *Federal Election Comm'n v. Massachusetts Citizens for Life, Inc. (MCFL)* (1986), we stated again "that 'the special characteristics of the corporate structure require particularly careful regulation' " (quoting *NRWC*), and again we acknowledged that the Government has a legitimate interest in "regulat[ing] the substantial aggregations of wealth amassed by the special advantages which go with the corporate form." Those aggregations can distort the "free trade in ideas" crucial to candidate elections at the expense of members or shareholders who may disagree with the object of the expenditures. What the Court held by a 5-to-4 vote was that a limited class of corporations must be allowed to use their general treasury funds for independent expenditures, because Congress' interests in protecting shareholders and "restrict[ing] 'the influence of political war chests funneled through the corporate form' " did not apply to corporations that were structurally insulated from those concerns.

It is worth remembering for present purposes that the four *MCFL* dissenters, led by Chief Justice Rehnquist, thought the Court was carrying the First Amendment *too far*. They would have recognized congressional authority to bar general treasury electioneering expenditures even by this class of nonprofits . . . . Not a single Justice suggested that regulation of corporate political speech could be no more stringent than of speech by an individual.

Four years later, in *Austin*, we considered whether corporations falling outside the *MCFL* exception could be barred from using general treasury funds to make independent expenditures in support of, or in opposition to, candidates. We held they could be. . . . In light of the corrupting effects such spending might have on the political process, we permitted the State of Michigan to limit corporate expenditures on candidate elections to corporations' PACs, which rely on voluntary contributions and thus "reflect actual public support for the political ideals espoused by corporations." . . .

In the 20 years since *Austin*, we have reaffirmed its holding and rationale a number of times, most importantly in *McConnell*, where we upheld the provision challenged here, § 203 of BCRA. Congress crafted § 203 in response to a problem created by *Buckley*. . . . After *Buckley*, corporations and unions figured out how to circumvent the limits on express advocacy by using sham "issue ads" that "eschewed the use of magic words" but nonetheless "advocate[d] the election or defeat of clearly identified federal candidates." . . . Congress passed § 203 to address this circumvention, prohibiting corporations and unions from using general treasury funds for electioneering communications that "refe[r] to a clearly identified candidate," whether or not those communications use the magic words.

When we asked in *McConnell* "whether a compelling governmental interest justifie[d]" § 203, we found the question "easily answered": "We have repeatedly sustained legislation aimed at 'the corrosive and distorting effects of immense aggregations of wealth that are accumulated with the help of the corporate form and that have little or no correlation to the public's support for the corporation's political ideas.' " . . .

3. *Buckley and Bellotti*

Against this extensive background of congressional regulation of corporate campaign spending, and our repeated affirmation of this regulation as constitutionally sound, the majority dismisses *Austin* as "a significant departure from ancient First Amendment principles." How does the majority attempt to justify this claim? Selected passages from two cases, *Buckley* and *First Nat. Bank of Boston v. Bellotti* (1978), do all of the work. In the Court's view, *Buckley* and *Bellotti* decisively rejected the possibility of distinguishing corporations from natural persons in the 1970's; it just so happens that in every single case in which the Court has reviewed campaign finance legislation in the decades since, the majority failed to grasp this truth. The Federal Congress and dozens of state legislatures, we now know, have been similarly deluded.

The majority emphasizes *Buckley*'s statement that "[t]he concept that government may restrict the speech of some elements of our society in order to enhance the relative voice of others is wholly foreign to the First Amendment." . . . It is not apparent why this is relevant to the case before us. The majority suggests that *Austin* rests on the foreign concept of speech equalization, but we made it clear in *Austin* (as in several cases before and since) that a restriction on the way corporations spend their money is no mere exercise in disfavoring the voice of some elements of our society in preference to others. Indeed, we *expressly* ruled that the compelling interest supporting Michigan's statute was not one of "equaliz[ing] the relative influence of speakers on elections," but rather the need to confront the distinctive corrupting potential of corporate electoral advocacy financed by general treasury dollars.

For that matter, it should go without saying that when we made this statement in *Buckley*, we could not have been casting doubt on the restriction on corporate expenditures in candidate elections, which had not been challenged as "foreign to the First Amendment," or for any other reason. *Buckley*'s independent expenditure analysis was focused on a very different statutory provision, 18 U.S.C. § 608(e)(1). It is implausible to think, as the majority suggests, that *Buckley* covertly invalidated FECA's separate corporate and union campaign expenditure restriction, § 610 (now codified at 2 U.S.C. § 441b), even though that restriction had been on the books for decades before *Buckley* and would remain on the books, undisturbed, for decades after.

The case on which the majority places even greater weight than *Buckley*, however, is *Bellotti*, claiming it "could not have been clearer" that *Bellotti*'s holding forbade distinctions between corporate and individual expenditures like the one at issue here. The Court's reliance is odd. The only thing about *Bellotti* that could not be clearer is that it declined to adopt the majority's position. *Bellotti* ruled, in an explicit limitation on the scope of its holding, that "our consideration of a corporation's right to speak on issues of general public interest implies no comparable right in the quite different context of participation in a political campaign for election to public office." *Bellotti* n.26. *Bellotti*, in other words, did not touch the question presented in *Austin* and *McConnell*, and the opinion squarely disavowed the proposition for which the majority cites it.

The majority attempts to explain away the distinction *Bellotti* drew — between general corporate speech and campaign speech intended to promote or prevent the election of specific candidates for office — as inconsistent with the rest of the opinion and with *Buckley*. Yet the basis for this distinction is perfectly coherent: The anticorruption interests that animate regulations of corporate participation in candidate elections, the "importance" of which "has never been doubted," do not apply equally to regulations of corporate participation in referenda. A referendum cannot owe a political debt to a corporation, seek to curry favor with a corporation, or fear the corporation's retaliation. The majority likewise overlooks the fact that, over the past 30 years, our cases have repeatedly recognized the candidate/issue distinction. The Court's critique of *Bellotti*'s footnote 26 puts it in the strange position of trying to elevate *Bellotti* to canonical status, while simultaneously disparaging a critical piece of its analysis as unsupported and irreconcilable with *Buckley*. *Bellotti*, apparently, is both the font of all wisdom and internally incoherent.

The *Bellotti* Court confronted a dramatically different factual situation from the one that confronts us in this case: a state statute that barred business corporations' expenditures on some referenda but not others. . . . The statute was a transparent attempt to prevent corporations from spending money to defeat [a state income tax] amendment, which was favored by a majority of legislators but had been repeatedly rejected by the voters. . . .

Bellotti thus involved a *viewpoint-discriminatory* statute, created to effect a particular policy outcome. . . . To make matters worse, the law at issue did not make any allowance for corporations to spend money through PACs. This really was a complete ban on a specific, pre-identified subject. See *MCFL* (stating that 2 U.S.C. § 441b's expenditure restriction "is *of course distinguishable* from the complete foreclosure of any opportunity for political speech that we invalidated in the state referendum context in . . . *Bellotti*").

The majority grasps a quotational straw from *Bellotti*, that speech does not fall entirely outside the protection of the First Amendment merely because it comes from a corporation. Of course not, but no one suggests the contrary and neither *Austin* nor *McConnell* held otherwise. They held that even though the expenditures at issue were subject to First Amendment scrutiny, the restrictions on those expenditures were justified by a compelling state interest. We acknowledged in *Bellotti* that numerous "interests of the highest importance" can justify campaign finance regulation. But we found no evidence that these interests were served by the Massachusetts law. We left open the possibility that our decision might have been different if there had been "record or legislative findings that corporate advocacy threatened imminently to undermine democratic processes, thereby denigrating rather than serving First Amendment interests."

Austin and *McConnell*, then, sit perfectly well with *Bellotti*. . . . The difference between the cases is not that *Austin* and *McConnell* rejected First Amendment protection for corporations whereas *Bellotti* accepted it. The difference is that the statute at issue in *Bellotti* smacked of viewpoint discrimination, targeted one class of corporations, and provided no PAC option; and the State has a greater interest in regulating independent corporate expenditures on candidate elections than on referenda, because in a functioning democracy the public must have faith that its representatives owe their positions to the people, not to the corporations with the deepest pockets. . . .

IV

. . . The majority recognizes that *Austin* and *McConnell* may be defended on anticorruption, antidistortion, and shareholder protection rationales. It badly errs both in explaining the nature of these rationales, which overlap and complement each other, and in applying them to the case at hand. [This portion of the opinion is summarized in the Note that follows.]

NOTE: (FURTHER) DISAGREEMENT IN *CITIZENS UNITED* ABOUT JUSTIFICATIONS FOR CAMPAIGN EXPENDITURE RESTRICTIONS

1.   Together, the opinions in *Citizens United* take up 175 pages in the advance sheets of the United States Reports. The excerpt just presented thus constitutes only a small portion of what the Justices said; it focuses on their views of what First Amendment precedent suggested about the constitutionality of restrictions on electoral expenditures by corporations and unions. This Note and the two that follow focus on different aspects of the Justices' opinions. This Note recounts how Justice Kennedy's majority opinion and Justice Stevens' dissent reprised earlier cases' disagreements about the various justifications for restrictions on corporate and union political speech. The next Note discusses the debate between Justice Scalia (who joined the majority and wrote a concurrence) and Justice Stevens about the likely views of the Framers about speech restrictions on corporations. The final Note considers the disclosure requirements that were upheld in *Citizens United*.

2.   Justice Kennedy renewed the *Austin* dissent's attack on the "antidistortion" rationale. He quoted *Buckley* as authority for rejecting "the premise that the Government has an interest 'in equalizing the relative ability of individuals and groups to influence the outcome of elections.' " He concluded that "[i]t is irrelevant

for purposes of the First Amendment that corporate funds may 'have little or no correlation to the public's support for the corporation's political ideas.' " (quoting *Austin*). He continued: "All speakers . . . use money amassed from the economic marketplace to fund their speech. The First Amendment protects the resulting speech, even if it was enabled by economic transactions with persons or entities who disagree with the speaker's ideas."

Justice Kennedy also repeated the concern expressed by Chief Justice Burger in his *Bellotti* concurrence that upholding the law would allow Congress to ban the political speech of media corporations. Again invoking *Austin*'s language, Justice Kennedy observed that "media corporations accumulate wealth with the help of the corporate form, the largest media corporations have 'immense aggregations of wealth,' and the views expressed by media corporations often 'have little or no correlation to the public's support' for those views."

Turning to the argument that BCRA's restrictions served the government interest in fighting corruption and its appearance, Justice Kennedy quoted *Buckley* to conclude that this interest was not served by BCRA: " 'The absence of prearrangement and coordination of an expenditure with the candidate . . . alleviates the danger that expenditures will be given as a *quid pro quo*.' " Turning to the government's interest in protecting shareholders, Justice Kennedy again observed that this interest would "would allow the Government to ban the political speech even of media corporations" and argued that "[t]he First Amendment does not allow that result." Quoting *Bellotti*, he also concluded that "[t]here is . . . little evidence of abuse that cannot be corrected by shareholders 'through the procedures of corporate democracy.' "

3.   Unsurprisingly, Justice Stevens took issue with nearly every aspect of the majority's analysis. With regard to the government's anti-corruption interest, he noted that the trial court that adjudicated the initial challenge to BCRA made numerous findings suggesting that candidates and office-holders knew who was making independent expenditures on their behalf, and that they expressed appreciation for those expenditures by lavishing attention and access on the speakers. Even with regard to the narrower concern for *quid pro quo* corruption, Justice Stevens argued that *Buckley* had discounted the possibility of independent expenditures implicating this interest only on the basis of the facts known to that Court. He concluded that in the years since *Buckley*, as corporations and unions became more adept at crafting issue ads, those expenditures had started to corrupt the political process more directly.

Turning to *Austin*'s anti-distortion rationale, Justice Stevens argued that the unique aspects of corporations made corporate speech uniquely threatening to electoral integrity and rendered restrictions on their speech less problematic under the First Amendment. Pivoting away from the rights of corporate speakers and toward the rights of listeners to hear political speech, he echoed *Austin* in arguing that, among other characteristics, the size the law allowed corporations to reach and their single-minded concern for profitability allowed them to "flood the market with advocacy that bears 'little or no correlation' to the ideas of natural persons or to any broader notion of the public good." He argued that the resulting corporate "domination" of electioneering could cause the citizenry to become cynical about the political process and unwilling to engage in self-government.

Finally, Justice Stevens considered the shareholder-protection rationale. He expressed doubt that corporate democracy would protect shareholders' interests in not funding speech with which they disagreed, given that so many shareholders hold their interests indirectly, via mutual funds and retirement plans. More fundamentally, he criticized the majority's discounting of this rationale as failing to appreciate how it fed into *Austin*'s anti-distortion idea. According to Justice Stevens, corporations' use of shareholder funds to finance speech with which shareholders may not agree might "compromise the views" of those dissenting shareholders.

4.   Consider the competing arguments summarized above as well as those made in earlier cases (particularly *Bellotti* and *Austin*). Which do you find more persuasive? If there are good arguments on both sides, is that a sufficient reason for deferring to the judgment of the political branches?

NOTE: CORPORATIONS' SPEECH RIGHTS AND THE ORIGINAL UNDERSTANDING OF THE FIRST AMENDMENT

1.   In *Citizens United* Justices Scalia and Stevens dueled over the question of what the Framers would have thought of restrictions on corporations' speech rights. Justice Stevens, dissenting from the Court's holding that government may not make identity-based distinctions with regard to the First Amendment right engage in political speech, argued in part that the original understanding of the First Amendment does not support that holding. He insisted that "there is not a scintilla of evidence to support the notion that anyone [in the framing generation] believed [the First Amendment] would preclude regulatory distinctions based on the corporate form." He continued that "[t]o the extent that the Framers' views are discernible . . . they would appear to cut strongly against the majority's position."

Justice Stevens contended that "the Framers . . . held very different views [from those held today] about the nature of the First Amendment right and the role of corporations in society." He noted that the first corporations in America "were authorized by grant of a special legislative charter," and thus "conceptualized as quasi-public entities designed to serve a social function for the state," rather than the profit-seeking entities created by general incorporation laws that we know today. Quoting a treatise on corporate law, he observed that these characteristics of early corporations as state-granted privileges helped explain "the cloud of disfavor" with which they were regarded. Thus, according to Justice Stevens, "[t]he Framers took it as a given that corporations could be comprehensively regulated in the service of the public welfare . . . [and] had little trouble distinguishing corporations from human beings," with the result that "when [the Framers] constitutionalized the right to free speech in the First Amendment it was the free speech of individual Americans that they had in mind." Based on these observations, he said that "it seems to me implausible that the Framers believed 'the freedom of speech' would extend equally to all corporate speakers, much less that it would preclude legislatures from taking limited measures to guard against corporate capture of elections."

Justice Scalia, while joining Justice Kennedy's opinion for the Court, also wrote a concurring opinion to address Justice Stevens' arguments. He asserted that even if the founding generation mistrusted early corporations, modern corporations "would probably have been favored by most of our enterprising Founders." He argued that founding-era "religious, educational and literary corporations were incorporated under general incorporation statutes, much as business corporations are today"; he asked why Justice Stevens had not discussed the framing era's views of those, more analogous organizations. He noted that such corporations "actively petitioned the Government and expressed their views in newspapers and pamphlets." He concluded by noting that the First Amendment "is written in terms of 'speech,' not speakers." He continued: "Its text offers no foothold for excluding any category of speaker. . . ."

2. Both Justices addressed the issue of media corporations and the applicability of the First Amendment to them. Justice Scalia observed that "[h]istorical evidence relating to the textually similar clause 'the freedom of . . . the press' also provides no support for the proposition that the First Amendment excludes conduct of artificial legal entities from the scope of its protection." He argued that the Press Clause was intended to protect "the publishing activities of individual editors and printers." He continued: "But these individual often acted through newspapers, which (much like corporations) had their own names, outlived the individuals who had founded them, could be bought and sold, were sometimes owned by more than one person, and were operated for profit."

Unsurprisingly, Justice Stevens analyzed the issue differently. In a footnote, he said:

> [T]he Free Press Clause might be turned against Justice Scalia, for two reasons. First, we learn from it that the drafters of the First Amendment did draw distinctions — explicit distinctions — between types of "speakers," or speech outlets or forms. Second, the Court's strongest historical evidence all relates to the Framers' views on the press, yet while the Court tries to sweep this evidence into the Free Speech Clause, the Free Press Clause provides a more natural textual home. The text and history highlighted by our colleagues suggests why one type of corporation, those that are part of the press, might be able to claim special First Amendment status, and therefore why some kinds of "identity"-based distinctions might be permissible after all.

3. During his discussion of the original understanding of corporations' speech rights, Justice Stevens wrote the following:

> This case sheds a revelatory light on the assumption of some that an impartial judge's application of an originalist methodology is likely to yield more determinate answers, or to play a more decisive role in the decisional process, than his or her views about sound policy.

Do you agree? Consider the competing versions of the founding-era history presented by Justice Stevens and Justice Scalia. How much guidance do they give in resolving the question presented in *Citizens United*?

NOTE: THE UPHOLDING OF CAMPAIGN SPEECH DISCLOSURE REQUIREMENTS IN *CITIZENS UNITED*

1. In *Citizens United* the Court upheld BCRA's disclosure requirements, enacted as BCRA §§ 201 and 311, as applied to the Citizens United group and its *Hillary* movie and ads for the movie. Section 311 requires, among other things, that the communication state the name of the party responsible for the ad and that it was not authorized by any candidate. It also requires that the communication display the name and address (or website) of the responsible party. Section 201 requires that parties spending more than $10,000 on electioneering communications within a calendar year file a disclosure statement with the FEC, including the person responsible for the expenditure, the amount spent, and the names of large contributors.

Writing for eight Justices, Justice Kennedy noted that, in the past, "[t]he Court has subjected [disclosure] requirements to 'exacting scrutiny,' which requires a 'substantial relation' between the disclosure statement and a 'sufficiently important' governmental interest.'" *Citizens United* (quoting *Buckley v. Valeo*). He described the government interest in disclosure as the "interest in 'provid[ing] the electorate with information' about the sources of election-related spending." *Citizens United* (quoting *Buckley*). He noted that the *McConnell* Court, in upholding the facial validity of these provisions, had found "evidence in the record that independent groups were running election-related advertisements 'while hiding behind dubious and misleading names.'" *Citizens United* (quoting *McConnell*). He then noted both *Buckley*'s and *McConnell*'s caveat that "as-applied challenges [to such requirements] would be available if a group could show a 'reasonable probability' that disclosure of its contributors' names 'will subject them to threats, harassment, or reprisals from either Government officials or private parties.'" *Citizens United* (quoting *McConnell* and *Buckley*).

Applying these principles, the Court upheld the requirements as applied to both the ads for *Hillary* and the movie itself. The Court rejected the argument that the government interests justifying disclosure did not apply to ads for a communication, as opposed to the communication itself, noting that the ads themselves fell within BCRA's definition of an "electioneering communication" and that the goals underlying disclosure were served by applying § 311's requirements to them.

Considering now both the ads and the movie itself, the Court rejected the group's argument that § 201's requirements must be limited to speech that is the functional equivalent of express advocacy, observing that "disclosure is a less restrictive alternative to more comprehensive regulation." The Court also concluded that Citizens United had "offered no evidence" that its members might face threats or reprisals if they were forced to disclose their identities.

2. Justice Stevens and the four dissenters from the rest of Justice Kennedy's opinion joined his analysis of the disclosure provisions. However, Justice Thomas,

who had joined the rest of the Court's opinion, dissented from the part of the opinion upholding those provisions. Justice Thomas described "the right of anonymous speech" as one whose infringement was not justified by "the simple interest in providing voters with additional relevant information." He discussed events in California during and after the campaign over Proposition 8 (the same-sex marriage rights initiative), where supporters and opponents received threats when their identities and addresses were disclosed as part of mandatory disclosure requirements for those contributing to initiative campaigns. He dismissed the possibility of an as-applied challenge to BCRA's disclosure requirements, arguing that speech would be chilled by the prospect of disclosure (and the possible threats that might ensue), "long before a plaintiff could prevail on an as-applied challenge." Quoting Justice Kennedy's analysis of the disclosure provisions, he noted: "now more than ever, [the disclosure provisions] will chill protected speech because — as California voters can attest — 'the advent of the Internet' enables 'prompt disclosure of expenditures,' which 'provide[s]' political opponents 'with the information needed' to intimidate and retaliate against their foes."

3. Tying together the two parts of his opinion (striking down the spending restrictions but upholding the disclosure), Justice Kennedy made the following observations about the campaign finance system that emerged after *Citizens United*:

> A campaign finance system that pairs corporate independent expenditures with effective disclosure has not existed before today. It must be noted, furthermore, that many of Congress' findings in passing BCRA were premised on a system without adequate disclosure. With the advent of the Internet, prompt disclosure of expenditures can provide shareholders and citizens with the information needed to hold corporations and elected officials accountable for their positions and supporters. . . . The First Amendment protects political speech; and disclosure permits citizens and shareholders to react to the speech of corporate entities in a proper way. This transparency enables the electorate to make informed decisions and give proper weight to different speakers and messages.

4. Recall Justice Kennedy's complaint, in a Note earlier in the chapter, about the system wrought by *Buckley*. Conceding that *Buckley*'s contribution/distinction remains in place, have he and his colleagues nevertheless succeeded in fundamentally altering the campaign finance regime in the United States?

5. In the paragraph set forth in item 3, above, Justice Kennedy summarizes the regulatory regime that he believes reflects a correct interpretation of the First Amendment. He implies that the combination of freedom of corporate speech and disclosure requirements is also sound policy. Do you agree?

PROBLEM: CORPORATE CONTRIBUTIONS TO AN INDEPENDENT SPENDER

Citizens for a Fantastic Economy ("CFE"), based in Chicago, is an association whose sole purpose is to make independent expenditures promoting political candidates who espouse CFE's views about sound government policy on the economy. Consolidated Megacorp, a leading American business corporation, wishes to contribute $5,000,000 to CFE. Illinois law prohibits for-profit corporations from contributing more than $10,000 to "any person, association, corporation or other entity whose primary purpose is to advocate the election or defeat of political candidates." Is the Illinois law valid?

Would the result be different if CFE made both independent expenditures and contributions? In answering this question, assume that Illinois law prohibits any person from contributing more than $10,000 to a candidate during an election cycle.

NOTE: BURDENING SPEECH, ENCOURAGING DEBATE, AND GOVERNMENT ASSISTANCE TO POLITICAL CANDIDATES

Most campaign finance cases focus on explicit limitations on either expenditures for campaign speech or campaign finance activities such as fund-raising. In two recent cases, however, the Supreme Court struck down government regulations that did not directly restrict campaign activities, but instead assisted a candidate in response to an opponent's use of personal funds. These cases raise the question of the extent to which such schemes serve purposes other than leveling the political playing field, and the extent to which they are at odds with the values underlying the First Amendment.

1.   In *Davis v. FEC*, 554 U.S. 724 (2008), the Court struck down a provision of the so-called "Millionaire's Amendment" to the Bipartisan Campaign Reform Act of 2002 (BCRA). In somewhat simplified terms, that provision trebled the maximum individual contribution a person could make to a congressional candidate if the candidate's opponent spent more than a specified amount of his own funds (*i.e.*, if he "self-funded"). When a self-funded congressional candidate challenged the law, the Court struck it down on a 5-4 vote, holding that the provision burdened the self-funder's political speech without satisfying strict scrutiny.

Writing for the majority, Justice Alito focused on the fact that the law raised contribution limits asymmetrically, i.e., it raised those limits for the self-funder's opponents, but not for the self-funder himself:

> If § 319(a) simply raised the contribution limits for all candidates, Davis' argument would plainly fail . . . Section 319(a), however, . . . raises the limits only for the non-self-financing candidate and does so only when the self-financing candidate's expenditure of personal funds [exceeds the statute's threshold]. We . . . agree with Davis that this scheme impermissibly burdens his First Amendment right to spend his own money for campaign speech.

After noting that *Buckley* had protected the right of individuals to spend their own money for campaign speech, the Court explained that "Section 319(a) requires a candidate to choose between the First Amendment right to engage in unfettered political speech and subjection to discriminatory fundraising limitations. . . . Under § 319(a), the vigorous exercise of the right to use personal funds to finance campaign speech produces fundraising advantages for opponents in the competitive context of electoral politics." The Court thus subjected the provision to strict scrutiny. The Government argued that "§ 319(a)'s asymmetrical limits are justified because they 'level electoral opportunities for candidates of different personal wealth.' " But the Court disagreed: "Our prior decisions . . . provide no support for the proposition that this is a legitimate government objective." The Court also rejected the argument that the provision was justified "because it ameliorates the deleterious effects that result from the tight limits that federal election law places on individual campaign contributions and coordinated party expenditures." In the Court's view, this argument essentially characterized the provision as "a legislative effort to mitigate the untoward consequences of Congress' own handiwork." The Court responded as follows:

> Whatever the merits of this argument as an original matter, it is fundamentally at war with the analysis of expenditure and contribution limits that this Court adopted in *Buckley* and has applied in subsequent cases. The advantage that wealthy candidates now enjoy and that § 319(a) seeks to reduce is an advantage that flows directly from *Buckley's* disparate treatment of expenditures and contributions. If that approach is sound . . . it is hard to see how undoing the consequences of that decision can be viewed as a compelling interest. . . . If the normally applicable limits on individual contributions . . . are seriously distorting the electoral process . . . then the obvious remedy is to raise or eliminate those limits.

Justice Stevens dissented. In the part of his opinion joined by Justices Souter, Ginsburg and Breyer, he wrote:

> [Davis] cannot show that the Millionaire's Amendment causes him — or any other self-financing candidate — any First Amendment injury whatsoever. The Millionaire's Amendment quiets no speech at all. On the contrary, it does no more than assist the opponent of a self-funding candidate in his attempts to make his voice heard; this amplification in no way mutes the voice of the millionaire, who remains able to speak as loud and as long as he likes in support of his campaign. Enhancing the speech of the millionaire's opponent, far from contravening the First Amendment, actually advances its core principles.

Relying on *Austin* and *MCFL* in this pre-*Citizens United* case, Justice Stevens concluded that the statute was justified by an interest in "reducing both the influence of wealth on the outcome of elections, and the appearance that wealth alone dictates those results."

2.   Three years later, in *Arizona Free Enterprise Club's Freedom Club PAC v. Bennett*, 2011 U.S. LEXIS 4992 (2011) (AFEC), the Court considered a challenge to Arizona's scheme of public funding of political campaigns. Under the Arizona scheme, when a self-funder spent a certain amount of money on his own campaign

those expenditures triggered additional payments by the state's public campaign finance program to the self-funder's opponents, with those payments approximately equaling the expenditures made by the self-funding candidate. In calculating the amount of money spent by the self-funding candidate the statute also included expenditures made by independent groups supporting the self-funder.

The Court, by a 5-4 vote, struck down the scheme. Writing for the majority, Chief Justice Roberts relied heavily on *Davis*. Quoting liberally from Justice Alito's opinion in that case, he wrote:

> The logic of *Davis* largely controls our approach to this case. Much like the burden placed on speech in *Davis*, the matching funds provision "imposes an unprecedented penalty on any candidate who robustly exercises [his] First Amendment right[s]." Under that provision, "the vigorous exercise of the right to use personal funds to finance campaign speech" leads to "advantages for opponents in the competitive context of electoral politics." . . . If the law at issue in *Davis* imposed a burden on candidate speech, the Arizona law unquestionably does so as well.

To the extent the Arizona law differed from the one struck down in *Davis*, the Chief Justice argued that those differences made the Arizona law even more problematic for purposes of First Amendment analysis:

> First . . . [t]he candidate who benefited from the increased limits still had to go out and raise the funds. He may or may not have been able to do so. The [self-funding] candidate, therefore, faced merely the possibility that his opponent would be able to raise additional funds, through contribution limits that remained subject to a cap.

Second, he argued that the Arizona law potentially created "a multiplier effect," because it gave additional public funds to each of the self-funder's opponents. Finally, he emphasized that the Arizona law counted as self-funding an independent group's expenditures supporting the self-funding candidate.

The Chief Justice rejected the State's arguments that the statute served the interests behind the First Amendment by enhancing political debate:

> The State argues that the matching funds provision actually results in more speech by increasing debate about issues of public concern in Arizona elections and promoting the free and open debate that the First Amendment was intended to foster. In the State's view, this promotion of First Amendment ideals offsets any burden the law might impose on some speakers.

> Not so. Any increase in speech resulting from the Arizona law is of one kind and one kind only — that of publicly financed candidates. The burden imposed on privately financed candidates and independent expenditure groups reduces their speech; "restriction[s] on the amount of money a person or group can spend on political communication during a campaign necessarily reduces the quantity of expression." *Buckley*. Thus, even if the matching funds provision did result in more speech by publicly financed candidates and more speech in general, it would do so at the expense of

impermissibly burdening (and thus reducing) the speech of privately financed candidates and independent expenditure groups. This sort of "beggar thy neighbor" approach to free speech — "restrict[ing] the speech of some elements of our society in order to enhance the relative voice of others" — is "wholly foreign to the First Amendment." *Buckley.*

He also rejected a similar argument made by the United States, as *amicus curiae*:

> The United States as *amicus* contends that "[p]roviding additional funds to petitioners' opponents does not make petitioners' own speech any less effective" and thus does not substantially burden speech. Of course it does. . . . All else being equal, an advertisement supporting the election of a candidate that goes without a response is often more effective than an advertisement that is directly controverted. And even if the publicly funded candidate decides to use his new money to address a different issue altogether, the end goal of that spending is to claim electoral victory over the opponent that triggered the additional state funding.

Turning to the interests supporting the law, the Chief Justice argued that the law appeared to have been aimed at leveling the field of political competition. As a foundational proposition of First Amendment law, he rejected the legitimacy of that goal:

> Leveling electoral opportunities means making and implementing judgments about which strengths should be permitted to contribute to the outcome of an election," *Davis* — a dangerous enterprise and one that cannot justify burdening protected speech.

He also rejected the argument that the law was justified by any general anti-corruption rationale, noting that neither self-funded speech nor truly independent speech in favor of a candidate raised this risk. Finally, he considered, and rejected, the state's argument that the matching funds provision served the state's anti-corruption interest indirectly, by making acceptance of public funds an attractive option for candidates by allowing candidates accepting public funds to mount effective campaigns:

> We have explained that the matching funds provision substantially burdens the speech of privately financed candidates and independent groups. It does so to an even greater extent than the law we invalidated in *Davis.* We have explained that those burdens cannot be justified by a desire to "level the playing field." We have also explained that much of the speech burdened by the matching funds provision does not, under our precedents, pose a danger of corruption. In light of the foregoing analysis, the fact that the State may feel that the matching funds provision is necessary to allow it to "find[ ] the sweet-spot" and "fine-tun[e]" its public funding system, *post*, (Kagan, J., dissenting), to achieve its desired level of participation without an undue drain on public resources, is not a sufficient justification for the burden.

Justice Kagan, joined by Justices Ginsburg, Breyer and Sotomayor, dissented. She described the matching funds provision as an attempt to calibrate the amount of the grants given to candidates accepting public financing. In particular, she explained that grants that are too large are wasteful, while grants that are too small discourage candidate participation in the program. She argued that using the amount of a self-funder's spending as a trigger for gradually increased public grants represented an attempt to find what she called "the sweet-spot" between these two extremes.

Turning to the plaintiff's First Amendment claim, Justice Kagan first argued that the Arizona law did not impose any burden on speech:

> Arizona's matching funds provision does not restrict, but instead subsidizes, speech. The law "impose[s] no ceiling on [speech] and do[es] not prevent anyone from speaking." *Citizens United.* The statute does not tell candidates or their supporters how much money they can spend to convey their message, when they can spend it, or what they can spend it on. Rather, the Arizona law, like the public financing statute in *Buckley*, provides funding for political speech, thus "facilitat[ing] communication by candidates with the electorate." *Buckley.* By enabling participating candidates to respond to their opponents' expression, the statute expands public debate, in adherence to "our tradition that more speech, not less, is the governing rule." *Citizens United.* What the law does — all the law does — is fund more speech.

She then directly addressed the majority's reasoning that the matching funds provision burdened the self-funded speaker:

> [The] very notion that additional speech constitutes a "burden" is odd and unsettling. . . . The only "burden" in this case comes from the grant of a subsidy to another person, and the opportunity that subsidy allows for responsive speech. . . . Yet in this case, the majority says that the prospect of more speech — responsive speech, competitive speech, the kind of speech that drives public debate — counts as a constitutional injury. That concept . . . is "wholly foreign to the First Amendment." *Buckley.*

She then attacked the majority's reliance on *Davis*:

> Under the First Amendment, the similarity between *Davis* and this case matters far less than the differences. Here is the similarity: In both cases, one candidate's campaign expenditure triggered . . . [*sic*] something. Now here are the differences: In *Davis*, the candidate's expenditure triggered a discriminatory speech restriction, which Congress could not otherwise have imposed consistent with the First Amendment; by contrast, in this case, the candidate's expenditure triggers a non-discriminatory speech subsidy, which all parties agree Arizona could have provided in the first instance. In First Amendment law, that difference makes a difference — indeed, it makes all the difference. As I have indicated before, two great fault lines run through our First Amendment doctrine: one, between speech restrictions and speech subsidies, and the other, between discriminatory and neutral government action. The Millionaire's Amendment fell on the disfavored side of both divides: To reiterate, it imposed a discriminatory speech restriction. The Arizona Clean Elections Act lands on the opposite side of both: It grants a non-discriminatory speech subsidy. So to say that

Davis "largely controls" this case is to decline to take our First Amendment doctrine seriously.

Justice Kagan continued:

> But what of the trigger mechanism — in *Davis*, as here, a candidate's campaign expenditures? That, after all, is the only thing that this case and *Davis* share. If *Davis* had held that the trigger mechanism itself violated the First Amendment, then the case would support today's holding. But *Davis* said nothing of the kind. It made clear that the trigger mechanism could not rescue the discriminatory contribution limits from constitutional invalidity; that the limits went into effect only after a candidate spent substantial personal resources rendered them no more permissible under the First Amendment. But *Davis* did not call into question the trigger mechanism itself. Indeed, *Davis* explained that Congress could have used that mechanism to activate a non-discriminatory (*i.e.*, across-the-board) increase in contribution limits; in that case, the Court stated, "Davis' argument would plainly fail." The constitutional infirmity in *Davis* was not the trigger mechanism, but rather what lay on the other side of it — a discriminatory speech restriction.

Finally, Justice Kagan argued that the provisions served a legitimate anti-corruption interest, by encouraging candidates to take advantage of public financing and thus eschew reliance on corruption-inducing and corrupt-appearing private contributions. She argued that that state interest was by itself sufficient to support the statute, regardless of whether or not the state also had made the case for an equalization goal in enacting the provision.

3. *AFEC*'s impact on public financing schemes more generally remains unclear, and we must await future cases. The Chief Justice's majority opinion did cite and quote *Buckley* for the proposition that "governments 'may engage in public financing of election campaigns' and that doing so can 'further significant governmental interest[s],' such as the state interest in preventing corruption." However, *AFEC* seems to make clear that the Court will carefully review the particular elements of public financing schemes, even when those elements are defended, as was the provision in *AFEC*, as necessary to ensure those schemes' overall success.

PROBLEM: ENCOURAGING SMALL CONTRIBUTORS

The elected leaders of the City of New Hague are concerned about low citizen participation in electoral politics in their city, and the perception that wealthy interests control access to elected leaders. The City already has contribution limits of $300 per person per candidate, which have been held by the courts to be sufficiently generous as to comply with the First Amendment. The City Council is considering the following amendment to that law:

> When any person contributes less than $100 to a candidate, and agrees to contribute nothing more to that candidate for that particular election, the City shall match the contribution.

Is the proposed law constitutional? Would the analysis change under either of these variations?

(1)   If the law allowed contributors to give up to the full legal limit, but simply limited the city's match to the first $99?

(2)   If the matching contributions were triggered by large expenditures of a candidate's own personal funds?

D. POLITICAL ASSOCIATION AND DISCLOSURE REQUIREMENTS

The attention (properly) given campaign finance regulation risks obscuring the other First Amendment issues that arise when citizens participate in the political process. For example, in *McIntyre v. Ohio Elections Comm'n*, 514 U.S. 334 (1995), the Court invalidated an Ohio law prohibiting the distribution of anonymous campaign literature. Disclosure of one's identity has remained an issue in the context of popular participation in the political process.

DOE v. REED
130 S. Ct. 2811 (2010)

CHIEF JUSTICE ROBERTS delivered the opinion of the Court.

The State of Washington allows its citizens to challenge state laws by referendum. Roughly four percent of Washington voters must sign a petition to place such a referendum on the ballot. That petition, which by law must include the names and addresses of the signers, is then submitted to the government for verification and canvassing, to ensure that only lawful signatures are counted. The Washington Public Records Act (PRA) authorizes private parties to obtain copies of government documents, and the State construes the PRA to cover submitted referendum petitions.

This case arises out of a state law extending certain benefits to same-sex couples, and a corresponding referendum petition to put that law to a popular vote. Respondent intervenors invoked the PRA to obtain copies of the petition, with the names and addresses of the signers. Certain petition signers and the petition sponsor objected, arguing that such public disclosure would violate their rights under the First Amendment.

The course of this litigation, however, has framed the legal question before us more broadly. The issue at this stage of the case is not whether disclosure of this particular petition would violate the First Amendment, but whether disclosure of referendum petitions in general would do so. We conclude that such disclosure does not as a general matter violate the First Amendment, and we therefore affirm the judgment of the Court of Appeals. We leave it to the lower courts to consider in the first instance the signers' more focused claim concerning disclosure of the information on this particular petition, which is pending before the District Court.

I

[The Washington State legislature enacted a bill expanding the rights of same-sex couples in Washington. A group opposed to the measure began collecting signatures to place a referendum on the ballot (which became known as R-71) that would repeal the law. After that group submitted its signatures to the secretary of state, a group opposed to the referendum brought a request under the PRA asking for a copy of the petition, which included the signatories' names and addresses.]

The referendum petition sponsor and certain signers filed a complaint and a motion for a preliminary injunction in the United States District Court for the Western District of Washington, seeking to enjoin the secretary of state from publicly releasing any documents that would reveal the names and contact information of the R-71 petition signers. Count I of the complaint alleges that "[t]he Public Records Act is unconstitutional as applied to referendum petitions." Count II of the complaint alleges that "[t]he Public Records Act is unconstitutional as applied to the Referendum 71 petition because there is a reasonable probability that the signatories of the Referendum 71 petition will be subjected to threats, harassment, and reprisals." Determining that the PRA burdened core political speech, the District Court held that plaintiffs were likely to succeed on the merits of Count I and granted them a preliminary injunction on that count, enjoining release of the information on the petition.

. . . Reviewing only Count I of the complaint, the Court of Appeals held that plaintiffs were unlikely to succeed on their claim that the PRA is unconstitutional as applied to referendum petitions generally. It therefore reversed the District Court's grant of the preliminary injunction. We granted certiorari.

II

It is important at the outset to define the scope of the challenge before us. As noted, Count I of the complaint contends that the PRA "violates the First Amendment as applied to referendum petitions." Count II asserts that the PRA "is unconstitutional as applied to the Referendum 71 petition." The District Court decision was based solely on Count I; the Court of Appeals decision reversing the District Court was similarly limited. Neither court addressed Count II.

The parties disagree about whether Count I is properly viewed as a facial or as-applied challenge. It obviously has characteristics of both: The claim is "as applied" in the sense that it does not seek to strike the PRA in all its applications, but only to the extent it covers referendum petitions. The claim is "facial" in that it is not limited to plaintiffs' particular case, but challenges application of the law more broadly to all referendum petitions.

The label is not what matters. The important point is that plaintiffs' claim and the relief that would follow — an injunction barring the secretary of state "from making referendum petitions available to the public" — reach beyond the particular circumstances of these plaintiffs. They must therefore satisfy our standards for a facial challenge to the extent of that reach.

III

A

The compelled disclosure of signatory information on referendum petitions is subject to review under the First Amendment. An individual expresses a view on a political matter when he signs a petition under Washington's referendum procedure. In most cases, the individual's signature will express the view that the law subject to the petition should be overturned. Even if the signer is agnostic as to the merits of the underlying law, his signature still expresses the political view that the question should be considered "by the whole electorate." In either case, the expression of a political view implicates a First Amendment right. . . .

Petition signing remains expressive even when it has legal effect in the electoral process. But that is not to say that the electoral context is irrelevant to the nature of our First Amendment review. We allow States significant flexibility in implementing their own voting systems. To the extent a regulation concerns the legal effect of a particular activity in that process, the government will be afforded substantial latitude to enforce that regulation. Also pertinent to our analysis is the fact that the PRA is not a prohibition on speech, but instead a *disclosure* requirement. "[D]isclosure requirements may burden the ability to speak, but they . . . do not prevent anyone from speaking." *Citizens United v. Federal Election Comm'n* (2010) [*supra* this supplement].

We have a series of precedents considering First Amendment challenges to disclosure requirements in the electoral context. These precedents have reviewed such challenges under what has been termed "exacting scrutiny." *See, e.g., Buckley v. Valeo* (1976) ("Since *NAACP v. Alabama* (1958) [Casebook p. 351], we have required that the subordinating interests of the State [offered to justify compelled disclosure] survive exacting scrutiny"); *Citizens United* ("The Court has subjected [disclosure] requirements to 'exacting scrutiny' " (quoting *Buckley*)); *Davis v. Federal Election Comm'n*, 554 U.S. 724 (2008) (governmental interest in disclosure " 'must survive exacting scrutiny' " (quoting *Buckley*)).

That standard "requires a 'substantial relation' between the disclosure requirement and a 'sufficiently important' governmental interest." *Citizens United* (quoting *Buckley*). To withstand this scrutiny, "the strength of the governmental interest must reflect the seriousness of the actual burden on First Amendment rights." *Davis* (citing *Buckley*).

B

Respondents assert two interests to justify the burdens of compelled disclosure under the PRA on First Amendment rights: (1) preserving the integrity of the electoral process by combating fraud, detecting invalid signatures, and fostering government transparency and accountability; and (2) providing information to the electorate about who supports the petition. Because we determine that the State's interest in preserving the integrity of the electoral process suffices to defeat the argument that the PRA is unconstitutional with respect to referendum petitions in general, we need not, and do not, address the State's "informational" interest.

The State's interest in preserving the integrity of the electoral process is undoubtedly important. . . . The State's interest is particularly strong with respect to efforts to root out fraud. . . .

But the State's interest in preserving electoral integrity is not limited to combating fraud. That interest extends to efforts to ferret out invalid signatures caused not by fraud but by simple mistake, such as duplicate signatures or signatures of individuals who are not registered to vote in the State. That interest also extends more generally to promoting transparency and accountability in the electoral process, which the State argues is "essential to the proper functioning of a democracy."

Plaintiffs contend that the disclosure requirements of the PRA are not "sufficiently related" to the interest of protecting the integrity of the electoral process. They argue that disclosure is not necessary because the secretary of state is already charged with verifying and canvassing the names on a petition, advocates and opponents of a measure can observe that process, and any citizen can challenge the secretary's actions in court. They also stress that existing criminal penalties reduce the danger of fraud in the petition process.

But the secretary's verification and canvassing will not catch all invalid signatures: The job is large and difficult (the secretary ordinarily checks "only 3 to 5% of signatures"), and the secretary can make mistakes, too. Public disclosure can help cure the inadequacies of the verification and canvassing process. . . .

Public disclosure thus helps ensure that the only signatures counted are those that should be, and that the only referenda placed on the ballot are those that garner enough valid signatures. Public disclosure also promotes transparency and accountability in the electoral process to an extent other measures cannot. In light of the foregoing, we reject plaintiffs' argument and conclude that public disclosure of referendum petitions in general is substantially related to the important interest of preserving the integrity of the electoral process.[2]

C

Plaintiffs' more significant objection is that "the strength of the governmental interest" does not "reflect the seriousness of the actual burden on First Amendment rights." According to plaintiffs, the objective of those seeking disclosure of the R-71 petition is not to prevent fraud, but to publicly identify those who had validly signed and to broadcast the signers' political views on the subject of the petition. Plaintiffs allege, for example, that several groups plan to post the petitions in searchable form on the Internet, and then encourage other citizens to seek out the R-71 signers. . . .

In related contexts, we have explained that those resisting disclosure can prevail under the First Amendment if they can show "a reasonable probability that the compelled disclosure [of personal information] will subject them to threats,

---

[2] Justice Thomas's contrary assessment of the relationship between the disclosure of referendum petitions generally and the State's interests in this case is based on his determination that strict scrutiny applies, rather than the standard of review that we have concluded is appropriate.

harassment, or reprisals from either Government officials or private parties." *Buckley*; see also *Citizens United*. The question before us, however, is not whether PRA disclosure violates the First Amendment with respect to those who signed the R-71 petition, or other particularly controversial petitions. The question instead is whether such disclosure in general violates the First Amendment rights of those who sign referendum petitions.

The problem for plaintiffs is that their argument rests almost entirely on the specific harm they say would attend disclosure of the information on the R-71 petition, or on similarly controversial ones. But typical referendum petitions "concern tax policy, revenue, budget, or other state law issues." Voters care about such issues, some quite deeply — but there is no reason to assume that any burdens imposed by disclosure of typical referendum petitions would be remotely like the burdens plaintiffs fear in this case. . . .

Faced with the State's unrebutted arguments that only modest burdens attend the disclosure of a typical petition, we must reject plaintiffs' broad challenge to the PRA. In doing so, we note — as we have in other election law disclosure cases — that upholding the law against a broad-based challenge does not foreclose a litigant's success in a narrower one. See *Buckley* ("minor parties" may be exempt from disclosure requirements if they can show "a reasonable probability that the compelled disclosure of a party's contributors' names will subject them to threats, harassment, or reprisals from either Government officials or private parties"); *Citizens United* (disclosure "would be unconstitutional as applied to an organization if there were a reasonable probability that the group's members would face threats, harassment, or reprisals if their names were disclosed") (citing *McConnell v. Federal Election Comm'n* (2003)). . . .

*   *   *

We conclude that disclosure under the PRA would not violate the First Amendment with respect to referendum petitions in general and therefore affirm the judgment of the Court of Appeals.

JUSTICE BREYER, concurring.

In circumstances where, as here, "a law significantly implicates competing constitutionally protected interests in complex ways," the Court balances interests. *Nixon v. Shrink Missouri Government PAC* (2000) (Breyer, J., concurring). . . . As I read their opinions, this is what both the Court and Justice Stevens do. And for the reasons stated in those opinions (as well as many of the reasons discussed by Justice Sotomayor), I would uphold the statute challenged in this case. With this understanding, I join the opinion of the Court and Justice Stevens' opinion.

JUSTICE ALITO, concurring.

The Court holds that the disclosure under the Washington Public Records Act (PRA) of the names and addresses of persons who sign referendum petitions does not as a general matter violate the First Amendment, and I agree with that conclusion. Many referendum petitions concern relatively uncontroversial matters, and plaintiffs have provided no reason to think that disclosure of signatory information in those contexts would significantly chill the willingness of voters to sign. Plaintiffs' facial challenge therefore must fail.

Nonetheless, facially valid disclosure requirements can impose heavy burdens on First Amendment rights in individual cases. Acknowledging that reality, we have long held that speakers can obtain as-applied exemptions from disclosure requirements if they can show "a reasonable probability that the compelled disclosure of [personal information] will subject them to threats, harassment, or reprisals from either Government officials or private parties." *Buckley v. Valeo* (1976); see also *Citizens United v. Federal Election Comm'n* (2010); *McConnell v. Federal Election Comm'n* (2003). Because compelled disclosure can "burden the ability to speak," *Citizens United*, and "seriously infringe on privacy of association and belief guaranteed by the First Amendment," *Buckley*, the as-applied exemption plays a critical role in safeguarding First Amendment rights.

I

The possibility of prevailing in an as-applied challenge provides adequate protection for First Amendment rights only if (1) speakers can obtain the exemption sufficiently far in advance to avoid chilling protected speech and (2) the showing necessary to obtain the exemption is not overly burdensome. . . . To avoid the possibility that a disclosure requirement might chill the willingness of voters to sign a referendum petition . . . voters must have some assurance *at the time when they are presented with the petition* that their names and identifying information will not be released to the public. The only way a circulator can provide such assurance, however, is if the circulator has sought and obtained an as-applied exemption from the disclosure requirement well before circulating the petition. . . .

Additionally, speakers must be able to obtain an as-applied exemption without clearing a high evidentiary hurdle. We acknowledged as much in *Buckley*, where we noted that "unduly strict requirements of proof could impose a heavy burden" on speech. Recognizing that speakers "must be allowed sufficient flexibility in the proof of injury to assure a fair consideration of their claim," we emphasized that speakers "need show only a *reasonable probability*" that disclosure will lead to threats, harassment, or reprisals. . . .

II

In light of those principles, the plaintiffs in this case have a strong argument that the PRA violates the First Amendment as applied to the Referendum 71 petition. . . .

As-applied challenges to disclosure requirements play a critical role in protecting First Amendment freedoms. To give speech the breathing room it needs to flourish, prompt judicial remedies must be available well before the relevant speech occurs and the burden of proof must be low. In this case — both through analogy and through their own experiences — plaintiffs have a strong case that they are entitled to as-applied relief, and they will be able to pursue such relief before the District Court.

JUSTICE SOTOMAYOR, with whom JUSTICE STEVENS and JUSTICE GINSBURG join, concurring.

. . . [I]n assessing the countervailing interests at stake in this case, we must be mindful of the character of initiatives and referenda. . . . States enjoy "considerable leeway" to choose the subjects that are eligible for placement on the ballot and to specify the requirements for obtaining ballot access. . . . As the Court properly recognizes, each of these structural decisions "inevitably affects — at least to some degree — the individual's right" to speak about political issues and "to associate with others for political ends." For instance, requiring petition signers to be registered voters or to use their real names no doubt limits the ability or willingness of some individuals to undertake the expressive act of signing a petition. Regulations of this nature, however, stand "a step removed from the communicative aspect of petitioning," and the ability of States to impose them can scarcely be doubted. . . . It is by no means necessary for a State to prove that such "reasonable, nondiscriminatory restrictions" are narrowly tailored to its interests.

The Court today confirms that the State of Washington's decision to make referendum petition signatures available for public inspection falls squarely within the realm of permissible election-related regulations. Public disclosure of the identity of petition signers, which is the rule in the overwhelming majority of States that use initiatives and referenda, advances States' vital interests in "[p]reserving the integrity of the electoral process, preventing corruption, and sustaining the active, alert responsibility of the individual citizen in a democracy for the wise conduct of government." *First Nat. Bank of Boston v. Bellotti* (1978); see also *Citizens United v. Federal Election Comm'n* (2010) ("[T]ransparency enables the electorate to make informed decisions and give proper weight to different speakers and messages").

On the other side of the ledger, I view the burden of public disclosure on speech and associational rights as minimal in this context. As this Court has observed with respect to campaign-finance regulations, "disclosure requirements . . . 'do not prevent anyone from speaking.' " *Citizens United.* . . .

Given the relative weight of the interests at stake and the traditionally public nature of initiative and referendum processes, the Court rightly rejects petitioners' constitutional challenge to the State of Washington's petition disclosure regulations. These same considerations also mean that any party attempting to challenge particular applications of the State's regulations will bear a heavy burden. . . . Case-specific relief may be available when a State selectively applies a facially neutral petition disclosure rule in a manner that discriminates based on the content of referenda or the viewpoint of petition signers, or in the rare circumstance in which disclosure poses a reasonable probability of serious and widespread harassment that the State is unwilling or unable to control. *Cf. NAACP v. Alabama* (1958) [Casebook p. 351]. . . .

JUSTICE STEVENS, with whom JUSTICE BREYER joins, concurring in part and concurring in the judgment.

This is not a hard case. It is not about a restriction on voting or on speech and does not involve a classic disclosure requirement. Rather, the case concerns a neutral, nondiscriminatory policy of disclosing information already in the State's possession that, it has been alleged, might one day indirectly burden petition signatories. The burden imposed by Washington's application of the Public Records Act (PRA) to referendum petitions in the vast majority, if not all, its applications is not substantial. And the State has given a more than adequate justification for its choice.

For a number of reasons, the application of the PRA to referendum petitions does not substantially burden any individual's expression. First, it is not "a regulation of pure speech." *McIntyre v. Ohio Elections Comm'n*, 514 U.S. 334 (1995); *cf. United States v. O'Brien* (1968) [Casebook p. 450]. It does not prohibit expression, nor does it require that any person signing a petition disclose or say anything at all. Nor does the State's disclosure alter the content of a speaker's message.

Second, any effect on speech that disclosure might have is minimal. The PRA does not necessarily make it more difficult to circulate or obtain signatures on a petition, or to communicate one's views generally. . . .

Weighed against the possible burden on constitutional rights are the State's justifications for its rule. In this case, the State has posited a perfectly adequate justification: an interest in deterring and detecting petition fraud. Given the pedigree of this interest and of similar regulations, the State need not produce concrete evidence that the PRA is the best way to prevent fraud. And there is more than enough evidence to support the State's election-integrity justification.

There remains the issue of petitioners' as-applied challenge. As a matter of law, the Court is correct to keep open the possibility that in particular instances in which a policy such as the PRA burdens expression "by the public enmity attending publicity," speakers may have a winning constitutional claim. " '[F]rom time to time throughout history,' " persecuted groups have been able " 'to criticize oppressive practices and laws either anonymously or not at all.' "

In my view, this is unlikely to occur in cases involving the PRA. . . . Just as we have in the past, I would demand strong evidence before concluding that an indirect and speculative chain of events imposes a substantial burden on speech. . . .

JUSTICE SCALIA, concurring in the judgment.

. . . I doubt whether signing a petition that has the effect of suspending a law fits within "the freedom of speech" at all. But even if, as the Court concludes, it does, a long history of practice shows that the First Amendment does not prohibit public disclosure.

I

We should not repeat and extend the mistake of *McIntyre v. Ohio Elections Comm'n*, 514 U.S. 334 (1995). There, with neither textual support nor precedents requiring the result, the Court invalidated a form of election regulation that had been widely used by the States since the end of the 19th century. The Court held that an Ohio statute prohibiting the distribution of anonymous campaign literature violated the First and Fourteenth Amendments.

Mrs. McIntyre sought a general right to "speak" anonymously about a referendum. Here, plaintiffs go one step further — they seek a general right to participate anonymously in the referendum itself. . . .

Today's opinion acknowledges such a right, finding that it can be denied here only because of the State's interest in "preserving the integrity of the electoral process." In my view this is not a matter for judicial interest-balancing. Our Nation's longstanding traditions of legislating and voting in public refute the claim that the First Amendment accords a right to anonymity in the performance of an act with governmental effect. . . . *McIntyre* (Scalia, J., dissenting). . . .

JUSTICE THOMAS, dissenting.

Just as "[c]onfidence in the integrity of our electoral processes is essential to the functioning of our participatory democracy," so too is citizen participation in those processes, which necessarily entails political speech and association under the First Amendment. In my view, compelled disclosure of signed referendum and initiative petitions under the Washington Public Records Act (PRA) severely burdens those rights and chills citizen participation in the referendum process. Given those burdens, I would hold that Washington's decision to subject all referendum petitions to public disclosure is unconstitutional because there will always be a less restrictive means by which Washington can vindicate its stated interest in preserving the integrity of its referendum process. I respectfully dissent. . . .

II

A

The Court correctly concludes that "an individual expresses" a "political view" by signing a referendum petition. The Court also rightly rejects the baseless argument that such expressive activity falls "outside the scope of the First Amendment" merely because "it has legal effect in the electoral process." Yet, the Court does not acknowledge the full constitutional implications of these conclusions.

The expressive political activity of signing a referendum petition is a paradigmatic example of "the practice of persons sharing common views banding together to achieve a common end." . . .

This Court has long recognized the "vital relationship between" political association "and privacy in one's associations," *NAACP v. Alabama* (1958) [Casebook p. 351], and held that "[t]he Constitution protects against the compelled disclosure of political associations and beliefs." This constitutional protection "yield[s] only to a subordinating interest of the State that is compelling, and then only if there is a substantial relation between the information sought and an overriding and compelling state interest." Thus, unlike the Court, I read our precedents to require application of strict scrutiny to laws that compel disclosure of protected First Amendment association. Under that standard, a disclosure requirement passes constitutional muster only if it is narrowly tailored — i.e., the least restrictive means — to serve a compelling state interest.

B

Washington's application of the PRA to a referendum petition does not survive strict scrutiny.

1

Washington first contends that it has a compelling interest in "transparency and accountability," which it claims encompasses several subordinate interests: preserving the integrity of its election process, preventing corruption, deterring fraud, and correcting mistakes by the secretary of state or by petition signers.

It is true that a State has a substantial interest in regulating its referendum and initiative processes "to protect the[ir] integrity and reliability." But Washington points to no precedent from this Court recognizing "correcting errors" as a distinct compelling interest that could support disclosure regulations. And our cases strongly suggest that preventing corruption and deterring fraud bear less weight in this particular electoral context: the signature-gathering stage of a referendum or initiative drive. . . .

Thus, I am not persuaded that Washington's interest in protecting the integrity and reliability of its referendum process, as the State has defined that interest, is compelling. But I need not answer that question here. Even assuming the interest is compelling, on-demand disclosure of a referendum petition to any person under the PRA is "a blunderbuss approach" to furthering that interest, not the least restrictive means of doing so. . . .

. . . Washington . . . could put the names and addresses of referendum signers into a similar electronic database that state employees could search without subjecting the name and address of each signer to wholesale public disclosure. . . . Doing so presumably would drastically reduce or eliminate possible errors or mistakes that Washington argues the secretary might make . . . .

2

Washington also contends that it has a compelling interest in "providing relevant information to Washington voters," and that on-demand disclosure to the public is a narrowly tailored means of furthering that interest. This argument is easily dispatched, since this Court has already rejected it in a similar context.

In *McIntyre v. Ohio Elections Comm'n*, 514 U.S. 334 (1995), the Court held that an Ohio law prohibiting anonymous political pamphleting violated the First Amendment. One of the interests Ohio had invoked to justify that law was identical to Washington's here: the "interest in providing the electorate with relevant information." The Court called that interest "plainly insufficient to support the constitutionality of [Ohio's] disclosure requirement." . . .

III

Significant practical problems will result from requiring as-applied challenges to protect referendum signers' constitutional rights.

The Court's approach will "require substantial litigation over an extended time" before a potential signer of any referendum will learn whether, if he signs a referendum, his associational privacy right will remain intact. *Citizens United v. Federal Election Comm'n* (2010). And the tenacious litigant's reward for trying to protect his First Amendment rights? An "interpretive process [that] itself would create an inevitable, pervasive, and serious risk of chilling protected speech pending the drawing of fine distinctions that, in the end, would themselves be questionable." *Id.* The large number of such fine and questionable distinctions in these types of cases reinforces my view that as-applied challenges provide no more than "a hollow assurance" that referendum signers' First Amendment rights will be protected. *Id.* (Thomas, J., concurring in part and dissenting in part). . . .

NOTE: ANONYMITY, SPEECH AND POLITICAL ACTIVITY

Doe v. Reed raises several important issues that remain unanswered, in part because of the (partially) facial nature of the challenge and in part because of the sheer novelty of some of the technological landscape. Consider the following questions:

1. In light of the different opinions in *Reed*, what are the plaintiffs' prospects for success in their as-applied challenge in the lower courts? What type of showing would they need to make?

2. Consider the context in which the asserted First Amendment harm arises. As Justice Alito noted in his concurrence, the harm to a would-be signatory arises at the time he or she considers signing the petition, which may be far in advance of any direct evidence of harassment of signatories by opposing groups. What special problems does this fact pose for would-be signatories who fear retaliation if they sign a referendum petition and wish to receive an assurance that their signatures will remain secret? How can a judge accurately predict such future events and weigh them against the claims of transparency in democratic self-government?

3. Today the Internet makes it possible to combine disclosed political speech information (such as the petition in *Doe v. Reed*) with other available data to create a detailed profile of who is engaging in what type of political speech. (See for yourself: go to fundrace.huffingtonpost.com, zero in on your neighborhood, and see

which of your neighbors is contributing money to which political candidate.) How should this type of technology affect the First Amendment analysis? Justice Brandeis, in a famous phrase about disclosure and transparency in government, commented that "sunlight is the best disinfectant." Does that change when the disinfectant is extra-strength?

Chapter 14

FREEDOM OF THE PRESS

A. SINGLING OUT THE PRESS

Page 831: *add after the Problem:*

PROBLEM: SAVE THE NEWSPAPERS!

As the public has become more and more accustomed to obtaining its news through online sites such as blogs, traditional newspapers have experienced a steep decline in their circulations, and thus, crucially, the rates they can charge for advertising. (Historically, advertisers have supplied upwards of 80% of newspaper revenues.) While most newspapers now also have online editions that feature additional advertising, the competitive nature of Internet advertising means that they are unable to charge enough to advertise on their online sites to offset their revenue declines in their print publications.

Newspapers' weakened market position has led to great concern about newsgathering in the United States. Many experts and observers argue that blogs and other Internet news sites are merely "aggregators" of news developed elsewhere — that is, they simply hyper-link to stories on other websites. Thus, these commentators do not believe that these sources are long-term substitutes for traditional media outlets, which are usually the only ones that employ teams of reporters and maintain physical presences ("bureaus") across the nation and around the world. The worrisome prediction is that newsgathering will suffer irremediably.

This state of affairs has led to some calls for governmental regulatory action. Among various possible responses that have been floated are the following:

1. An exemption from federal antitrust laws that would allow newspapers to demand, as a group acting together, payment every time a blog links to a newspaper story. Ordinarily, such a united negotiating position would violate federal antitrust laws; this proposal would specifically exempt newspapers from those laws for this limited purpose.

2. A direct tax on all commercial blogs (that is, blogs that accept advertising), based on the number of times per year they link to a newspaper article.

3. A tax on Internet Service Provider (ISP) services, the proceeds of which would be paid as a direct subsidy to newspapers. The theory behind this proposal is that the tax is an implicit and indirect tax on Internet users who (presumably) patronize the Internet news sites that are harming newspapers.

What constitutional issues would these government actions raise?

PROBLEM: (NON-)TAXATION OF ONLINE INFORMATION

For the last seventy years, the State of Texas has imposed a 2% sales tax on all retail sales in the state, including sales of newspapers and all other periodicals. Two years ago the State revamped its sales tax scheme to bring it in line with the growth in online retailing. The State enacted a law that reads as follows:

> Any sale made over the Internet to a Texas purchaser shall be subject to the same sales tax as would be applied if the sale had been made through non-Internet means, *provided however*, that no sales tax shall be imposed on any Internet purchase when the subject of the transaction is online delivery of information rather than delivery of a tangible item.

America Today is a daily newspaper that is distributed across the country, including Texas. Like many newspapers, it has a website. Again like many newspapers, it has considered charging for website-delivered content. However, it has decided not to do so. It is concerned that the exemption for sales tax charged on purchases of online-delivered information — such as purchases of subscriptions to online periodicals — will substantially disadvantage it in the marketplace as it will have to either absorb the sales tax, thus losing revenue, or build the tax into its sale price, thus losing price competitiveness. It sues, alleging a violation of the Press Clause. What result?

1. Does your analysis differ if most traditional print newspapers have online versions to which they sell subscriptions?

2. Does your analysis differ if most traditional print newspapers have online versions to which they sell subscriptions, but a growing number of media entities exist only as online information outlets?

3. Does your analysis differ if, in addition to the facts assumed above, there is a legislative finding attached to the bill that reads as follows: "The State of Texas hereby finds that new, online-only publications provide fresh perspectives on local and national issues"?

Chapter 16

THE ESTABLISHMENT CLAUSE

A. FINANCIAL AID TO RELIGION

[1] Basic Principles

Page 898: *insert new Note before subsection [2]:*

NOTE: STANDING DOCTRINE

1. Under the Constitution, there is a foundational proposition that "the judicial power of the United States" extends only to "cases" and "controversies." U.S. CONST. art. III, §§ 1 & 2. One of the controlling requirements is standing to sue: "A plaintiff must allege personal injury fairly traceable to the defendant's allegedly unlawful conduct and likely to be redressed by the requested relief." *Allen v. Wright*, 468 U.S. 737, 751 (1984). In an Establishment Clause case, these considerations take on a peculiar meaning in the context of taxpayer standing.

2. In *Frothingham v. Mellon*, 262 U.S. 447 (1923), the plaintiff sued as a federal taxpayer, not merely as a citizen. The Supreme Court ruled that the plaintiff lacked standing to bring a Tenth Amendment challenge against the Federal Maternity Act, which provided financial grants to the states to reduce maternal and infant mortality. The Court reasoned that the federal taxpayer's "interest in the moneys of the treasury — partly realized from taxation and partly from other sources — is shared with millions of others, is comparatively minute and indeterminable, and the effect upon future taxation, of any payment out of the funds, so remote, fluctuating and uncertain" that she lacked the requisite standing to bring the lawsuit. Thus, the general rule is there is no federal taxpayer standing to challenge federal programs.

3. The landmark decision in *Flast v. Cohen*, 392 U.S. 83 (1968), established an important exception to the long-standing general rule against taxpayer standing. The Supreme Court held that a federal taxpayer did have standing to bring a lawsuit to enjoin federal subsidies to parochial schools under the Elementary and Secondary Education Act as a violation of the Establishment Clause. First, there was a logical link between the status of being a taxpayer and the expenditure of funds under the Taxing and Spending Clause of the Constitution, U.S. CONST. art. I, § 8, cl. 1. Second, there was a constitutional nexus between the status of being a taxpayer and the particular infringement being alleged, i.e., a violation of the Establishment Clause. The Establishment Clause was understood to limit the taxing and spending power of Congress. This precedent is significant for making it procedurally possible to bring many of the federal Establishment Clause cases that are found in this Chapter.

4. In *Valley Forge Christian College v. Americans United for Separation of Church and State*, 454 U.S. 464 (1982), the Supreme Court was careful to

distinguish but not to overrule *Flast v. Cohen* on two bases. First, the plaintiff was challenging a decision of the Department of Health, Education and Welfare, not a congressional statute. Second, the challenged action was a transfer of real property pursuant to the congressional power over government property, U.S. CONST. art. IV, § 3, not an exercise of the taxing and spending power. Therefore, the Court held that the plaintiff organization — whose raison d'tre was the separation of church and state — did not have standing to challenge a grant of surplus real property by the federal government to a church-related college. The case did not fit the narrow exception for taxpayer standing to challenge congressional expenditures under the Establishment Clause.

5.   In *Hein v. Freedom from Religion Foundation, Inc.*, 551 U.S. 587 (2007), the Justices revisited the *Flast v. Cohen* standing doctrine for federal taxpayer suits based on the Establishment Clause. The President, by executive orders, had created a White House office and corresponding centers within various federal agencies to ensure that faith-based community groups were eligible to compete successfully for federal funding. Significantly, no congressional legislation specifically authorized these entities, which were created entirely within the Executive Branch, nor did Congress enact any law specifically appropriating money for their activities, which were funded through general Executive Branch appropriations. Plaintiffs, an organization opposed to Government endorsement of religion and three of its members, brought suit alleging a violation of the Establishment Clause. Plaintiffs particularly alleged that the directors of these centers had organized conferences that were designed to promote, and had had the effect of promoting and funding, and thus advantaging, religious community groups over secular ones. The only asserted basis for standing was that the individual plaintiffs were federal taxpayers opposed to the Executive Branch spending of congressional appropriations for these conferences.

The Supreme Court held that the plaintiffs lacked standing to pursue their constitutional challenge, but there was no majority opinion. Justice Alito, joined by the Chief Justice and Justice Kennedy, concluded that the plaintiffs failed to satisfy the narrow exception of *Flast v. Cohen*. That precedent and later cases applying the exception require that the Establishment Clause challenge be directed at an exercise of congressional power under the Taxing and Spending Clause. The expenditures being challenged here were pursuant to general appropriations to the Executive Branch. The exception for federal taxpayer standing applies only when plaintiffs challenge congressional legislation. The plurality understood this doctrine to be the proper interpretation of the Establishment Clause, and one that comported with the separation of powers concern that the judicial branch ought not intrude unduly on Executive Branch prerogatives.

Justice Scalia, joined by Justice Thomas, concurred in the Court's judgment, but argued that *Flast v. Cohen* should be overruled. They insisted that the federal taxpayer standing exception is neither logical as a matter of Article III standing doctrine nor proper as an interpretation of the Establishment Clause.

Justice Souter filed a dissenting opinion, joined by Justices Stevens, Ginsburg, and Breyer. The dissenters endorsed the *Flast v. Cohen* exception both as a doctrine of standing and as an interpretation of the Establishment Clause. They would have applied the exception to allow the plaintiffs to bring this lawsuit.

6.   In *Arizona Christian School Tuition Organization v. Winn*, 131 S. Ct. 1436 (2011), Arizona taxpayers sued the Director of the State Department of Revenue challenging state statutes on Establishment Clause grounds. The challenged statutes provided state income tax credits for contributions to school tuition organizations ("STOs"), which then used the contributions to provide scholarships to students attending private schools, including private religious schools. Thus, state taxpayers could contribute up to $500 per person or $1,000 per married couple to an authorized STO and qualify for a dollar-for-dollar credit reducing their Arizona income tax liability. An STO was required to be a federally tax-exempt organization and could not limit its scholarships to students attending only one qualified school. A qualified school was defined to be a private school that did not discriminate on the basis of race, color, handicap, familial status, or national origin. However, as the dissenters noted, many of the STOs did in fact discriminate on the basis of a child's religion when awarding scholarships. According to the State's own estimates, since 1997, the private-school-tuition tax credit diverted a total of $350 million in state tax revenues. And the portion that went to religious schools was estimated by some to be as high as ninety percent. The District Court dismissed the suit for failure to state a claim. The Ninth Circuit held that plaintiffs had standing under *Flast v. Cohen* and reversed on the merits.

The Supreme Court in turn reversed the Ninth Circuit on the standing question, but did not reach the merits. Justice Kennedy authored the majority opinion joined by Chief Justice Roberts and Justices Scalia, Thomas, and Alito. The Court held that because the plaintiffs challenged a tax credit, as opposed to a governmental expenditure, they lacked standing under the taxpayer exception recognized in *Flast v. Cohen*. According to the majority, the Arizona state income tax credit does not visit the kind of injury identified in *Flast v. Cohen*, i.e., the constitutionally particularized injury of using the taxing and spending power to transfer an individual taxpayer's property through the government's treasury to a sectarian entity in violation of the consciences of objecting taxpayers. In contrast, Arizona taxpayers remain free to pay their own tax bills without contributing to an STO, to contribute to a religious or secular STO of their choice, or to contribute to other charitable organizations as they see fit. Under the Arizona statutes: private citizens create STOs; STOs designate beneficiary schools; and individual taxpayers contribute to STOs to obtain a tax credit. The tax credit does not extract and spend the actual funds of objecting taxpayers. Therefore, the tax credit is not tantamount to the imposition of a religious tax.

Justice Scalia, joined by Justice Thomas, concurred separately to once again call for the overruling of *Flast v. Cohen*.

In her first dissenting opinion, Justice Kagan was joined by Justices Ginsburg, Breyer, and Sotomayor. The dissent argued that the plaintiffs properly fit into the exception for taxpayer standing in *Flast v. Cohen*. The dissent squarely rejected the majority's distinction between an appropriation and a tax credit as being constitutionally facile as a matter of precedent and economically unsound as a matter of principle. The dissent reasoned that targeted tax breaks accomplish the very same unconstitutional mischief as direct governmental financial aid; both are effective methods of financing religion in violation of the First Amendment. The dissent cited and quoted extensively from the Supreme Court's Establishment Clause jurisprudence to try to make its case that the majority was mistaken and wrong. By the dissent's research count, five Supreme Court cases and at least twenty different appellate and district courts previously had reached the merits in similar challenges. In perhaps a telling lament, the dissent concluded:

> Today's decision devastates taxpayer standing in Establishment Clause cases. The government, after all, often uses tax expenditures to subsidize favored persons and activities. Still more, the government almost *always* has this option. Appropriations and tax subsidies are readily interchangeable; what is a cash grant today can be a tax break tomorrow. The Court's opinion thus offers a roadmap — more truly, just a one-step instruction — to any government that wishes to insulate its financing of religious activity from legal challenge. Structure the funding as a tax expenditure [or tax credit], and *Flast* will not stand in the way. No taxpayer will have standing to object. However blatantly the government may violate the Establishment Clause, taxpayers cannot gain access to the federal courts.

Do you think the dissent's worry is justified: does the majority opinion effectively allow the government to "end-run *Flast*'s guarantee of access to the Judiciary" in Establishment Clause challenges to state financial aid to religion?

Suppose that a similar state tax credit provision were challenged on federal Establishment Clause grounds in state court and the state supreme court rejected the federal rules on standing and reached the merits under the First and Fourteenth Amendments. What are the arguments for and against finding the provision constitutional on the merits? How are the arguments on the merits different, if at all, from the arguments over standing?

[2]   The *Lemon* Test as Modified

Page 926: *insert new Problems after the Note:*

PROBLEM: IS THE NATIONAL DAY OF PRAYER STATUTE A "LAW RESPECTING AN ESTABLISHMENT OF RELIGION"?

How would you answer the above question if you were a U.S. District Judge applying the Supreme Court precedents in a case challenging that federal statute? Here is a summary of its legislative history.

In 1952, evangelist Billy Graham led a six-week religious revival in Washington, D.C. The campaign culminated in a speech delivered on the steps of the U.S. Capitol in which he called for a national day of prayer:

> Ladies and gentlemen, our Nation was founded upon God, religion, and the church. . . .

> What a thrilling, glorious thing it would be to see the leaders of our country today kneeling before Almighty God in prayer. What a thrill would sweep this country. What renewed hope and courage would grip Americans at this hour of peril. . . .

We have dropped our pilot, the Lord Jesus Christ, and are sailing on blindly without divine chart or compass, hoping somehow to find our desired haven. We have certain leaders who are rank materialists; they do not recognize God nor care for Him. . . .

My brothers and sisters, I warn you, if this state of affairs continues, the end of the course is national shipwreck and ruin.

The next day, Representative Priest introduced a bill to establish a "National Day of Prayer." In addressing the House of Representatives, he noted that the country had been "challenged yesterday by the suggestion made on the east steps of the Capitol by Billy Graham that the Congress call on the President for the proclamation of a day of prayer." In support of the bill, Representative Brooks stated that "the national interest would be much better served if we turn aside for a full day of prayer for spiritual help and guidance from the Almighty during these troublous times. I hope that all denominations, Catholics, Jews, and Protestants, will join us in this day of prayer." Representative Rodino added that "it is fitting and timely that the people of America, in approaching the Easter season, as God-fearing men and women, devote themselves to a day of prayer in the interest of peace." The committee report in the House of Representatives stated that the purpose of the bill "is to direct the President to proclaim a National Day of Prayer each year."

Senator Robertson introduced the bill in the Senate, describing it as a measure against "the corrosive forces of communism which seek simultaneously to destroy our democratic way of life and the faith in an Almighty God on which it is based." The Senate committee report included the following statement:

From its beginning the United States of America has been a nation fully cognizant of the value and power of prayer. In the early days of colonization, the Pilgrims frequently engaged in prayer. When the delegates to the Constitutional Convention encountered difficulties in writing and formation of a Constitution for this Nation, prayer was suggested and became an established practice at succeeding sessions. Today, both Houses of Congress are opened daily with prayer.

Prayer has indeed been a vital force in the growth and development of this Nation. It would certainly be appropriate if, pursuant to this resolution and the proclamation it urges, the people of this country were to unite in a day of prayer each year, each in accordance with his own religious faith, thus reaffirming in a dramatic manner the deep religious conviction which has prevailed throughout the history of the United States.

On April 17, 1952, Congress passed Pub. L. No. 82-324, 66 Stat. 64:

The President shall set aside and proclaim a suitable day each year, other than a Sunday, as a National Day of Prayer, on which the people of the United States may turn to God in prayer and meditation at churches, in groups, and as individuals.

In 1988, the founders of the Campus Crusade for Christ and the members of the National Day of Prayer Commission lobbied Congress to amend the National Day of Prayer statute urging that "we should have a day in this country where we cover this nation and its leaders in prayer." During the floor debate, Representative Hall, the bill's sponsor, stated that its purpose was to "bring more certainty to the scheduling of events related to the National Day of Prayer and permit more effective long-range planning." He quoted the statement of Pat Boone, the co-chairperson of the National Day of Prayer Commission, that the law in existence at the time "offered little advance notice to adequately inform the grassroots constituencies."

Senator Thurmond introduced the bill in the Senate. He stated that because the National Day of Prayer has "a date that changes each year, it is difficult for religious groups to give advance notice to the many citizens who would like to make plans for their church and community. Maximum participation in the public knowledge of this event could be achieved if, in addition to its being proclaimed annually, it were established as a specific, annual, calendar day." Senator Helms stated that the bill would allow "Americans . . . to plan and prepare to intercede as a corporate body on behalf of the Nation and its leaders from year to year with certainty." He proclaimed that "America must return to the spiritual source of her greatness and reclaim her religious heritage. Our prayer should be that — like the Old Testament nation of Israel — Americans would once again 'humble themselves, and pray, and seek God's face, and turn from [our] wicked ways' so that God in heaven will hear and forgive our sins and heal our land."

On May 5, 1988, Congress approved Pub. L. No. 100-307, 112 Stat. 456 and President Reagan promptly signed the bill into law. The statute was included without change in the Patriotic and National Observances Codification Act of 1998 — along with, *inter alia*, Citizenship Day, Columbus Day, Constitution Week, Father's Day, Flag Day, Law Day, Mother's Day, Grandparents Day, Hispanic Heritage Month, Korean War Veterans Armistice Day, Pearl Harbor Remembrance Day, Safe Boating Week, School Lunch Week, Peace Officers Memorial Day, Thomas Jefferson's birthday, and Wright Brothers Day. Pub. L. No. 105-225, 112 Stat. 1258. The current version of the statute, 36 U.S.C. § 119, provides:

> The President shall issue each year a proclamation designating the first Thursday in May as a National Day of Prayer on which the people of the United States may turn to God in prayer and meditation at churches, in groups, and as individuals.

All Presidents since 1952 have issued proclamations designating the National Day of Prayer each year. Since 1988, the National Day of Prayer has been held on the first Thursday in May. The President's proclamations are released by the Office of the Press Secretary to the President. Presidents typically have hosted an ecumenical event in the White House to celebrate the National Day of Prayer by inviting representatives of various religions and religious denominations to an interdenominational prayer service. All 50 governors also issue proclamations annually in support of the day.

The National Day of Prayer Commission is a private organization with a mission to "proselytize every individual about the need for personal repentance and prayer, mobilizing the Judeo-Christian community to intercede for America and its leadership in the seven centers of power: Government, Military, Media, Business, Education, Church and Family." It offers "draft" proclamations for the President to consider and it chooses a theme each year with supporting scripture from the Bible. For example, in 2001, the President incorporated the Commission's theme of "One Nation under God"; in 2008, he adopted the Commission's theme of "Prayer! America's Strength and Shield." The chairperson for the Commission has spoken at eight White House prayer services on the National Day of Prayer. The Commission organizes and supports between 30,000 and 40,000 local prayer gatherings across the country in conjunction with the National Day of Prayer.

Carefully parse this summary — and the applicable Supreme Court precedents — to decide whether the National Day of Prayer statute is constitutional or unconstitutional.

PROBLEM: "I BELIEVE" IN LICENSE PLATES

The Legislature of the State of Florida has added another specialty license plate to the approved plates available that features the words "I BELIEVE" set against a sunrise along with a cross in front of a stained-glass window — see the illustration below. You are a U.S. District Judge being asked to enjoin the sale of this plate under the First and Fourteenth Amendments. How do you rule and why?

Florida has more than one hundred approved specialty plates. The specialty plates feature some aspect of Florida life and culture, such as one of its professional sports teams, one of the state or private universities, the Challenger space shuttle, popular state animals, including the panther and the manatee, *etc.* Those who propose a new plate must pay a $60,000 one-time fee to the State and conduct a survey that demonstrates a sufficient level of demand. Final approval requires the passage of a statute by the Legislature authorizing the particular plate. *See* FLA. STAT. §§ 320.08053 & 320.08056. Motorists pay an extra $25 for the specialty plates that is earmarked to a designated nonprofit organization; for this new plate, the designated private charity will use the funds to provide scholarships to in-state students attending faith-based high schools. Two other previously-approved specialty plates arguably have a quasi-religious content: "In God We Trust" (funding college scholarships for the children of "first responders") and "Choose Life!" (funding an organization that promotes adoption for unplanned pregnancies).

*   *   *

(The actual plate will be in color.)

D. DISPLAYS IN PUBLIC PLACES

Page 1013: *insert new Note before the Problem:*

NOTE: WHEN IS A CROSS NOT A CROSS?

A. Background

1. In 2010, the Supreme Court decided *Salazar v. Buono*, 130 S. Ct. 1803 (2010), a case with a lengthy litigation history and a complicated procedural posture, as demonstrated by the fact that there were six separate opinions which merely resulted in a remand to the lower court. There was no majority opinion.

2. Back in 1934, members of the Veterans of Foreign Wars (VFW) placed a Latin cross on federal land in the Mojave National Preserve (Preserve) to honor American soldiers who died in World War I. The Preserve spans 1.6 million acres. The cross rests on Sunrise Rock, a granite outcropping within the Preserve located near two private ranches. The cross has been repaired and replaced several times, most recently in 1998 by Henry Sandoz, who owns land elsewhere in the Preserve that he is willing to transfer to the Government, so long as the Government transfers the land on which the cross rests to the VFW. The cross is eight feet tall and consists of four-inch diameter metal pipes painted white. It cannot be seen from the nearest state highway, but it is visible from a local paved road. The cross is a gathering place for Easter services and the Sunrise Rock area is not infrequently used as a remote camping site. Wooden signs identified the VFW as the sponsor of the original cross, but they disappeared and the cross now stands unmarked. Before any litigation, Congress had passed an appropriations act with a provision that forbade the use of Government funds to remove the cross.

3. Alleging that he was offended by a religious symbol's presence on federal land, Frank Buono, a retired Park Service employee and a regular visitor to the Preserve, filed suit alleging a violation of the Establishment Clause and seeking an

injunction requiring the Government to remove the cross. While the case was pending in the District Court, Congress designated the cross and adjoining land a national memorial commemorating veterans of World War I and directed the Secretary of the Interior to expend up to $10,000 to acquire and install an accurate replica of the original cross and sign from 1934. The District Court eventually found that Buono had standing to sue and concluded that the presence of the cross on federal land conveyed an impression of governmental endorsement of religion; it granted injunctive relief ("2002 injunction") permanently forbidding the Government from "permitting the display" of the cross.

4.   While the Government's appeal was pending, Congress passed the Department of Defense Appropriations Act of 2004, which directed the Secretary of the Interior to transfer the cross and the land on which it stands to the VFW in exchange for a plot of privately owned land elsewhere in the Preserve ("land-transfer statute"). Affirming the District Court's judgment both as to standing and on the merits, the Ninth Circuit declined to address the land-transfer statute's effect on Buono's suit or the statute's constitutionality. The Government did not seek review in the Supreme Court. Thereafter, Buono returned to the District Court specifically seeking injunctive relief against the land transfer, either through enforcement or modification of the 2002 injunction. In 2005, the District Court rejected the Government's claim that the land-transfer statute was a *bona fide* attempt to comply with the injunction, concluding instead that the statute was actually an invalid attempt to keep the cross on display. The District Court granted Buono's motion to enforce the 2002 injunction and permanently enjoined the Government from implementing the land-transfer statute. The Ninth Circuit again affirmed. The Supreme Court granted *certiorari*.

B. The Divided Majority

5.   Justice Kennedy wrote the plurality opinion, joined in full by Chief Justice Roberts and in part by Justice Alito. That opinion concluded that Buono had standing to bring the original law suit and to seek application of the 2002 injunction to the land-transfer statute. The plurality held that the District Court erred, however, in treating Congress's motives in enacting the land-transfer statute as an illicit attempt to evade the injunction, and instead was required to consider the context in which the statute was enacted and the reasons for its passage. On remand, the District Court was instructed to take into account the land-transfer statute's significance as a substantial change in circumstances bearing on the propriety of the requested injunctive relief. This included the possibility that the public's awareness of the land-transfer statute and the eventual actual transfer of the land would change the alleged public perception that the Government was endorsing religion — that alleged perception was the announced legal basis for the 2002 injunction. According to Justice Kennedy, even assuming that the land-transfer statute was an attempt by Congress to prevent the removal of the cross, an injunction against the implementation of the statute was not automatic. Indeed, reading between the lines, he seems to suggest that the land-transfer statute likely ought to be sustained, although he was careful not to expressly instruct the District Court to reach that result:

By dismissing Congress's motives as illicit, the District Court took insufficient account of the context in which the statute was enacted and the reasons for its passage. Private citizens put the cross on Sunrise Rock to commemorate American servicemen who had died in World War I. Although certainly a Christian symbol, the cross was not emplaced on Sunrise Rock to promote a Christian message. *County of Allegheny v. American Civil Liberties Union, Greater Pittsburgh Chapter* (1989) (Kennedy, J., concurring in judgment in part and dissenting in part) [Casebook p. 974] ("[T]he [Establishment] Clause forbids a city to permit the permanent erection of a large Latin cross on the roof of city hall . . . because such an obtrusive year-round religious display would place the government's weight behind an obvious effort to proselytize on behalf of a particular religion"). Placement of the cross on Government-owned land was not an attempt to set the *imprimatur* of the state on a particular creed. Rather, those who erected the cross intended simply to honor our Nation's fallen soldiers.

Time also has played its role. The cross had stood on Sunrise Rock for nearly seven decades before the statute was enacted. By then, the cross and the cause it commemorated had become entwined in the public consciousness. Members of the public gathered regularly at Sunrise Rock to pay their respects. Rather than let the cross deteriorate, community members repeatedly took it upon themselves to replace it. Congress ultimately designated the cross as a national memorial, ranking it among those monuments honoring the noble sacrifices that constitute our national heritage. . . . It is reasonable to interpret the congressional designation as giving recognition to the historical meaning that the cross had attained. *Cf. Van Orden v. Perry* (2005) (Breyer, J., concurring in judgment) [Casebook p. 998]. . . .

The land-transfer statute embodies Congress's legislative judgment that this dispute is best resolved through a framework and policy of accommodation for a symbol that, while challenged under the Establishment Clause, has complex meaning beyond the expression of religious views. . . . The goal of avoiding governmental endorsement does not require eradication of all religious symbols in the public realm. . . . The Constitution does not oblige government to avoid any public acknowledgment of religion's role in society. . . . Rather, it leaves room to accommodate divergent values within a constitutionally permissible framework. . . .

The District Court failed to consider whether, in light of the change in law and circumstances effected by the land-transfer statute, the "reasonable observer" standard continued to be the appropriate framework through which to consider the Establishment Clause concerns invoked to justify the requested relief. As a general matter, courts considering Establishment Clause challenges do not inquire into "reasonable observer" perceptions with respect to objects on private land. Even if, however, this standard were the appropriate one, it is not clear that Buono's claim is meritorious. That test requires the hypothetical construct of an objective observer who knows all of the pertinent facts and circumstances surrounding the symbol and its placement. Applying this test here, the message conveyed by the cross would be assessed in the context of all relevant factors.

The District Court did not attempt to reassess the findings [in] light of the policy of accommodation that Congress had embraced. Rather, the District Court concentrated solely on the religious aspects of the cross, divorced from its background and context. But a Latin cross is not merely a reaffirmation of Christian beliefs. It is a symbol often used to honor and respect those whose heroic acts, noble contributions, and patient striving help secure an honored place in history for this Nation and its people. Here, one Latin cross in the desert evokes far more than religion. It evokes thousands of small crosses in foreign fields marking the graves of Americans who fell in battles, battles whose tragedies are compounded if the fallen are forgotten.

. . . . Even if, contrary to the congressional judgment, the land transfer were thought an insufficient accommodation in light of the earlier finding of religious endorsement, it was incumbent upon the District Court to consider less drastic relief than complete invalidation of the land-transfer statute. For instance, if there is to be a conveyance, the question might arise regarding the necessity of further action, such as signs to indicate the VFW's ownership of the land. As we have noted, Congress directed the Secretary of the Interior to install near the cross a replica of its original memorial plaque. One of the signs that appears in early photographs of the cross specifically identifies the VFW as the group that erected it.

Noting the possibility of specific remedies, however, is not an indication of agreement about the continued necessity for injunctive relief. The land-transfer statute's bearing on this dispute must first be determined. To date, this Court's jurisprudence in this area has refrained from making sweeping pronouncements, and this case is ill suited for announcing categorical rules. In light of the finding of unconstitutionality, and the highly fact-specific nature of the inquiry, it is best left to the District Court to undertake the analysis in the first instance. On remand, if Buono continues to challenge implementation of the statute, the District Court should conduct a proper inquiry as described above.

6.   Justice Alito joined Justice Kennedy's opinion in all respects but one: he would have reversed and remanded with express instructions to vacate the District Court's order prohibiting the implementation of the land-transfer statute:

. . . The Sunrise Rock monument was located on land belonging to the Federal Government, but in this part of the country, where much of the land is federally owned, boundaries between Government and private land are often not marked, and private citizens are permitted to go on and to use federal land for a variety of purposes. Although Sunrise Rock was federally owned, [the World War I] veterans took it upon themselves to place their monument on that spot, apparently without obtaining approval from any federal officials, and this use of federal land seems to have gone largely unnoticed for many years, in all likelihood due to the spot's remote and rugged location.

Sunrise Rock is situated far from any major population center; temperatures often exceed 100 degrees Fahrenheit in the summer; and visitors are warned of the dangers of traveling in the area. As a result, at least until this litigation, it is likely that the cross was seen by more rattlesnakes than humans. Those humans who made the trip to see the monument appear to have viewed it as conveying at least two significantly different messages. *See Pleasant Grove City, Utah v. Summum* (2009) [Casebook p. 801]. The cross is of course the preeminent symbol of Christianity, and Easter services have long been held on Sunrise Rock. But . . . the original reason for the placement of the cross was to commemorate American war dead and, particularly for those with searing memories of The Great War, the symbol that was selected, a plain unadorned white cross, no doubt evoked the unforgettable image of the white crosses, row on row, that marked the final resting places of so many American soldiers who fell in that conflict.

If Congress had done nothing [after the 2002 injunction], the Government would have been required to take down the cross, which had stood on Sunrise Rock for nearly 70 years, and this removal would have been viewed by many as a sign of disrespect for the brave soldiers whom the cross was meant to honor. The demolition of this venerable if unsophisticated, monument would also have been interpreted by some as an arresting symbol of a Government that is not neutral but hostile on matters of religion and is bent on eliminating from all public places and symbols any trace of our country's religious heritage. *Cf. Van Orden v. Perry* (2005) (Breyer, J., concurring in judgment) [Casebook p. 998]. . . .

Congress chose an alternative approach that was designed to eliminate any perception of religious sponsorship stemming from the location of the cross on federally owned land, while at the same time avoiding the disturbing symbolism associated with the destruction of the historic monument. The mechanism that Congress selected is one that is quite common in the West, a "land exchange." . . . Although Justice Stevens characterizes this land exchange as one that endorses "a particular religious view," it is noteworthy that Congress, in which our country's religious diversity is well represented, passed this law by overwhelming majorities: 95-0 in the Senate and 407-15 in the House. In my view, there is no legal ground for blocking the implementation of this law. . . .

There is also no merit in Justice Stevens' contention that implementation of the statute would constitute an endorsement of Christianity and would thus violate the Establishment Clause. Assuming that it is appropriate to apply the so-called "endorsement test," this test would not be violated by the land exchange. The endorsement test views a challenged display through the eyes of a hypothetical reasonable observer who is deemed to be aware of the history and all other pertinent facts relating to a challenged display. Here, therefore, this observer would be familiar with the origin and history of the monument and would also know both that the land on which the monument is located is privately owned and that the new owner is under no obligation to preserve the monument's present design. With this knowledge, a reasonable observer would not view the land exchange as the equivalent of the construction of an official World War I memorial on the National Mall. Rather, a well-informed observer would appreciate that the transfer represents an effort by Congress to address a unique situation and to find a solution that best accommodates conflicting concerns.

Finally, I reject Justice Stevens' suggestion that the enactment of the land-transfer law was motivated by an illicit purpose. . . . I would not jump to the conclusion that Congress' aim in enacting the land-transfer law was to embrace the religious message of the cross; rather, I see no reason to doubt that Congress' consistent goal, in legislating with regard to the Sunrise Rock monument, has been to commemorate our Nation's war dead and to avoid the disturbing symbolism that would have been created by the destruction of the monument.

7.　Justice Scalia, joined by Justice Thomas, concluded that Buono did not have Article III standing to seek the expansion of the 2002 injunction to invalidate the land-transfer statute because the Establishment Clause injury he alleged arose from the display of the cross on public property. Therefore, once the land was transferred and privately owned, he would not suffer an injury. The opinion concurring in the judgment did lament that "the litigants have lost considerable time and money" and that the Supreme Court was "forced to forgo an opportunity to clarify the law." Their two votes made for a 5-to-4 determination to reverse the Court of Appeals decision upholding the District Court's ruling that the land-transfer statute violated the 2002 injunction.

C. The Dissent

8.　Justice Stevens, joined by Justices Ginsburg and Sotomayor, dissented. The thrust of the dissent, to paraphrase Gertrude Stein, is that "a cross is a cross is a cross":

"The Establishment Clause, if nothing else, prohibits government from 'specifying details upon which men and women who believe in a benevolent, omnipotent Creator and Ruler of the world are known to differ.' " *Van Orden v. Perry* (2005) (Stevens, J., dissenting) [Casebook p. 998]. A Latin cross necessarily symbolizes one of the most important tenets upon which believers in a benevolent Creator, as well as nonbelievers, are known to differ. In my view, the District Court was right to enforce its prior judgment by enjoining Congress' proposed remedy — a remedy that was engineered to leave the cross intact and that did not alter its basic meaning. I certainly agree that the Nation should memorialize the service of those who fought and died in World War I, but it cannot lawfully do so by continued endorsement of a starkly sectarian message. . . .

A government practice violates the Establishment Clause if it "either has the purpose or effect of 'endorsing' religion." *County of Allegheny v. American Civil Liberties Union, Greater Pittsburgh Chapter* (1989) [Casebook p. 974]. "Whether the key word is 'endorsement,' 'favoritism,' or 'promotion,' the essential principle remains the same. The Establishment Clause, at the very least, prohibits government from appearing to take a position on questions of religious belief or from 'making adherence to a religion relevant in any way to a person's standing in the political community.' " *Id.*

The 2002 injunction was based on a finding that display of the cross had the effect of endorsing religion. . . . The determination that the Government had endorsed religion necessarily rested on two premises: first, that the Government endorsed the cross, and second, that the cross "takes a position on questions of religious belief" or " 'makes adherence to religion relevant . . . to a person's standing in the political community.' " *County of Allegheny.* . . .

In my view, the transfer ordered by [the land-transfer statute] would not end government endorsement of the cross for two independently sufficient reasons. First, after the transfer it would continue to appear to any reasonable observer that the Government has endorsed the cross, notwithstanding that the name has changed on the title to a small patch of underlying land. . . . Second, the transfer continues the existing government endorsement of the cross because the purpose of the transfer is to preserve its display. Congress' intent to preserve the display of the cross maintains the Government's endorsement of the cross. . . .

After the transfer, a well-informed observer would know that the cross was no longer on public land, but would additionally be aware of the following facts: the cross was once on public land, the Government was enjoined from permitting its display, Congress transferred it to a specific purchaser in order to preserve its display in the same location, and the Government maintained a reversionary interest in the land. From this chain of events, in addition to the factors that remain the same after the transfer, he would perceive government endorsement of the cross.

Particularly important to this analysis is that although the transfer might remove the implicit endorsement that presence on public land signifies, it would not change the fact that the Government has taken several explicit actions to endorse this cross. . . . [Before the litigation] and again after the District Court had entered its initial injunction, Congress passed legislation prohibiting the use of any federal funds to remove the cross from its location on federal property. . . . [Congress] passed legislation officially designating the "five-foot-tall white cross" in the Mojave Desert "as a national memorial commemorating United States participation in World War I and honoring the American veterans of that war." Thereafter, the cross was no longer just a local artifact; it acquired a formal national status of the highest order. Once that momentous step was taken, changing the identity of the owner of the underlying land could no longer change the public or private character of the cross. The Government has expressly adopted the cross as its own.

Even though Congress recognized this cross for its military associations, the solitary cross conveys an inescapably sectarian message. As the District Court observed, it is undisputed that the "Latin cross is the preeminent symbol of Christianity. It is exclusively a Christian symbol, and not a symbol of any other religion." We have recognized the significance of the Latin cross as a sectarian symbol, and no participant in this litigation denies that the cross bears that social meaning. Making a plain, unadorned Latin cross a war memorial does not make the cross secular. It makes the war memorial sectarian. . . .

. . . All we are debating at this juncture is whether the shift from public to private ownership of the land sufficiently distanced the Government from the cross; we are no longer debating the message the cross conveys to a reasonable observer. In arguing that Congress can legitimately favor the cross because of its purported double meaning, the plurality implicitly tries to reopen what is closed. [In a footnote, Justice Stevens added:] For the record, I cannot agree that a bare cross such as this conveys a nonsectarian meaning simply because crosses are often used to commemorate "heroic acts, noble contributions, and patient striving" and to honor fallen soldiers. The cross is not a universal symbol of sacrifice. It is the symbol of one particular sacrifice, and that sacrifice carries deeply significant meaning for those who adhere to the Christian faith. The cross has sometimes been used, it is true, to represent the sacrifice of an individual, as when it marks the grave of a fallen soldier or recognizes a state trooper who perished in the line of duty. Even then, the cross carries a religious meaning. But the use of the cross in such circumstances is linked to, and shows respect for, the individual honoree's faith and beliefs. I, too, would consider it tragic if the Nation's fallen veterans were to be forgotten. But there are countless different ways, consistent with the Constitution, that such an outcome may be averted. . . .

[Even] assuming (wrongly) that the cross would be purely private speech after the transfer, and even assuming (quite implausibly) that the transfer statute is neutral with respect to the cross, it would still be appropriate for the District Court to apply the reasonable observer standard. . . . [The] reasonable observer "who knows all of the pertinent facts and circumstances surrounding the symbol and its placement," would perceive that the Government has endorsed the cross. . . . Changing the ownership status of the underlying land in the manner required by [the land-transfer statute] would not change the fact that the cross conveys a message of government endorsement of religion. . . .

Even setting aside that the effect of the post-transfer cross would still be to convey a message of government endorsement of religion, the District Court was correct to conclude that [the land-transfer statute] would not cure the Establishment Clause violation because the very purpose of the transfer was to preserve the display of the cross. That evident purpose maintains government endorsement of the cross. . . .

I believe that most judges would find it to be a clear Establishment Clause violation if Congress had simply directed that a solitary Latin cross be erected on the Mall in the Nation's Capital to serve as a World War I Memorial. Congress did not erect this cross, but it commanded that the cross remain in place, and it gave the cross the imprimatur of Government. Transferring the land . . . would perpetuate rather than cure that unambiguous endorsement of a sectarian message. . . .

9.   Justice Breyer dissented for procedural reasons only. He approved the District Court's ruling, based on the law of injunctions, without reaching the merits of the constitutional questions. He would have dismissed the writ of *certiorari* as having been improvidently granted.

10.   Thus, this case had a somewhat curious lineup and outcome. Only the three Justices in the plurality favored the remand to the District Court for reconsideration of the land-transfer statute under the Establishment Clause. The remaining six Justices — Justices Stevens, Scalia, Thomas, Ginsburg, Breyer, and Sotomayor — deemed that to be unnecessary or inappropriate, albeit for different and opposing sets of reasons.

D. Some Possible Implications

11.   In something of a postscript, Chief Justice Roberts added a separate one-paragraph concurring opinion to say Congress should be allowed to require the land transfer if the interpretation of the 2002 injunction that Respondent Buono's attorney asserted at oral argument was sound, namely that the Government could take down the cross, sell the land to the VFW, and turn over the cross to allow the VFW to put it back up. In his dissent, Justice Stevens took issue with that conclusion. Would that hypothetical sequence be constitutional under the Establishment Clause?

12.   In his concurring opinion, Justice Alito speculated, "One possible solution would have been to supplement the monument on Sunrise Rock so that it appropriately recognized the religious diversity of the American soldiers who gave their lives in the First World War. In American military cemeteries overseas, the graves of soldiers who perished in that war were marked with either a white cross or a white Star of David . . . and Congress might have chosen to place a Star of David on Sunrise Rock so that the monument would duplicate those two types of headstones." Would that "solution" violate the Establishment Clause?

13.   A few days after the Supreme Court announced its decision, some unknown person or persons surreptitiously took down the cross before the District Court could reconsider the case on remand. Then, a few days after that happened, some unknown person or persons surreptitiously put up a replacement cross. But the National Park Service officials inspected the replacement cross and concluded that it was not the cross erected by Henry Sandoz in 1998, which had been the subject of the 2002 injunction, so they removed it. Under the Establishment Clause, could the National Park Service officials have replaced the stolen cross with their own replacement cross that was an accurate facsimile? Could they have kept in place the replacement cross?

14.　In an understated aside, Justice Kennedy observed in his plurality opinion: "To date, this Court's jurisprudence in this area has refrained from making sweeping pronouncements, and this case is ill suited for announcing categorical rules." For the benefit of the District Court on remand, however, the plurality opinion unmistakably invoked the imagery of World War I graveyards — depicted famously and most poignantly in John McCrae's 1915 poem, *In Flanders Fields* — to imply that a cross is not always a cross:

> In Flanders fields the poppies blow
> Between the crosses, row on row,
> That mark our place; and in the sky
> The larks, still bravely singing, fly
> Scarce heard amid the guns below.
>
> We are the Dead. Short days ago
> We lived, felt dawn, saw sunset glow,
> Loved, and were loved, and now we lie
> In Flanders fields.
>
> Take up our quarrel with the foe:
>
> To you from failing hands we throw
> The torch; be yours to hold it high.
>
> If ye break faith with us who die
> We shall not sleep, though poppies grow
> In Flanders fields.

As we have seen, Justice Stevens resisted this equivalency of meaning. So, when is a cross a cross and when is it something else? How does a religious symbol become a symbol for something else? What does the cross at Sunrise Rock symbolize for purposes of Establishment Clause analysis? What kinds of religious symbols and images may be incorporated into the design of a Government war memorial to fallen soldiers erected on public property?

15.　If you were the District Judge, on remand, does the land-transfer statute cure the Establishment Clause violation? Why or why not?

Chapter 17

THE FREE EXERCISE CLAUSE

C. DISCRIMINATION AGAINST RELIGION

Page 1065: *insert new Problem after the Problem:*

PROBLEM: DORM LIFE VERSUS A CHRISTIAN LIFE

The State University ("SU") requires full-time freshman students to live on campus. This parietal policy ostensibly is designed to foster diversity, promote tolerance, increase academic achievement, and improve the graduation rate. It also ensures full occupancy of residence halls. Simon Peters has filed suit in the U.S. district court seeking an injunction against enforcement of the policy on the ground that it violates his right to free exercise of religion. SU's parietal policy provides:

> The State University requires all full-time freshman students to live on campus their entire freshman year. Established exceptions to the policy are only: (a) the student will be living with his/her parents, (b) the student is twenty years old or older as of the first day of classes, or (c) the student is married. All freshman students not living on campus are required to submit a petition for exception to this policy.

If a freshman student meets one of the foregoing criteria, he or she is not required to live on campus. Further exceptions are granted on an *ad hoc* basis at the discretion of SU administrators. If a freshman student fails to sign a valid housing contract without obtaining an exception to the policy, SU may suspend the student's course registration and all other University services. Approximately 2,500 full-time freshmen attend SU; 1,600 reside on campus and the remaining 900 live off campus.

Simon Peters is an eighteen-year-old incoming freshman student. He was raised by his parents in a distinctly religious environment and is a member of the non-denominational Christian Church of Eden County. Peters and his family believe that the Bible is the word of God which instructs them to live every aspect of their daily lives in a way that brings glory to God. Peters' religious beliefs require him to abstain from smoking, premarital sex, the consumption of alcohol or drugs, and the use of profanity. Peters chose SU over other universities because it offered him a rowing scholarship and he was interested in its fisheries management program.

Peters petitioned SU for an exception to the policy on the ground that his religious convictions exhort him to live in an environment that encourages "moral excellence during college and for the rest of my life." Peters detailed the misbehavior he believes occurs in SU residence halls: "I have heard from many of my classmates and friends of the wild lifestyles allowed in the dormitories at SU. . . . The obnoxious alcohol parties in the dormitories, the immoral atmosphere, and the intolerance towards those who profess to be Christians would severely hinder my free exercise of religion and be a definite hardship for me." He compared his request to the example of Jesus Christ who, he explained, associated with "sinners" but lived among his apostles and disciples. His petition concluded: "I respectfully request that I be allowed to live in alternate housing at the Christian Student Fellowship ("CSF"), which is an organization my church and my family have supported for many years."

According to its organizational charter, CSF is a non-denominational Christian ministry with the stated mission to "foster the Lordship of Jesus Christ on the SU campus." CSF operates a three-story residential facility across the street from the campus for students who wish to share "a lifestyle which glorifies Christ." The facility offers residents regular fellowship activities, weekly Bible studies, counseling, prayer support, and leadership and evangelism training. A full-time minister lives in residence and coordinates the religious activities. Although a student does not have to be a member of a particular denomination to reside at CSF, the twenty-five students who live in the facility are all Christians who profess beliefs similar to those of Peters. Students reside on the top two floors of the building and are segregated according to sex. A kitchen, meeting room, Christian library, and administrative offices are located on the first floor. All residents agree to keep the doors of their rooms open while entertaining guests of the opposite sex and also agree to abstain from the use of alcohol, drugs, tobacco, and profanity. A violation of the facility's rules will result in expulsion; however, that has never been actually necessary.

Simon Peters' request for an exemption from the parietal policy was rejected by SU housing administrators. He thereafter brought suit asking for injunctive relief and a declaration that the policy is unconstitutional on its face and as applied to him. How should the district court rule and why?

Chapter 18

INTERRELATIONSHIPS AMONG THE CLAUSES

C. RELIGIOUS SPEECH

Page 1137: *add new case before the Problem:*

CHRISTIAN LEGAL SOCIETY v. MARTINEZ
130 S. Ct. 2971 (2010)

JUSTICE GINSBURG delivered the opinion of the Court.

. . . This case concerns a novel question regarding student activities at public universities: May a public law school condition its official recognition of a student group — and the attendant use of school funds and facilities — on the organization's agreement to open eligibility for membership and leadership to all students? . . .

I

Like many institutions of higher education, Hastings College of the Law (Hastings or Law School) encourages students to form extracurricular associations that "contribute to the Hastings community and experience." . . . Through its "Registered Student Organization" (RSO) program, Hastings extends official recognition to student groups. Several benefits attend this school-approved status. RSOs are eligible to seek financial assistance from the Law School, which subsidizes their events using funds from a mandatory student-activity fee imposed on all students. RSOs may also use Law-School channels to communicate with students: They may place announcements in a weekly Office-of-Student-Services newsletter, advertise events on designated bulletin boards, send e-mails using a Hastings-organization address, and participate in an annual Student Organizations Fair designed to advance recruitment efforts. In addition, RSOs may apply for permission to use the Law School's facilities for meetings and office space. Finally, Hastings allows officially recognized groups to use its name and logo.

. . . [All] RSOs must undertake to comply with Hastings' "Policies and Regulations Applying to College Activities, Organizations and Students." The Law School's Policy on Nondiscrimination (Nondiscrimination Policy), which binds RSOs, states:

> Hastings is committed to a policy against legally impermissible, arbitrary or unreasonable discriminatory practices. All groups, including administration, faculty, student governments, Hastings-owned student residence facilities and programs sponsored by Hastings, are governed by this policy of nondiscrimination. Hastings's policy on nondiscrimination is to comply fully with applicable law.

Hastings shall not discriminate unlawfully on the basis of race, color, religion, national origin, ancestry, disability, age, sex or sexual orientation. This nondiscrimination policy covers admission, access and treatment in Hastings-sponsored programs and activities.

Hastings interprets the Nondiscrimination Policy, as it relates to the RSO program, to mandate acceptance of all comers: School-approved groups must "allow any student to participate, become a member, or seek leadership positions in the organization, regardless of [her] status or beliefs."[2] . . .

. . . [The] leaders of a predecessor Christian organization — which had been an RSO at Hastings for a decade — formed the Christian Legal Society (CLS) by affiliating with the national Christian Legal Society (CLS-National). CLS-National, an association of Christian lawyers and law students, charters student chapters at law schools throughout the country. CLS chapters must adopt bylaws that, *inter alia*, require members and officers to sign a "Statement of Faith" and to conduct their lives in accord with prescribed principles.[3] Among those tenets is the belief that sexual activity should not occur outside of marriage between a man and a woman; CLS thus interprets its bylaws to exclude from affiliation anyone who engages in "unrepentant homosexual conduct." CLS also excludes students who hold religious convictions different from those in the Statement of Faith.

[CLS] submitted to Hastings an application for RSO status, accompanied by all required documents, including the set of bylaws mandated by CLS-National. Several days later, the Law School rejected the application; CLS's bylaws, Hastings explained, did not comply with the Nondiscrimination Policy because CLS barred students based on religion and sexual orientation.

CLS formally requested an exemption from the Nondiscrimination Policy, but Hastings declined to grant one. . . . If CLS instead chose to operate outside the RSO program, Hastings stated, the school "would be pleased to provide CLS the use of Hastings facilities for its meetings and activities." . . . In other words, Hastings would do nothing to suppress CLS's endeavors, but neither would it lend

---

[2] "This policy," Hastings clarifies, "does not foreclose neutral and generally applicable membership requirements unrelated to 'status or beliefs.' " Brief for Hastings. So long as all students have the *opportunity* to participate on equal terms, RSOs may require them, *inter alia*, to pay dues, maintain good attendance, refrain from gross misconduct, or pass a skill-based test, such as the writing competitions administered by law journals. The dissent trumpets these neutral, generally applicable membership requirements, arguing that, in truth, Hastings has a "some-comers," not an all-comers, policy. Hastings' open-access policy, however, requires only that student organizations open eligibility for membership and leadership regardless of a student's status or beliefs; dues, attendance, skill measurements, and comparable uniformly applied standards are fully compatible with the policy. . . .

[3] The Statement of Faith provides:

Trusting in Jesus Christ as my Savior, I believe in:
- One God, eternally existent in three persons, Father, Son and Holy Spirit.
- God the Father Almighty, Maker of heaven and earth.
- The Deity of our Lord, Jesus Christ, God's only Son conceived of the Holy Spirit, born of the virgin Mary; His vicarious death for our sins through which we receive eternal life; His bodily resurrection and personal return.
- The presence and power of the Holy Spirit in the work of regeneration.
- The Bible as the inspired Word of God.

RSO-level support for them. Refusing to alter its bylaws, CLS . . . operate[d] independently during the 2004-2005 academic year. . . .

[CLS] filed suit . . . [alleging] that Hastings' refusal to grant the organization RSO status violated CLS's First and Fourteenth Amendment rights to free speech, expressive association, and free exercise of religion. . . . On cross-motions for summary judgment, the [District Court] ruled in favor of Hastings. . . . On appeal, the Ninth Circuit affirmed in an opinion that stated, in full [citations omitted]:

> The parties stipulate that Hastings imposes an open membership rule on all student groups — all groups must accept all comers as voting members even if those individuals disagree with the mission of the group. The conditions on recognition are therefore viewpoint neutral and reasonable.

We granted certiorari, and now affirm the Ninth Circuit's judgment.

II

. . . [CLS] urges us to review the Nondiscrimination Policy as written — prohibiting discrimination on several enumerated bases, including religion and sexual orientation — and not as a requirement that all RSOs accept all comers. The written terms of the Nondiscrimination Policy, CLS contends, "target solely those groups whose beliefs are based on religion or that disapprove of a particular kind of sexual behavior," and leave other associations free to limit membership and leadership to individuals committed to the group's ideology. . . . For example, "[a] political . . . group can insist that its leaders support its purposes and beliefs," CLS alleges, but "a religious group cannot."

CLS's assertion runs headlong into the stipulation of facts it jointly submitted with Hastings at the summary-judgment stage. In that filing, the parties specified:

> Hastings requires that registered student organizations allow *any* student to participate, become a member, or seek leadership positions in the organization, regardless of [her] status or beliefs. Thus, for example, the Hastings Democratic Caucus cannot bar students holding Republican political beliefs from becoming members or seeking leadership positions in the organization. Joint Stipulation ¶ 18.

Under the District Court's local rules, stipulated facts are deemed "undisputed."[6] . . . In light of the joint stipulation, both the District Court and the Ninth Circuit trained their attention on the constitutionality of the all-comers requirement, as described in the parties' accord. . . . This opinion, therefore, considers only whether conditioning access to a student-organization forum on compliance with an all-comers policy violates the Constitution.[10]

---

[6] The dissent spills considerable ink attempting to create uncertainty about when the all-comers policy was adopted. What counts, however, is the parties' unqualified agreement that the all-comers policy *currently* governs. CLS's suit, after all, seeks only declaratory and injunctive — that is, prospective — relief.

[10] The dissent, in contrast, devotes considerable attention to CLS's arguments about the Nondis-

III

A

In support of the argument that Hastings' all-comers policy treads on its First Amendment rights to free speech and expressive association, CLS draws on two lines of decisions. First, in a progression of cases, this Court has employed forum analysis to determine when a governmental entity, in regulating property in its charge, may place limitations on speech.[12] . . . Second, as evidenced by another set of decisions, this Court has rigorously reviewed laws and regulations that constrain associational freedom. . . .

CLS would have us engage each line of cases independently, but its expressive-association and free-speech arguments merge: *Who* speaks on its behalf, CLS reasons, colors *what* concept is conveyed. It therefore makes little sense to treat CLS's speech and association claims as discrete. Instead, three observations lead us to conclude that our limited-public-forum precedents supply the appropriate framework for assessing both CLS's speech and association rights.

First, the same considerations that have led us to apply a less restrictive level of scrutiny to speech in limited public forums as compared to other environments, apply with equal force to expressive association occurring in limited public forums. . . .

Second, and closely related, the strict scrutiny we have applied in some settings to laws that burden expressive association would, in practical effect, invalidate a defining characteristic of limited public forums — the State may "reserv[e] [them] for certain groups." *Rosenberger.* The same ground rules must govern both speech and association challenges in the limited-public-forum context, lest strict scrutiny trump a public university's ability to "confin[e] a [speech] forum to the limited and legitimate purposes for which it was created." *Id.*

Third, this case fits comfortably within the limited-public-forum category, for CLS, in seeking what is effectively a state subsidy, faces only indirect pressure to modify its membership policies; CLS may exclude any person for any reason if it forgoes the benefits of official recognition. The expressive-association precedents on which CLS relies, in contrast, involved regulations that *compelled* a group to include unwanted members, with no choice to opt out. . . . Application of the less-restrictive limited-public-forum analysis better accounts for the fact that Hastings, through its RSO program, is dangling the carrot of subsidy, not wielding the stick of prohibition.

. . . We turn to the merits of the instant dispute, therefore, with the limited-public-forum decisions as our guide.

---

crimination Policy as written. We decline to address these arguments, not because we agree with the dissent that the Nondiscrimination Policy is "plainly" unconstitutional, but because that constitutional question is not properly presented.

[12] Our decisions make clear, and the parties agree, that Hastings, through its RSO program, established a limited public forum. *See Rosenberger v. Rector and Visitors of Univ. of Va.* (1995) [Casebook p. 1112].

B

Most recently and comprehensively, in *Rosenberger*, we reiterated that a university generally may not withhold benefits from student groups because of their religious outlook. . . . The constitutional constraints on the boundaries the State may set bear repetition here: "The State may not exclude speech where its distinction is not reasonable in light of the purpose served by the forum, . . . nor may it discriminate against speech on the basis of . . . viewpoint."

C

We first consider whether Hastings' policy is reasonable taking into account the RSO forum's function and "all the surrounding circumstances."

1

. . . This Court is the final arbiter of the question whether a public university has exceeded constitutional constraints, and we owe no deference to universities when we consider that question. . . . [However,] we have cautioned courts in various contexts to resist "substitut[ing] their own notions of sound educational policy for those of the school authorities which they review." A college's commission — and its concomitant license to choose among pedagogical approaches — is not confined to the classroom, for extracurricular programs are, today, essential parts of the educational process. . . .

2

[We] review the justifications Hastings offers in defense of its all-comers requirement. First, the open-access policy "ensures that the leadership, educational, and social opportunities afforded by [RSOs] are available to all students." . . . RSOs, we count it significant, are eligible for financial assistance drawn from mandatory student-activity fees, the all-comers policy ensures that no Hastings student is forced to fund a group that would reject her as a member.[18]

Second, the all-comers requirement helps Hastings police the written terms of its Nondiscrimination Policy without inquiring into an RSO's motivation for membership restrictions . . . [CLS] proposes that Hastings permit exclusion because of *belief* but forbid discrimination due to *status*. But that proposal would impose on Hastings a daunting labor. . . . This case itself is instructive in this regard. CLS contends that it does not exclude individuals because of sexual orientation, but rather "on the basis of a conjunction of conduct and the belief that the conduct is not wrong." Our decisions have declined to distinguish between status and conduct in this context. *See Lawrence v. Texas*, 539 U.S. 558, 575 (2003) ("When homosexual *conduct* is made criminal by the law of the State, that

---

[18] CLS notes that its "activities — its Bible studies, speakers, and dinners — are open to all students," even if attendees are barred from membership and leadership. Welcoming all comers as guests or auditors, however, is hardly equivalent to accepting all comers as full-fledged participants.

declaration in and of itself is an invitation to subject homosexual *persons* to discrimination." (emphasis added)).

Third, the Law School reasonably adheres to the view that an all-comers policy, to the extent it brings together individuals with diverse backgrounds and beliefs, "encourages tolerance, cooperation, and learning among students." . . .

Fourth, Hastings' policy, which incorporates — in fact, subsumes — state-law proscriptions on discrimination, conveys the Law School's decision "to decline to subsidize with public monies and benefits conduct of which the people of California disapprove." . . .

In sum, the several justifications Hastings asserts in support of its all-comers requirement are surely reasonable in light of the RSO forum's purposes.

3

. . . [When] access barriers are viewpoint neutral, our decisions have counted it significant that other available avenues for the group to exercise its First Amendment rights lessen the burden created by those barriers. In this case, Hastings offered CLS access to school facilities to conduct meetings and the use of chalkboards and generally available bulletin boards to advertise events. Although CLS could not take advantage of RSO-specific methods of communication, the advent of electronic media and social-networking sites reduces the importance of those channels (CLS maintained a Yahoo! message group to disseminate information to students). Private groups, from fraternities and sororities to social clubs and secret societies, commonly maintain a presence at universities without official school affiliation. Based on the record before us, CLS was similarly situated: It hosted a variety of activities the year after Hastings denied it recognition, and the number of students attending those meetings and events doubled. . . . It is beyond dissenter's license, constantly to maintain that non-recognition of a student organization is equivalent to prohibiting its members from speaking.

4

. . . "There can be no diversity of viewpoints in a forum," [CLS and the dissent both] assert, "if groups are not permitted to form around viewpoints." This catchphrase confuses CLS's preferred policy with constitutional limitation — the *advisability* of Hastings' policy does not control its *permissibility*.[22]

CLS also assails the reasonableness of the all-comers policy in light of the RSO forum's function by forecasting that the policy will facilitate hostile takeovers; if organizations must open their arms to all, CLS contends, saboteurs will infiltrate groups to subvert their mission and message. This supposition strikes us as more

---

[22] CLS's concern, shared by the dissent, that an all-comers policy will squelch diversity has not been borne out by Hastings' experience. In the 2004-2005 academic year, approximately 60 student organizations, representing a variety of interests, registered . . . . Three of these 60 registered groups had a religious orientation: Hastings Association of Muslim Law Students, Hastings Jewish Law Students Association, and Hastings Koinonia.

hypothetical than real. CLS points to no history or prospect of RSO-hijackings at Hastings. . . .

RSOs, moreover, in harmony with the all-comers policy, may condition eligibility for membership and leadership on attendance, the payment of dues, or other neutral requirements designed to ensure that students join because of their commitment to a group's vitality, not its demise. . . .

Hastings, furthermore, could reasonably expect more from its law students than the disruptive behavior CLS hypothesizes — and to build this expectation into its educational approach. A reasonable policy need not anticipate and preemptively close off every opportunity for avoidance or manipulation. If students begin to exploit an all-comers policy by hijacking organizations to distort or destroy their missions, Hastings presumably would revisit and revise its policy.

Finally, CLS asserts (and the dissent repeats) that the Law School lacks any legitimate interest — let alone one reasonably related to the RSO forum's purposes — in urging "religious groups not to favor co-religionists for purposes of their religious activities." CLS's analytical error lies in focusing on the benefits it must forgo while ignoring the interests of those it seeks to fence out: Exclusion, after all, has two sides. Hastings, caught in the crossfire between a group's desire to exclude and students' demand for equal access, may reasonably draw a line in the sand permitting *all* organizations to express what they wish but *no* group to discriminate in membership.

D

We next consider whether Hastings' all-comers policy is viewpoint neutral.

1

Although this aspect of limited-public-forum analysis has been the constitutional sticking point in our prior decisions, we need not dwell on it here. It is, after all, hard to imagine a more viewpoint-neutral policy than one requiring *all* student groups to accept *all* comers. In contrast to *Rosenberger*, in which [the university] singled out [an] organization for disfavored treatment because of [its] point of view, Hastings' all-comers requirement draws no distinction between groups based on their message or perspective. An all-comers condition on access to RSO status, in short, is textbook viewpoint neutral.

2

Conceding that Hastings' all-comers policy is "nominally neutral," CLS attacks the regulation by pointing to its effect: The policy is vulnerable to constitutional assault, CLS contends, because "it systematically and predictably burdens most heavily those groups whose viewpoints are out of favor with the campus mainstream." Brief of Petitioner; *cf. post*, (Alito, J., dissenting) (charging that Hastings' policy favors "political[ly] correc[t]" student expression). This argument stumbles from its first step because "[a] regulation that serves purposes unrelated to the content of expression is deemed neutral, even if it has an incidental effect on some speakers or messages but not others." . . .

Hastings' requirement that student groups accept all comers, we are satisfied, "is justified without reference to the content [or viewpoint] of the regulated speech." *Ward v. Rock Against Racism* (1989) [Casebook p. 395]. The Law School's policy aims at the *act* of rejecting would-be group members without reference to the reasons motivating that behavior: Hastings' "desire to redress the perceived harms" of exclusionary membership policies "provides an adequate explanation for its [all-comers condition] over and above mere disagreement with [any student group's] beliefs or biases." *Wisconsin v. Mitchell* (1993) [Casebook p. 646]. CLS's conduct — not its Christian perspective — is, from Hastings' vantage point, what stands between the group and RSO status. "In the end," as Hastings observes [in its Brief], "CLS is simply confusing its *own* viewpoint-based objections to . . . nondiscrimination laws (which it is entitled to have and [to] voice) with viewpoint *discrimination*."

Finding Hastings' open-access condition on RSO status reasonable and viewpoint neutral, we reject CLS' free-speech and expressive-association claims.[27]

IV

In its reply brief, CLS contends that "[t]he peculiarity, incoherence, and suspect history of the all-comers policy all point to pretext." Neither the District Court nor the Ninth Circuit addressed an argument that Hastings selectively enforces its all-comers policy, and this Court is not the proper forum to air the issue in the first instance. On remand, the Ninth Circuit may consider CLS's pretext argument if, and to the extent, it is preserved.

For the foregoing reasons, we affirm the Court of Appeals' ruling that the all-comers policy is constitutional and remand the case for further proceedings consistent with this opinion.

It is so ordered.

JUSTICE STEVENS, concurring.

. . . Because the dissent has volunteered an argument that the school's general Nondiscrimination Policy would be "plainly" unconstitutional if applied to this case, a brief response is appropriate. . . .

The Hastings College of Law's (Hastings) Nondiscrimination Policy contains boilerplate language used by institutions and workplaces across the country: It prohibits "unlawfu[l]" discrimination "on the basis of race, color, religion, national origin, ancestry, disability, age, sex or sexual orientation." . . . CLS, in short,

---

[27] CLS briefly argues that Hastings' all-comers condition violates the Free Exercise Clause. Our decision in *Employment Division v. Smith* (1990) [Casebook p. 1039], forecloses that argument. In *Smith*, the Court held that the Free Exercise Clause does not inhibit enforcement of otherwise valid regulations of general application that incidentally burden religious conduct. In seeking an exemption from Hastings' across-the-board all-comers policy, CLS, we repeat, seeks preferential, not equal, treatment; it therefore cannot moor its request for accommodation to the Free Exercise Clause.

wanted to receive the school's formal recognition — and the benefits that attend formal recognition — while continuing to exclude gay and non-Christian students (as well as, it seems, students who advocate for gay rights). . . .

As written, the Nondiscrimination Policy is content and viewpoint neutral. It does not reflect a judgment by school officials about the substance of any student group's speech. Nor does it exclude any would-be groups on the basis of their convictions. Indeed, it does not regulate expression or belief at all. . . . Those who hold religious beliefs are not "singled out" [as the dissent claims]; those who engage in discriminatory *conduct* based on someone else's religious status and belief are singled out.[1] Regardless of whether they are the product of secular or spiritual feeling, hateful or benign motives, all acts of religious discrimination are equally covered. The discriminator's beliefs are simply irrelevant. . . . The policy's religion clause was plainly meant to promote, not to undermine, religious freedom.

To be sure, the policy may end up having greater consequence for religious groups — whether and to what extent it will is far from clear *ex ante* — inasmuch as they are more likely than their secular counterparts to wish to exclude students of particular faiths. But there is likewise no evidence that the policy was intended to cause harm to religious groups, or that it has in practice caused significant harm to their operations. . . . The dissent has thus given no reason to be skeptical of the basic design, function, or rationale of the Nondiscrimination Policy. . . .

It is critical, in evaluating CLS's challenge to the Nondiscrimination Policy, to keep in mind that an RSO program is a *limited* forum — the boundaries of which may be *delimited* by the proprietor. When a religious association, or a secular association, operates in a wholly public setting, it must be allowed broad freedom to control its membership and its message, even if its decisions cause offense to outsiders. Profound constitutional problems would arise if the State of California tried to "demand that all Christian groups admit members who believe that Jesus was merely human." *Post* (Alito, J., dissenting). But the CLS chapter that brought this lawsuit does not want to be just a Christian group; it aspires to be a recognized student organization. . . .

The campus is, in fact, a world apart from the public square in numerous respects, and religious organizations, as well as all other organizations, must abide by certain norms of conduct when they enter an academic community. . . . These are not legal questions but policy questions; they are not for the Court but for the university to make. . . .

In this case, petitioner excludes students who will not sign its Statement of Faith or who engage in "unrepentant homosexual conduct." The expressive

---

[1] The dissent appears to accept that Hastings may prohibit discrimination on the basis of religious *status*, though it rejects the notion that Hastings may do the same for religious *belief*. If CLS sought to exclude a Muslim student in virtue of the fact that he "is" Muslim, the dissent suggests, there would be no problem in Hastings forbidding that. But if CLS sought to exclude the same student in virtue of the fact that he subscribes to the Muslim faith, Hastings must stand idly by. This proposition is not only unworkable in practice but also flawed in conception. A person's religion often simultaneously constitutes or informs a status, an identity, a set of beliefs and practices, and much else besides. (So does sexual orientation for that matter, notwithstanding the dissent's view that a rule excluding those who engage in "unrepentant homosexual conduct," does not discriminate on the basis of status or identity.)

association argument it presses, however, is hardly limited to these facts. Other groups may exclude or mistreat Jews, blacks, and women — or those who do not share their contempt for Jews, blacks, and women. A free society must tolerate such groups. It need not subsidize them, give them its official imprimatur, or grant them equal access to law school facilities.

JUSTICE KENNEDY, concurring.

. . . *Rosenberger* is distinguishable from the instant case in various respects. Not least is that here the school policy in question is not content based either in its formulation or evident purpose; and were it shown to be otherwise, the case likely should have a different outcome. Here, the policy applies equally to all groups and views. And, given the stipulation of the parties, there is no basis for an allegation that the design or purpose of the rule was, by subterfuge, to discriminate based on viewpoint.

An objection might be that the all-comers policy, even if not so designed or intended, in fact makes it difficult for certain groups to express their views in a manner essential to their message. A group that can limit membership to those who agree in full with its aims and purposes may be more effective in delivering its message or furthering its expressive objectives; and the Court has recognized that this interest can be protected against governmental interference or regulation. . . . In the instant case, however, if the membership qualification were enforced, it would contradict a legitimate purpose for having created the limited forum in the first place. Many educational institutions, including respondent Hastings College of Law, have recognized that the process of learning occurs both formally in a classroom setting and informally outside of it. Students may be shaped as profoundly by their peers as by their teachers. . . .

Law students come from many backgrounds and have but three years to meet each other and develop their skills. They do so by participating in a community that teaches them how to create arguments in a convincing, rational, and respectful manner and to express doubt and disagreement in a professional way. A law school furthers these objectives by allowing broad diversity in registered student organizations. But these objectives may be better achieved if students can act cooperatively to learn from and teach each other through interactions in social and intellectual contexts. A vibrant dialogue is not possible if students wall themselves off from opposing points of view.

The school's objectives thus might not be well served if, as a condition to membership or participation in a group, students were required to avow particular personal beliefs or to disclose private, off-campus behavior. Students whose views are in the minority at the school would likely fare worse in that regime. . . . A school quite properly may conclude that allowing an oath or belief-affirming requirement, or an outside conduct requirement, could be divisive for student relations and inconsistent with the basic concept that a view's validity should be tested through free and open discussion. The school's policy therefore represents a permissible effort to preserve the value of its forum.

. . . [CLS] would have a substantial case on the merits if it were shown that the all-comers policy was either designed or used to infiltrate the group or challenge its leadership in order to stifle its views. But that has not been shown to be so likely or self-evident as a matter of group dynamics in this setting that the Court can declare the school policy void without more facts; and if there were a showing that in a particular case the purpose or effect of the policy was to stifle speech or make it ineffective, that, too, would present a case different from the one before us. . . .

JUSTICE ALITO, with whom THE CHIEF JUSTICE, JUSTICE SCALIA, and JUSTICE THOMAS join, dissenting.

The proudest boast of our free speech jurisprudence is that we protect the freedom to express "the thought that we hate." *United States v. Schwimmer* (1929) (Holmes, J., dissenting) [Casebook p. 65]. Today's decision rests on a very different principle: no freedom for expression that offends prevailing standards of political correctness in our country's institutions of higher learning. The Hastings College of the Law . . . [currently] has more than 60 registered groups and, in all its history, has denied registration to exactly one: the Christian Legal Society (CLS). . . . The Court's treatment of this case is deeply disappointing. . . .

I

The Court provides a misleading portrayal of this case. . . . I begin by correcting the picture.

A

The Court bases all of its analysis on the proposition that the relevant Hastings' policy is the so-called accept-all-comers policy. This frees the Court from the difficult task of defending the constitutionality of either the policy that Hastings actually — and repeatedly — invoked when it denied registration, i.e., the school's written Nondiscrimination Policy, or the policy that Hastings belatedly unveiled when it filed its brief in this Court. Overwhelming evidence, however, shows that Hastings denied CLS's application pursuant to the Nondiscrimination Policy and that the accept-all-comers policy was nowhere to be found until it was mentioned by a former dean in a deposition taken well after this case began. [Here the dissent cited and quoted from the trial court stipulation, the pleadings, the lower court briefs and opinions, the record on appeal, the Supreme Court briefs, and applicable procedural precedents to argue its claim that the Nondiscrimination Policy — instead of the all-comers policy — should be the subject of review in this case.] . . .

B

The Court also distorts the record with respect to the effect on CLS of Hastings' decision to deny registration. [Here the dissent detailed several examples of the practical ways that, according to CLS, it was disadvantaged and harmed by the Law School's decision to deny it RSO status.] . . . And since one of CLS's principal claims is that it was subjected to discrimination based on its viewpoint, the majority's emphasis on CLS's ability to endure that discrimination — by using private facilities and means of communication — is quite amazing.

This Court does not customarily brush aside a claim of unlawful discrimination with the observation that the effects of the discrimination were really not so bad. We have never before taken the view that a little viewpoint discrimination is acceptable. . . .

C

Finally, I must comment on the majority's emphasis on funding. According to the majority, CLS is "seeking what is effectively a state subsidy." . . . In fact, funding plays a very small role in this case. Most of what CLS sought and was denied — such as permission to set up a table on the law school patio — would have been virtually cost free. If every such activity is regarded as a matter of funding, the First Amendment rights of students at public universities will be at the mercy of the administration. . . .

III

The Court . . . focuses solely on the question whether Hastings' registration policy represents a permissible regulation in a limited public forum. . . . [I] am content to address the constitutionality of Hastings' actions under our limited public forum cases . . . .

In this case, the forum consists of the RSO program. Once a public university opens a limited public forum, it "must respect the lawful boundaries it has itself set." *Rosenberger v. Rector and Visitors of Univ. of Va.* (1995) [Casebook p. 1112]. The university "may not exclude speech where its distinction is not 'reasonable in light of the purpose served by the forum.' " And the university must maintain strict viewpoint neutrality. *Id.*

This requirement of viewpoint neutrality extends to the expression of religious viewpoints. In an unbroken line of decisions analyzing private religious speech in limited public forums, we have made it perfectly clear that "[r]eligion is [a] viewpoint from which ideas are conveyed." *Good News Club v. Milford Central School* (2001) [Casebook p. 1128]. We have applied this analysis in cases in which student speech was restricted because of the speaker's religious viewpoint, and we have consistently concluded that such restrictions constitute viewpoint discrimination. We have also stressed that the rules applicable in a limited public forum are particularly important in the university setting, where "the State acts against a background of tradition of thought and experiment that is at the center of our intellectual and philosophic tradition." *Rosenberger.*

IV

Analyzed under this framework, Hastings' refusal to register CLS pursuant to its Nondiscrimination Policy plainly fails. . . . [When] Hastings refused to register CLS, it claimed that the CLS bylaws impermissibly discriminated on the basis of religion and sexual orientation. As interpreted by Hastings and applied to CLS, both of these grounds constituted viewpoint discrimination.

Religion. . . . [The Hastings Nondiscrimination Policy] singled out one category of expressive associations for disfavored treatment: groups formed to express a religious message. Only religious groups were required to admit students who did not share their views. An environmentalist group was not required to admit students who rejected global warming. An animal rights group was not obligated to accept students who supported the use of animals to test cosmetics. But CLS was required to admit avowed atheists. This was patent viewpoint discrimination. . . . It is no wonder that the Court makes no attempt to defend the constitutionality of the Nondiscrimination Policy. . . .

Justice Stevens [in his concurring opinion] argues that the Nondiscrimination Policy is viewpoint neutral because it "does not regulate expression or belief at all" but instead regulates conduct. This Court has held, however, that the particular conduct at issue here constitutes a form of expression that is protected by the First Amendment. It is now well established that the First Amendment shields the right of a group to engage in expressive association by limiting membership to persons whose admission does not significantly interfere with the group's ability to convey its views. . . .

Justice Stevens also maintains that the Nondiscrimination Policy is viewpoint neutral because it prohibits all groups, both religious and secular, from engaging in religious speech. This argument is also contrary to established law. In *Rosenberger*, the dissent, which Justice Stevens joined, made exactly this argument. The Court disagreed, holding that a policy that treated secular speech more favorably than religious speech discriminated on the basis of viewpoint. The Court reaffirmed this holding in *Good News Club*.

Here, the Nondiscrimination Policy permitted membership requirements that expressed a secular viewpoint. (For example, the Hastings Democratic Caucus and the Hastings Republicans were allowed to exclude members who disagreed with their parties' platforms.) But religious groups were not permitted to express a religious viewpoint by limiting membership to students who shared their religious viewpoints. Under established precedent, this was viewpoint discrimination.

It bears emphasis that permitting religious groups to limit membership to those who share the groups' beliefs would not have the effect of allowing other groups to discriminate on the basis of religion. It would not mean, for example, that fraternities or sororities could exclude students on that basis. . . . But for religious groups, the situation is very different. . . .

Sexual orientation. The Hastings Nondiscrimination Policy, as interpreted by the law school, also discriminated on the basis of viewpoint regarding sexual morality. CLS has a particular viewpoint on this subject, namely, that sexual conduct outside marriage between a man and a woman is wrongful. Hastings would not allow CLS to express this viewpoint by limiting membership to persons willing to express a sincere agreement with CLS's views. By contrast, nothing in the Nondiscrimination Policy prohibited a group from expressing a contrary viewpoint by limiting membership to persons willing to endorse that group's beliefs. A Free Love Club could require members to affirm that they reject the traditional view of sexual morality to which CLS adheres. It is hard to see how this can be viewed as anything other than viewpoint discrimination. . . .

VI

I come now to the version of Hastings' policy that the Court has chosen to address. . . . [It] is clear that the accept-all-comers policy is not reasonable in light of the purpose of the RSO forum, and it is impossible to say on the present record that it is viewpoint neutral.

A

. . . The accept-all-comers policy is antithetical to the design of the RSO forum for the same reason that a state-imposed accept-all-comers policy would violate the First Amendment rights of private groups if applied off campus. . . . There can be no dispute that this standard would not permit a generally applicable law mandating that private religious groups admit members who do not share the groups' beliefs. Religious groups like CLS obviously engage in expressive association, and no legitimate state interest could override the powerful effect that an accept-all-comers law would have on the ability of religious groups to express their views. The State of California surely could not demand that all Christian groups admit members who believe that Jesus was merely human. Jewish groups could not be required to admit anti-Semites and Holocaust deniers. Muslim groups could not be forced to admit persons who are viewed as slandering Islam. . . . [However,] the Court now holds that Hastings, a state institution, may impose these very same requirements on students who wish to participate in a forum that is designed to foster the expression of diverse viewpoints. . . .

The Court first says that the accept-all-comers policy is reasonable because it helps Hastings to ensure that " 'leadership, educational, and social opportunities' " are afforded to all students. The RSO forum, however, is designed to achieve these laudable ends in a very different way — by permitting groups of students, no matter how small, to form the groups they want. . . .

Second, the Court approves the accept-all-comers policy because it is easier to enforce than the Nondiscrimination Policy that it replaced. . . . This is a strange argument, since the Nondiscrimination Policy prohibits discrimination on substantially the same grounds as the antidiscrimination provisions of many States, including California . . .

Third, the Court argues that the accept-all-comers policy, by bringing together students with diverse views, encourages tolerance, cooperation, learning, and the development of conflict-resolution skills. These are obviously commendable goals, but they are not undermined by permitting a religious group to restrict membership to persons who share the group's faith. Many religious groups impose such restrictions. . . .

Fourth, the Court observes that Hastings' policy "incorporates . . . state-law proscriptions on discrimination." Because the First Amendment obviously takes precedence over any state law, this would not justify the Hastings policy even if it were true — but it is not. . . . Neither Hastings nor the Court claims that California law demands that state entities must accept all comers. Hastings itself certainly does not follow this policy in hiring or student admissions. Nor is it at all clear that California law requires Hastings to deny registration to a religious group that limits membership to students who share the group's religious beliefs. . . .

In sum, Hastings' accept-all-comers policy is not reasonable in light of the stipulated purpose of the RSO forum: to promote a diversity of viewpoints *"among"* — not within — "registered student organizations."

B

The Court is also wrong in holding that the accept-all-comers policy is viewpoint neutral. . . . The adoption of a facially neutral policy for the purpose of suppressing the expression of a particular viewpoint is viewpoint discrimination. . . . Here, CLS has made a strong showing that Hastings' sudden adoption and selective application of its accept-all-comers policy was a pretext for the law school's unlawful denial of CLS's registration application under the Nondiscrimination Policy. . . . [Here the dissent goes into some factual detail to attempt to corroborate this conclusion.] . . .

C

. . . [In] response to the argument that the accept-all-comers-policy would permit a small and unpopular group to be taken over by students who wish to silence its message, the Court states that the policy would permit a registered group to impose membership requirements "designed to ensure that students join because of their commitment to a group's vitality, not its demise." With this concession, the Court tacitly recognizes that Hastings does not really have an accept-all-comers policy — it has an accept-some-dissident-comers policy — and the line between members who merely seek to change a group's message (who apparently must be admitted) and those who seek a group's "demise" (who may be kept out) is hopelessly vague. . . .

In the end, the Court refuses to acknowledge the consequences of its holding. A true accept-all-comers policy permits small unpopular groups to be taken over by students who wish to change the views that the group expresses. . . . The possibility of such takeovers, however, is by no means the most important effect of the Court's holding. There are religious groups that cannot in good conscience agree in their bylaws that they will admit persons who do not share their faith, and for these groups, the consequence of an accept-all-comers policy is marginalization. This is where the Court's decision leads. . . .

Even those who find CLS's views objectionable should be concerned about the way the group has been treated — by Hastings, the Court of Appeals, and now this Court. I can only hope that this decision will turn out to be an aberration.

NOTE: UNRESOLVED AND IRRESOLVABLE DIFFERENCES

There are unresolved and seemingly irresolvable differences in this set of opinions. The majority opinion by Justice Ginsburg focuses exclusively on the all-comers policy and holds it is constitutional under the limited public forum doctrine — a win for Hastings Law School. The dissent by Justice Alito focuses on the nondiscrimination policy and would strike it down under that doctrine and, in the alternative, argues that the all-comers policy likewise is unconstitutional. The two concurring opinions, by Justices Stevens and Kennedy, attempt to respond to the dissent in some particulars. Furthermore, the two main opinions dispute the record on appeal in important respects, such as the legal significance of the parties' stipulation of facts and whether Hastings adopted the all-comers policy in good faith and what issues are left open on remand. On the common denominator between the majority and the dissent, i.e., the application of the limited public forum doctrine to the all-comers policy, who has the better argument and why? *See* Note: The Free Speech — Public Forum Overlay (Casebook p. 1111).

Page 1139: *add new Problem after the Problem:*

PROBLEM: "OPEN YOUR HYMNALS TO THE FIRST AMENDMENT" — RELIGIOUS MUSIC IN THE PUBLIC SCHOOLS

You are a law clerk serving in the chambers of a U.S. Circuit Judge who has assigned you to write a bench memo on two cases on the docket for her upcoming panel sitting. Your memo should outline the casebook cases on which you rely to make your recommendations either to affirm or reverse the two District Courts.

In No. 11-123, *George Bailey v. Bedford Falls School District*, the District Court upheld a recently-promulgated school district policy which provides, in part: "Religious music, like any other music, can only be used if it achieves specific goals of the music curriculum. Music programs prepared or presented by student groups as an outcome of the curriculum shall not have a religious orientation or focus on religious holidays." This new policy was interpreted by the principal and the superintendent of the public school district to disallow traditional Christmas holiday music that in previous years had been performed at year-end concerts by the high school's choir, including "Joy to the World," "O' Come All Ye Faithful," "Hark, the Herald Angels Sing," and "Silent Night." The choir director, some students in the choir, and some students' parents brought suit against the principal, the superintendent, and the school district. The District Court rejected their First and Fourteenth Amendment claims under the Free Speech Clause, the Free Exercise Clause, and the Establishment Clause.

In No. 11-345, *Ralphie Parker v. Hammond School District*, the District Court upheld the junior high school's practice to allow the seventh and eighth grade choir to choose an annual theme song, which is sung at the end of each performance. This year, a majority of the student members voted for "The Lord Bless You and Keep You." Plaintiffs Ralphie Parker and his parents brought suit against the choir director, the principal, the superintendent, and the school district. Plaintiffs

— who do not profess any religious belief — had argued unsuccessfully that their First and Fourteenth Amendment rights were violated each and every time Ralphie was required to sing that religious composition as a member of the choir enrolled for academic credit in a public school. The lyrics of the hymn, adapted from Numbers 6:24-26 (KJV), are:

> The Lord bless you and keep you,
> The Lord lift His countenance upon you,
> And give you peace, and give you peace,
> The Lord make His face to shine upon you,
> And be gracious unto you, be gracious,
> The Lord be gracious, gracious unto you.
> Amen.

Appendix B

THE JUSTICES OF THE UNITED STATES SUPREME COURT, 1946–2010 TERMS

U.S. Reports	Term[*]	The Court[**]
329-332[1]	1946	**Vinson**, Black, Reed, Frankfurter, Douglas, Murphy, Jackson, Rutledge, Burton
332[1]-335[2]	1947	"
335[2]-338[3]	1948	"
338[3]-339	1949	Vinson, Black, Reed, Frankfurter, Douglas, Jackson, Burton, Clark, Minton
340-341	1950	"
342-343	1951	"
344-346[4]	1952	"
346[4]-347	1953	**Warren**, Black, Reed, Frankfurter, Douglas, Jackson, Burton, Clark, Minton
348-349	1954	Warren, Black, Reed, Frankfurter, Douglas, Burton, Clark, Minton, Harlan[5]
350-351	1955	"
352-354	1956	Warren, Black, Reed,[6] Frankfurter, Douglas, Burton, Clark, Harlan, Brennan, Whittaker[7]
355-357	1957	Warren, Black, Frankfurter, Douglas, Burton, Clark, Harlan, Brennan, Whittaker
358-360	1958	Warren, Black, Frankfurter, Douglas, Clark, Harlan, Brennan, Whittaker, Stewart
361-364[8]	1959	"
364[8]-367	1960	"

---

[*] Rule 3 of the Supreme Court's Rules provides in part: "The Court holds a continuous annual Term commencing on the first Monday in October and ending on the day before the first Monday in October of the following year."

[**] Justices are listed in order of seniority. Boldface indicates a new Chief Justice.

[1] The 1947 Term begins at 332 U.S. 371.

[2] The 1948 Term begins at 335 U.S. 281.

[3] The 1949 Term begins at 338 U.S. 217.

[4] The 1953 Term begins at 346 U.S. 325.

[5] Participation begins with 349 U.S.

[6] Participation ends with 352 U.S. 564.

[7] Participation begins with 353 U.S.

[8] The 1960 Term begins with 364 U.S. 285.

U.S. Reports	Term	The Court[*]
368-370	1961	Warren, Black, Frankfurter,[9] Douglas, Clark, Harlan, Brennan, Whittaker,[10] Stewart, White[11]
371-374	1962	"
375-378	1963	"
379-381	1964	"
382-384	1965	Warren, Black, Douglas, Clark, Harlan, Brennan, Stewart, White, Fortas
385-388	1966	"
389-392	1967	Warren, Black, Douglas, Harlan, Brennan, Stewart, White, Fortas, Marshall
393-395	1968	Warren, Black, Douglas, Harlan, Brennan, Stewart, White, Fortas,[12] Marshall
396-399	1969	**Burger**, Black, Douglas, Harlan, Brennan, Stewart, White, Marshall, [vacancy]
400-403	1970	Burger, Black, Douglas, Harlan, Brennan, Stewart, White, Marshall, Blackmun
404-408	1971	Burger, Douglas, Brennan, Stewart, White, Marshall, Blackmun, Powell,[13] Rehnquist[13]
409-413	1972	"
414-418	1973	"
419-422	1974	"
423-428	1975	Burger, Brennan, Stewart, White, Marshall, Blackmun, Powell, Rehnquist, Stevens[14]
429-433	1976	"
434-438	1977	"
439-443	1978	"
444-448	1979	"
449-453	1980	"
454-458	1981	Burger, Brennan, White, Marshall, Blackmun, Powell, Rehnquist, Stevens, O'Connor
459-463	1982	"
464-468	1983	"
469-473	1984	"
474-478	1985	"

---

[*] Justices are listed in order of seniority. Boldface indicates a new Chief Justice.

[9] Participation ends with 369 U.S. 422.

[10] Participation ends with 369 U.S. 120.

[11] Participation begins with 370 U.S.

[12] Participation ends with 394 U.S.

[13] Participation begins with 405 U.S.

[14] Participation begins with 424 U.S.

U.S. Reports	Term	The Court*
479-483	1986	**Rehnquist**, Brennan, White, Marshall, Blackmun, Powell, Stevens, O'Connor, Scalia
484-487	1987	"
488-492	1988	Rehnquist, Brennan, White, Marshall, Blackmun, Stevens, O'Connor, Scalia, Kennedy
493-497	1989	"
498-501	1990	Rehnquist, White, Marshall, Blackmun, Stevens, O'Connor, Scalia, Kennedy, Souter
502-505	1991	Rehnquist, White, Blackmun, Stevens, O'Connor, Scalia, Kennedy, Souter, Thomas
506-509	1992	"
510-512	1993	Rehnquist, Blackmun, Stevens, O'Connor, Scalia, Kennedy, Souter, Thomas, Ginsburg
513-515	1994	Rehnquist, Stevens, O'Connor, Scalia, Kennedy, Souter, Thomas, Ginsburg, Breyer
516-518	1995	"
519-521	1996	"
522-524	1997	"
525-527	1998	"
528-530	1999	"
531-533	2000	"
534-536	2001	"
537-539	2002	"
540-542	2003	"
543-545	2004[15]	Rehnquist, Stevens, O'Connor, Scalia, Kennedy, Souter, Thomas, Ginsburg, Breyer
546-548	2005	**Roberts**, Stevens, O'Connor,[16] Scalia, Kennedy, Souter, Thomas, Ginsburg, Breyer, Alito[17]
549-551	2006	Roberts, Stevens, Scalia, Kennedy, Souter, Thomas, Ginsburg, Breyer, Alito
552-554	2007	"
555-557	2008	"
558-561	2009	Roberts, Stevens, Scalia, Kennedy, Thomas, Ginsburg, Breyer, Alito, Sotomayor
562-564	2010	Roberts, Scalia, Kennedy, Thomas, Ginsburg, Breyer, Alito, Sotomayor, Kagan

---

[15] Chief Justice Rehnquist died on Sept. 3, 2005, shortly before the 2004 Term officially concluded, but after all opinions from that Term had been delivered.

[16] Participation ends with 546 U.S. 417.

[17] Participation begins with 547 U.S.